THE BOTANICAL PALETTE

Colour for the Botanical Painter

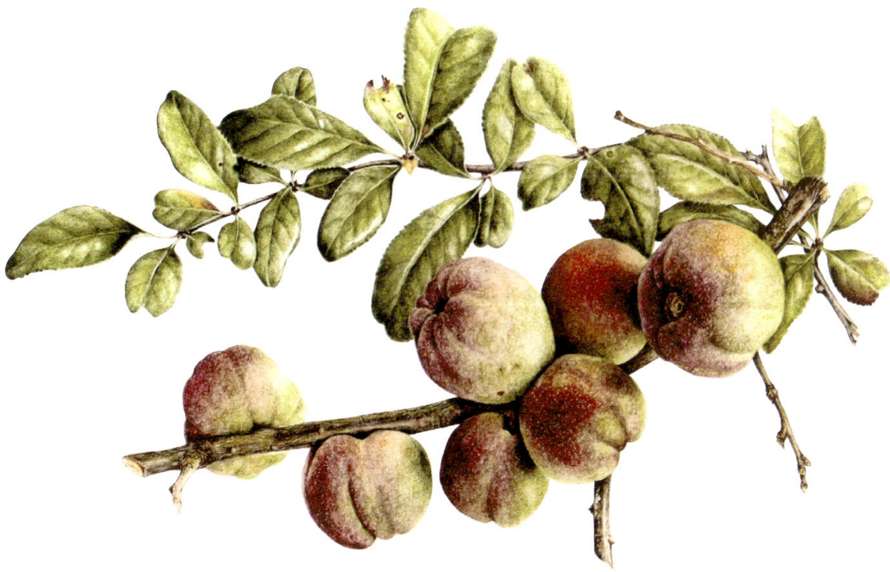

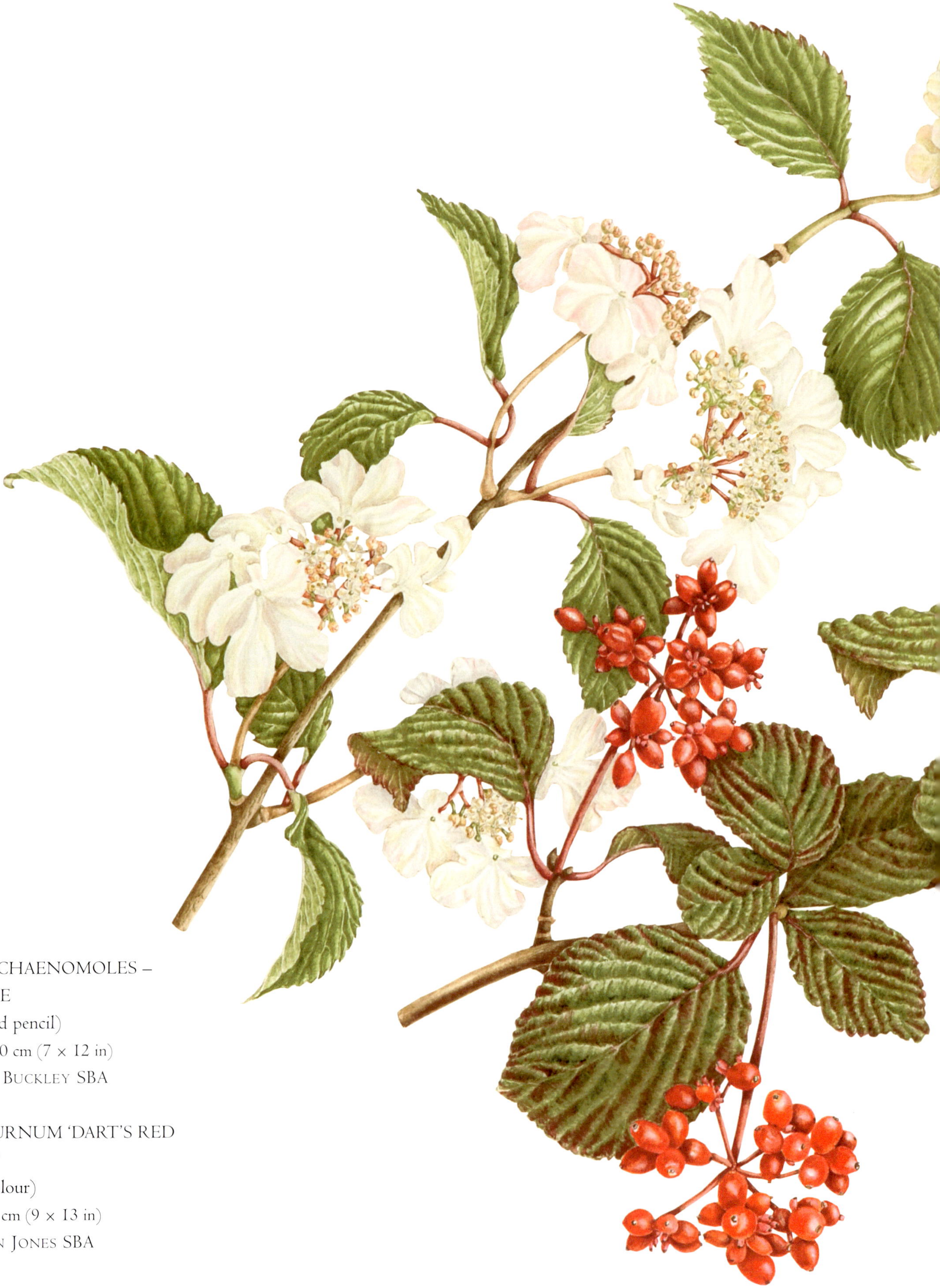

Page I CHAENOMOLES –
QUINCE
(coloured pencil)
18.5 × 30 cm (7 × 12 in)
Hilary Buckley SBA

▷ VIBURNUM 'DART'S RED
ROBIN'
(watercolour)
24 × 33 cm (9 × 13 in)
Doreen Jones SBA

THE BOTANICAL PALETTE

Colour for the Botanical Painter

in association with

THE SOCIETY OF BOTANICAL ARTISTS

MARGARET STEVENS PSBA

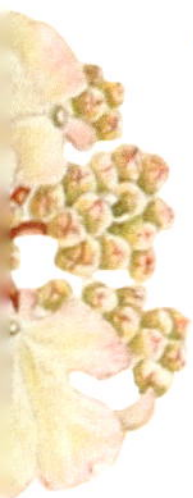

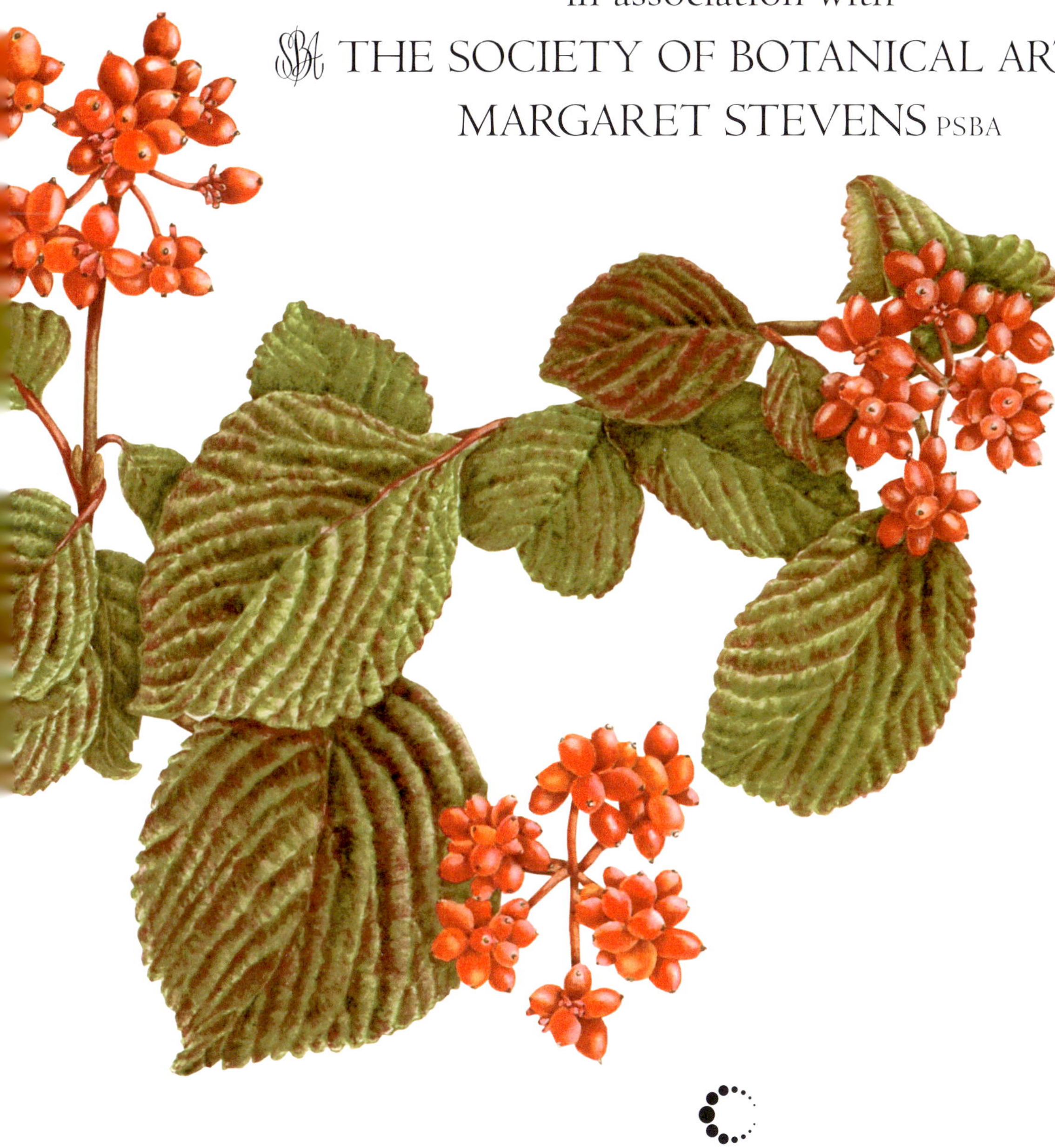

Collins

Dedication

In memory of my father and husband who both encouraged me to paint.

First published in 2007 by
Collins, an imprint of
HarperCollins Publishers
77–85 Fulham Palace Road
London W6 8JB

The Collins website address is www.collins.co.uk

12 11 10 09 08
10 9 8 7 6 5 4 3 2

A catalogue record for this book is available from the British Library

ISBN 978 0 00 724785 1

Designer: Caroline Hill
Editor: Geraldine Christy
Indexer: Ingrid Lock
Photographer: Richard Palmer
Photographer: Andrew Bennison (pages 1, 9, 118, 122, 125, 126, 135, 138, 140, 141)

Colour reproduction by Colourscan, Singapore
Printed and bound by Printing Express Ltd, Hong Kong

Jacket painting:
PHALAENOPSIS
(watercolour)
54 × 51 cm (21¼ × 20 in)
Libby Carreck SBA

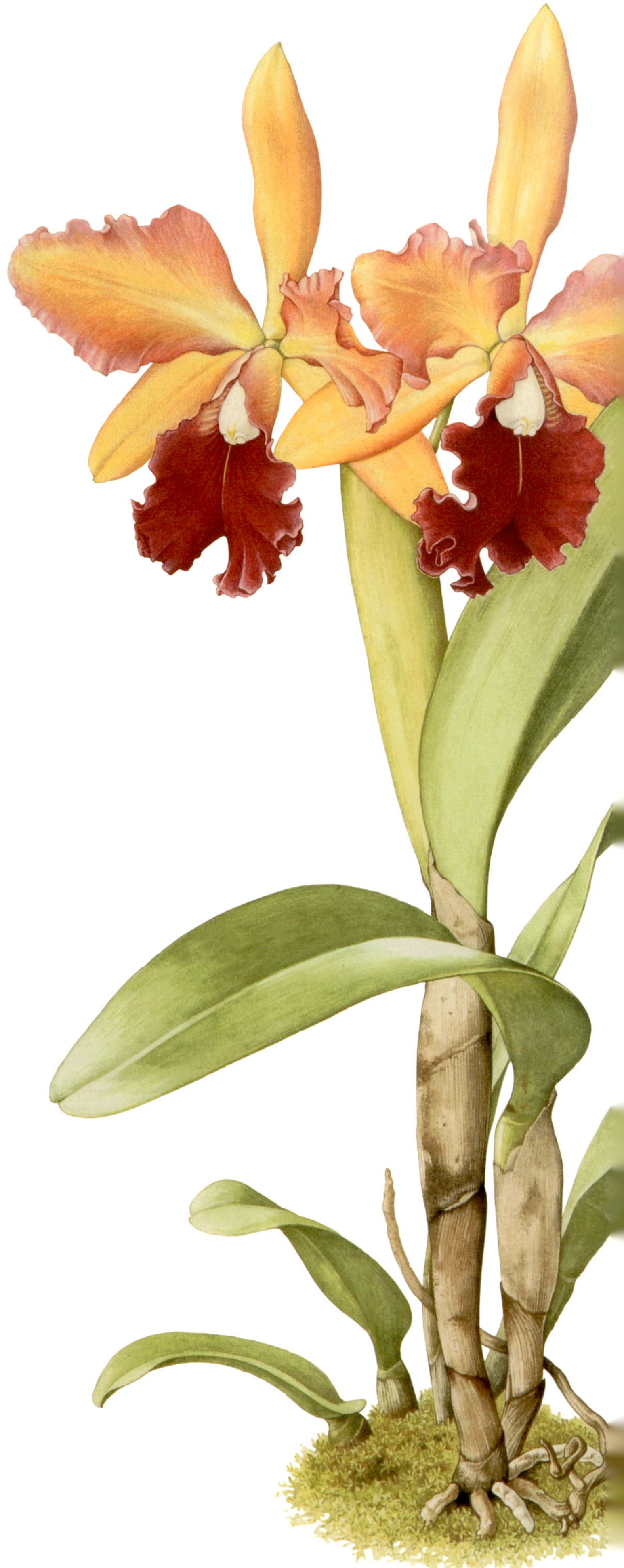

▷ LAELIOCATTLEYA
'VALDEMOSA BOISSY'
(watercolour)
25 × 20 cm (10 × 8 in)
Eileen Maddison SBA

CONTENTS

NAMES OF COLOURS

Paint manufacturers constantly upgrade their colours, so research current options before planning your palette. All the paints used in this book are Winsor & Newton unless otherwise stated. Names given to coloured pencils frequently change, but numbers usually remain the same.

FOREWORD

THERE IS AN innate fascination in watching an expert at work. Whether they are cabinetmaker or charcoal burner, seeing a person with the ability to produce something of interest, use or beauty makes for compelling viewing and inspires deep admiration. But experts can be either born or made and I believe there is artistic ability in all of us, even though it may lie deeply buried. Nonetheless, the right guidance, from accomplished experts, can bring it out. This book does that. The immense skills of Margaret Stevens as artist and teacher are widely recognized, and here, in association with the Society of Botanical Artists, she has harnessed her own and others' talents for the benefit of all.

This is not the first or the only book on botanical painting techniques, but it is the only one I know where the use of colour is so carefully explained. Among the features that make this new work so valuable is the attention it gives to colour mixing and layering. It takes a very special ability to explain this in the way Margaret Stevens and her colleagues have done here. Moreover by following the very personal guidance these inspirational artists provide, it is possible for students the world over to participate in the Society's Distance Learning Diploma Course.

Botany and art have always been closely linked. Many of the most knowledgeable botanists, from Leonhart Fuchs to Joseph Hooker, were also wonderful artists, while the finest of botanical painters have a profound appreciation of why plants are as they are. Margaret Stevens and her colleagues are the admirable inheritors of this great tradition and I warmly commend this magnificent book to all lovers of plants and fine painting; and to all prospective botanical artists.

Stefan Buczacki DPhil, FIHort
June 2007

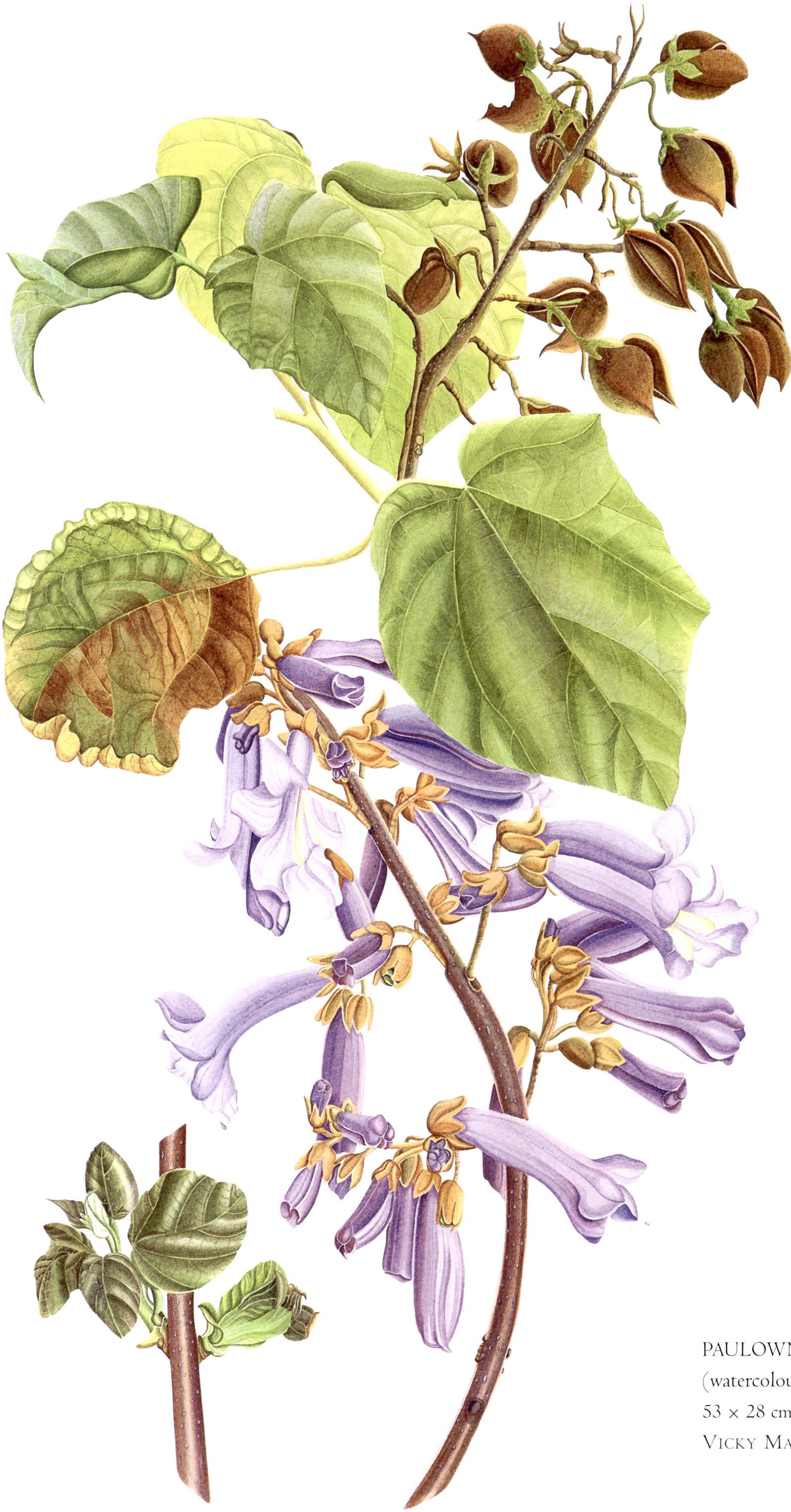

PAULOWNIA ELONGATA
(watercolour)
53 × 28 cm (21 × 11 in)
Vicky Mappin SBA

THE SOCIETY OF BOTANICAL ARTISTS

FOUNDED IN 1985 by Suzanne Lucas MBE, FLS, herself an artist of repute and holder of numerous Gold Medals awarded by the Royal Horticultural Society, the SBA made history by being the first Society devoted to the art of botanical painting.

In the past two decades there has been a renaissance in this branch of the arts with increasing public awareness and appreciation both in the United Kingdom and overseas. Contributing to this have been the efforts made by the SBA in promoting this beautiful art form, both by its annual exhibition at Westminster Central Hall, London, and occasional exhibitions in other parts of the country.

More recently the publication of *The Art of Botanical Painting* written by Margaret Stevens, as now, on behalf of the Society, has helped to spread interest to many corners of the world. Following publication it was decided to set up a course so that anyone interested in learning some of the skills that the SBA Members have at their disposal may do so, no matter where they live.

So the Distance Learning Diploma Course was born and soon proved to be enormously popular, with students enrolling from Australia and Japan to America, Canada and throughout Europe as well as much closer to home. As a registered charity with education as one of its principal aims, this twenty-seven-month course is enabling many people to find a new interest as well as refining the techniques of more advanced students. The twenty-five tutors drawn from the Society membership are selected because of their particular strengths, be it precise drawing skills, a matchless eye for

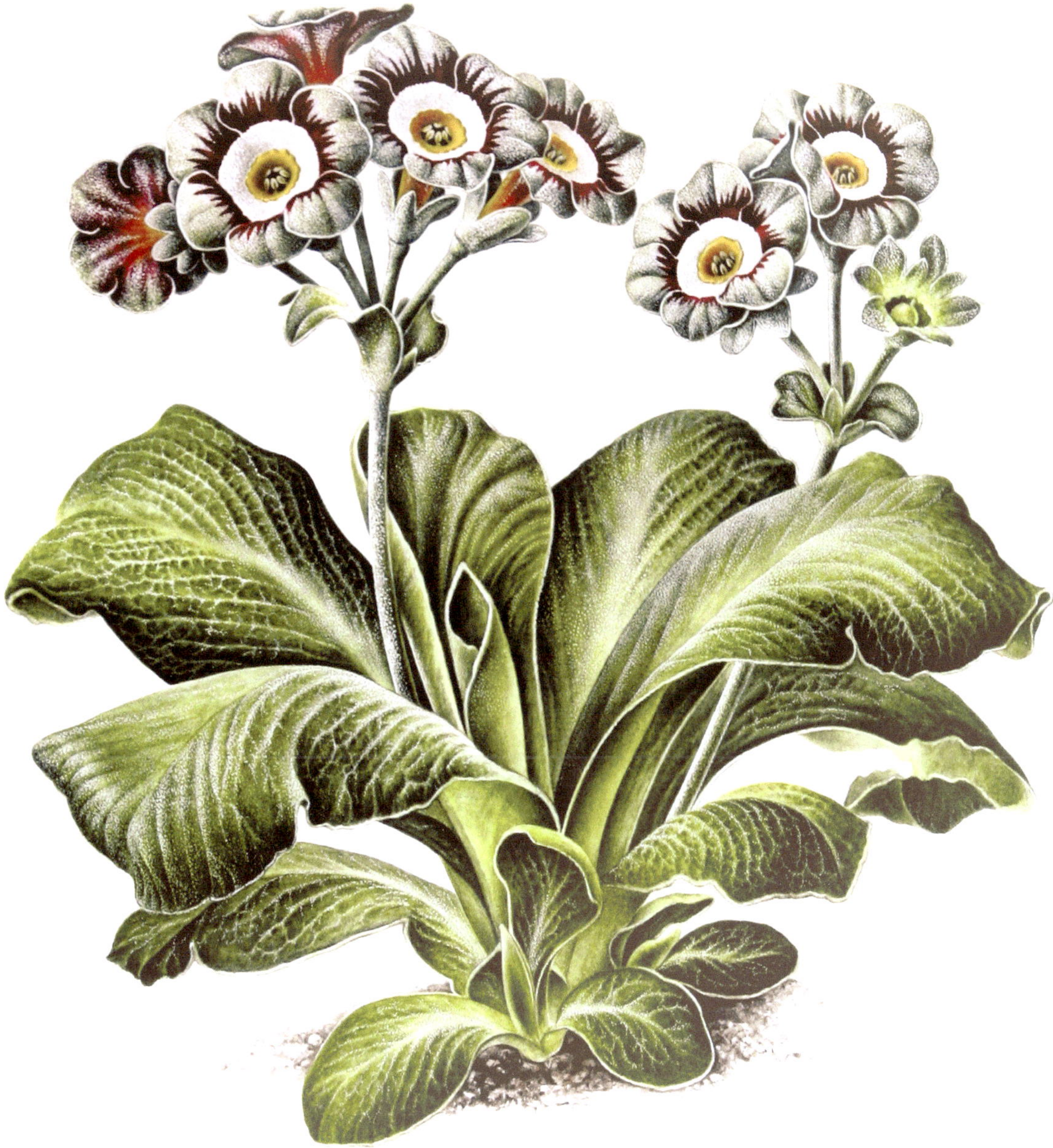

composition, or the ease with which they handle the techniques required for creating stunning work in watercolour or coloured pencil.

△ AURICULA 'OLD ENGLAND' (watercolour) 19 × 17 cm (7½ × 7 in) BRIGITTE E M DANIEL SBA

Anyone with an interest in exhibiting at an SBA Open Exhibition, perhaps with the hope of becoming a Member, or requiring details of the DLDC should contact the Executive Secretary and Course Administrator SBA, 1 Knapp Cottages, Wyke, Gillingham, Dorset, SP8 4NQ, or email pam@soc-botanical-artists.org. Further information and other examples of Members' work may also be found on our website www.soc-botanical-artists.org (Charity Registration Number 1110869).

INTRODUCTION

In over twenty years of my teaching botanical painting one source of worry seemed to arise more frequently than any other – colour and just about everything that relates to it. This seems particularly unfortunate since scarcely any other subject demands such a wide-ranging palette and the confidence to use it. The landscape painter can settle before his or her easel and capture a vista, which may spread for many miles, using a mere six pigments. Sometimes the botanical painter can work the same magic, as you will see later in the book, but more often than not he or she will need to be in command of a much wider spectrum.

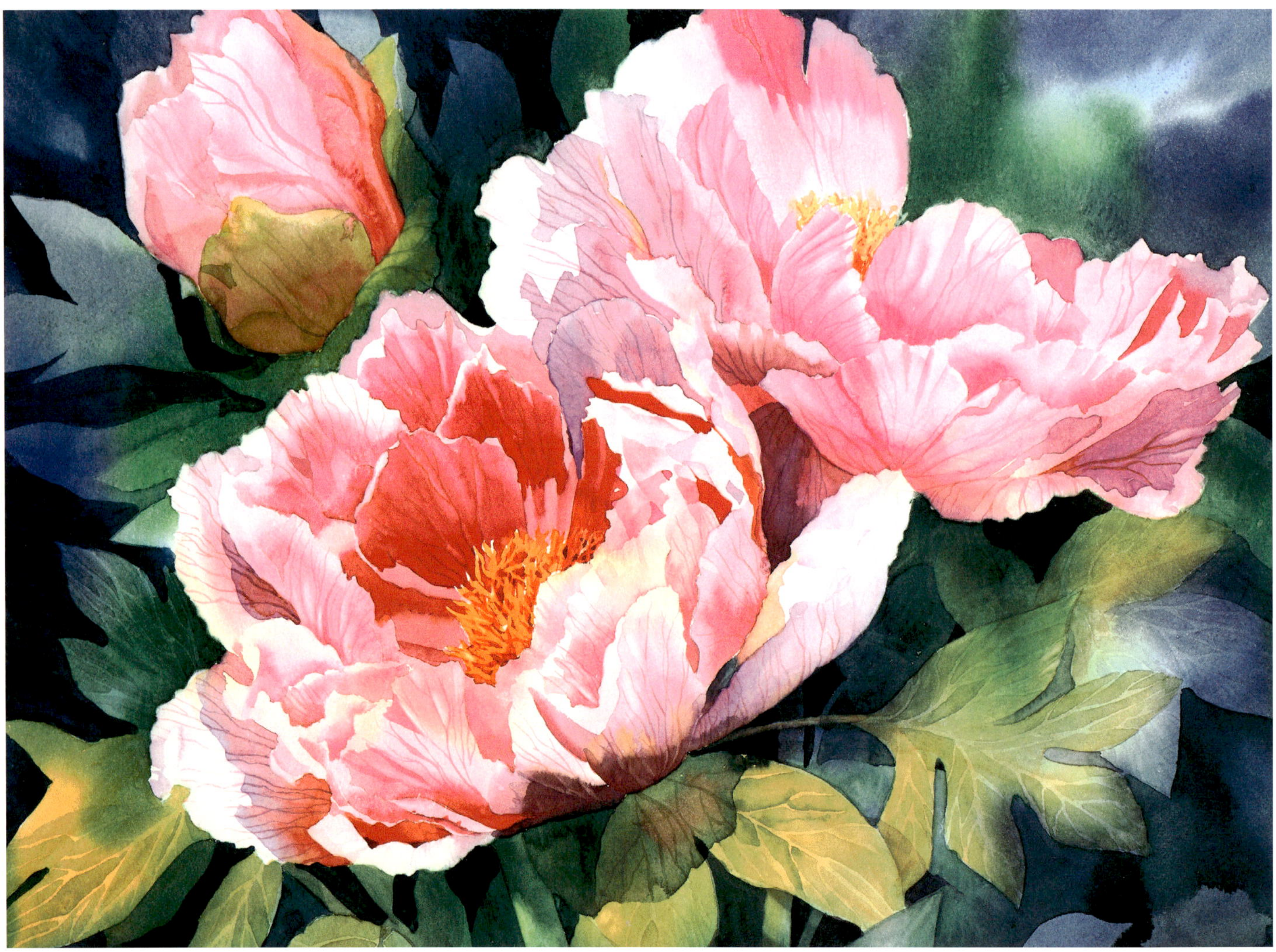

Most 'How to Do' books contain a colour wheel, but even so students still ask the difference between warm and cool colours, and shadow colours cause endless confusion. These are the sort of practical everyday questions that crop up time and again, not the chemical components of Cadmium Yellow or Sap Green, which now can be easily found on the internet. It is hardly surprising, therefore, that when I was approached to write another book, colour was the obvious choice for its theme.

CLEAN, STRONG COLOUR

I sent a questionnaire to one hundred students taking part on the SBA Distance Learning Diploma Course, and much of what follows is based on their replies. Shadow colours, particularly on white and yellow, figured frequently in the problem analysis and how to create shadows without making the work appear dirty. Deep and bright colours were just plain scary to many people. In fact, from their answers it appears we are lucky that anyone paints anything other than pale pink sweet peas and lavender clematis, with the odd poppy or sunflower thrown in for good measure!

There is safety in trying to reproduce a flower of pastel hue because it requires less pigment and fewer washes or glazes to achieve the desired result. On the other hand, a flower of intense colour needs a build-up of stronger pigmented glazes and without care this can become muddy. The solution may be simple, and work is often spoilt by the student's impatience. Wet-in-wet is not always the answer. Sometimes the first glaze needs to be totally dry before the next one is applied, particularly where there is a shift in colour, such as changing a bright red to a more purple burgundy on the shadow side of a bloom.

◁ PEONIES
(watercolour)
31 × 38 cm (12 × 15 in)
JANET WHITTLE SBA

Even the word watercolour can create the wrong mental image – it does not mean 'watery colour', yet often one sees a wishy-washy piece of work where the ratio of pigment to water is insufficient. When the tutor points this out the usual reply is 'I was afraid to add more paint in case I spoilt it'.

Impatience can also cause overworking; the student may not allow sufficient drying time before adding detail such as veins on a leaf. Instead of looking crisply drawn with the brush, details blur into the wash beneath, so in goes the brush again to try and rescue the situation. This probably only succeeds in dirtying what was a clear colour, so sometimes a piece of kitchen paper is used to blot the offending area and the whole process starts again. Do this two or three times and the result will surely be mud, and it is unlikely that a rescue job will be possible.

TRANSPARENCY AND FASTNESS

Watercolour properly used enables the artist to achieve a freshness and clarity with both pale and strong colours that is second to none. Many watercolours are transparent, which means that when glazed one on top of the other the underlying colour gleams through. A transparent pigment on top of an opaque pigment provides a window for the opaque colour beneath. Reverse this, however, and, the opaque colour blocks the underlying transparent one, making this a pretty useless exercise. Therefore students need to get to know their paints thoroughly and to be aware of or check their transparency rating.

Lightfastness is also important, but as all paints are clearly marked, albeit in code, it should enable the artist to make an educated decision as to the use of individual pigments. It has to be said that the owners of watercolour paintings, including some that have cost a great deal of money, often hang them in places that are totally inappropriate.

Gone are the days when they were kept in portfolios and brought out to be admired as cherished items. Now they are just as likely to be hung in a conservatory, as have some of mine, at least until I pointed out the error of the owner's ways. To hang a watercolour or work in coloured pencil in strong sunlight is expecting much of a pigment. Protecting with conservation glass is one alleviating remedy.

MANUFACTURERS' COLOURS

Another major cause of bewilderment is the sheer quantity of different paints available from a number of reputable manufacturers. Confusion arises when students are using Colour A, but their tutor or a fellow student recommends Colour B from a different manufacturer. The student buys Colour B only to find that it seems to be identical to Colour A. Paint is expensive as an initial purchase, so naturally the student feels aggrieved.

I recommend any artist to obtain the manufacturers' shade cards, but it has to be appreciated that one cannot hope for totally accurate colour reproduction, and jumping around from one card to the next makes it even harder to reach a true colour assessment. With that in mind, towards the end of the book you will find a reference series of colour charts showing a range of swatches that link to the text. My colleague and SBA Member Kay Rees-Davies and I have tested around two hundred watercolours by several leading manufacturers, concentrating on those most likely to be of interest to the botanical painter. Naturally we cannot say for certain that the colour printing is one hundred per cent accurate, but if we say that Red A is almost identical to Red B, but with a slightly bluer tinge, the reader can take this to be the case.

Paints that are identical will be made from exactly the same constituents, although marketed under a different name. Even so the binder or filler might vary, causing the paint to feel different on the brush. By experience the artist finds which make suits him or her best; most use paints from several manufacturers while keeping on the alert for colours that will add an extra touch of magic to their work.

USING THIS BOOK

The aim of this book is to provide guidance through the rainbow of the botanical palette and to help the aspiring artist and student to gain confidence. The book starts with white, then runs through varying shades of yellow, green, blue, purple, red, and brown, ending with black – yes, black. Demonstration step-by-steps are a familiar feature in many art books, but here you are encouraged to try out at least some of those featured and there are eight projects throughout the book. The projects provide a simplified ink drawing that students can trace, and a chart of suggested colours to use. The charts, together with the demonstration of a particular artist's working method should enable you to try out the projects. Instead of just looking and thinking 'if only', have a go. Follow the artist's method and you may well be surprised at the result.

Trace off the drawing and transfer it to good watercolour paper, either HP or Not; it should not be less than 300 gsm (140 lb) as a lighter paper would not adequately support the paint. Prepare your palette with the colours required, making sure that you can identify them easily. If you substitute the brands or colours the accuracy of the result cannot be guaranteed. Remember, too, that depth of colour is easily varied depending on the ratio of water to pigment. No one can give you precise guidelines for this, so experiment on spare paper before using a mix on your work.

In more recent years coloured pencils have become increasingly popular, and the CP artists now have an even wider palette than the watercolourists. Therefore I have included five demonstrations for coloured-pencil students that will help to show the technique used.

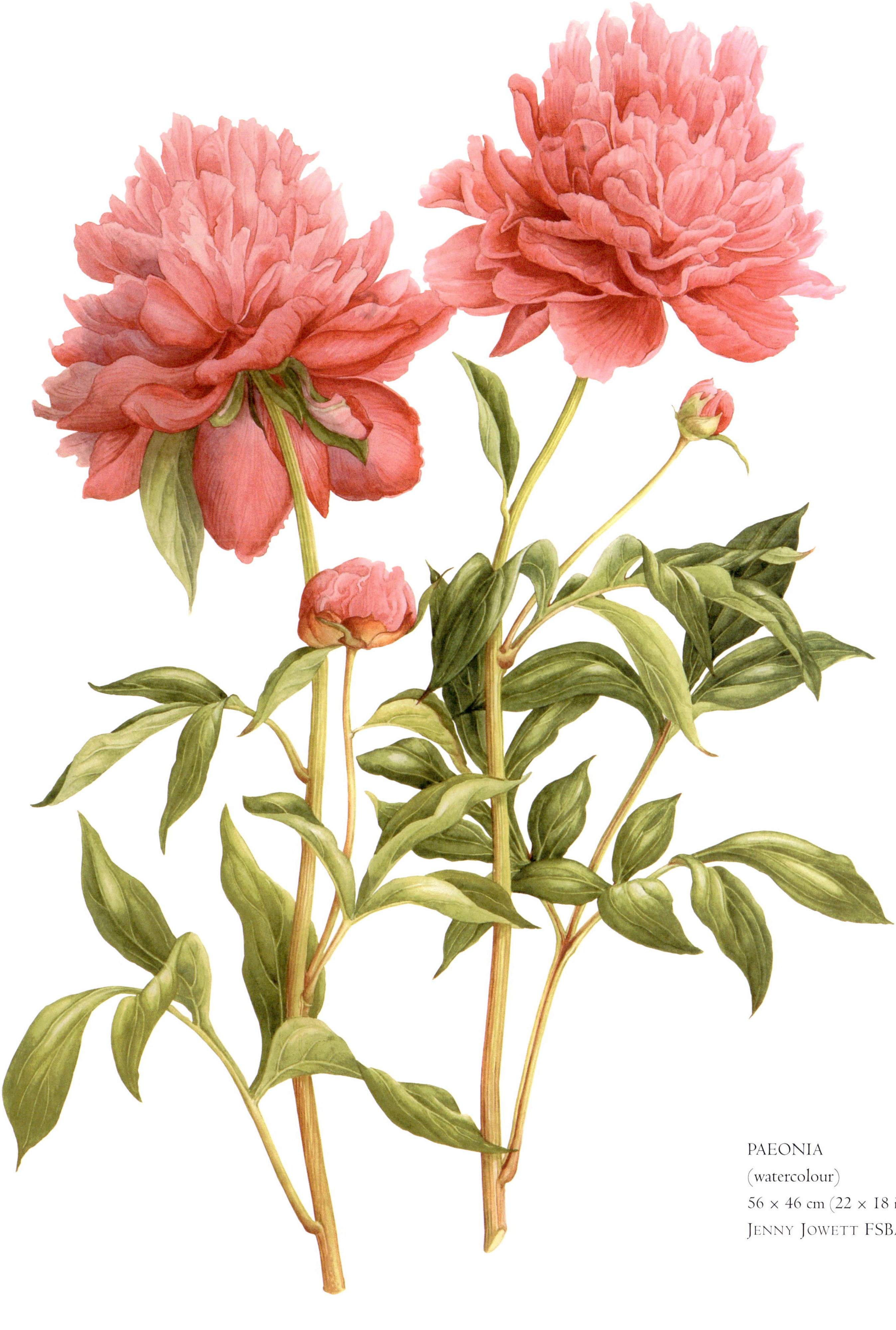

PAEONIA
(watercolour)
56 × 46 cm (22 × 18 in)
JENNY JOWETT FSBA

CHAPTER I

WHITE

For artists working in pure watercolour white is a non-colour since they will depend on the whiteness of the paper to provide the highest and brightest tone. Painters in gouache or other media will rely on zinc, lead or titanium to supply their body colour. In spite of the absence of colour it can be quite a challenge to capture the subtleties of reflected light and shadow that enable the image to come to life in a three-dimensional manner.

Much depends on the time of day when the painting of a white flower is started, assuming you are not working in an unchanging north light. Sunlight will warm the petals with a golden reflection that would not be apparent on a dull day. This may seem obvious, but it is surprising how factors that contribute to the overall appearance of the flower can easily be overlooked. The room in which you are working will also have a bearing on the tints that are visible; walls, curtains, and even your clothes, are likely to be reflected, albeit in the smallest degree. These are the hints of colour that need to merge with shadow tone. Unless the artist makes the most of these nuances of colour and tone the flower will look flat, and would be as well illustrated by a good line drawing. For the less experienced painter it is helpful to draw the flower in some detail as a preparatory exercise, carefully noting the shaded areas and the depth of tone needed to give form.

Artists all arrive at their favourite mixes by trial and error and never is it more important than for the grey tones on any flower, particularly a white one. If you paint the project on page 20 based on *Lilium auratum* 'Virginale' you might like to try your own grey mixes rather than the Light Red/ Ultramarine mix used in the demonstration on page 16.

▷ SORBUS CINEREOPUBESCENS McALLISTER
48.5 x 33 cm
(19 x 13 in)
GILLIAN DUDLEY-SMITH SBA

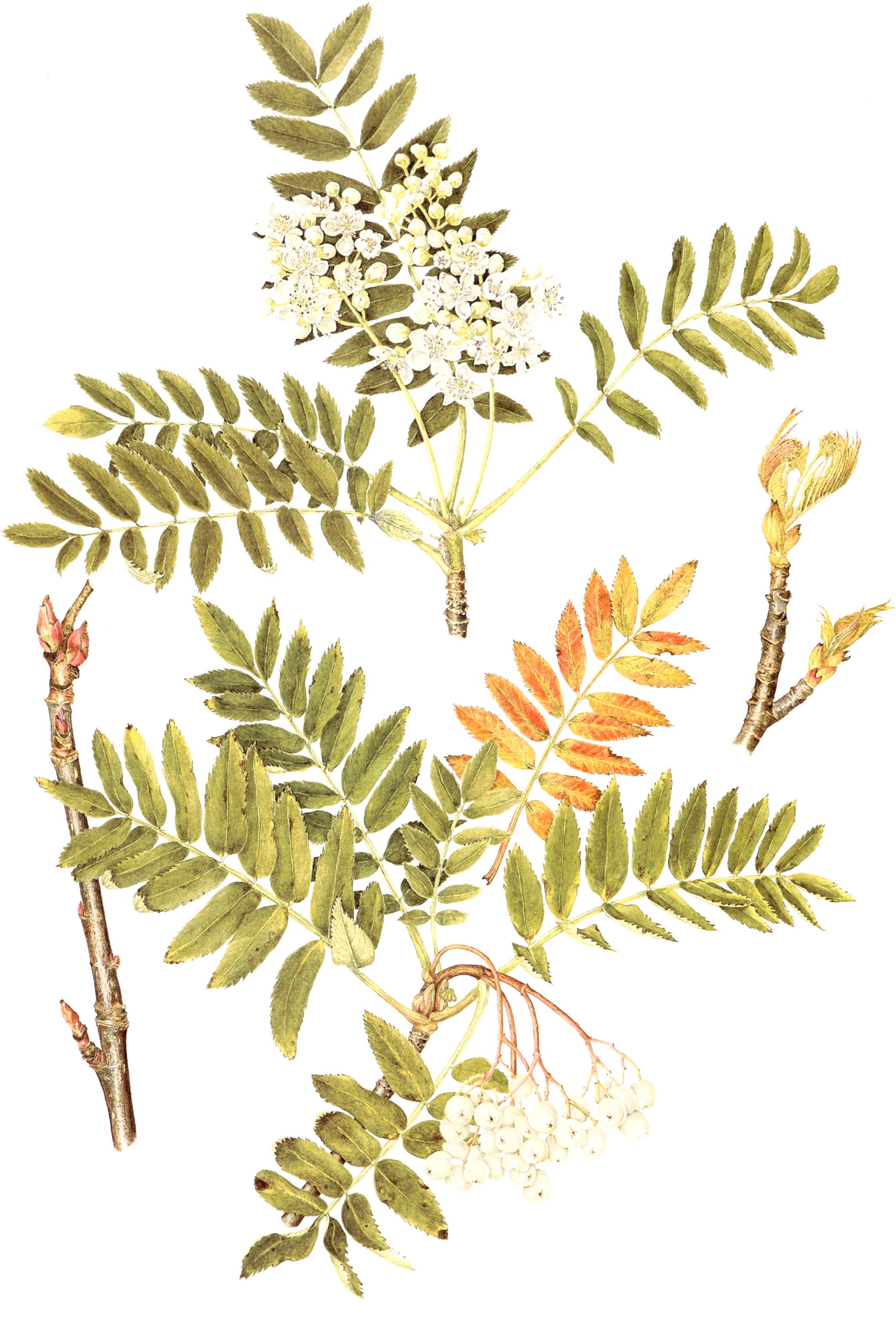

LILY

Lilium auratum 'Virginale'

Margaret Stevens PSBA

This perfect flower is best admired at twilight when it seems to glow with a magical quality. I grow it in pots near my front door where it cannot possibly be missed. As this study was painted for reproduction I have strengthened the shading. Had it been solely for exhibition slightly lighter tones would have been appropriate.

PAINTS

WINSOR & NEWTON
Transparent Yellow
Aureolin
Light Red
French Ultramarine
Perylene Green
Burnt Sienna
Burnt Umber

DALER-ROWNEY
Sap Green
Olive Green

SCHMINCKE
Glowing Violet
Gold Brown
Olive Green

BRUSHES

RAPHAEL
Kolinsky sable size 4

DALER-ROWNEY
Diana Kolinsky sable sizes 3 and 2

SURFACE

FABRIANO
Classico 5 HP 300 gsm (140 lb)

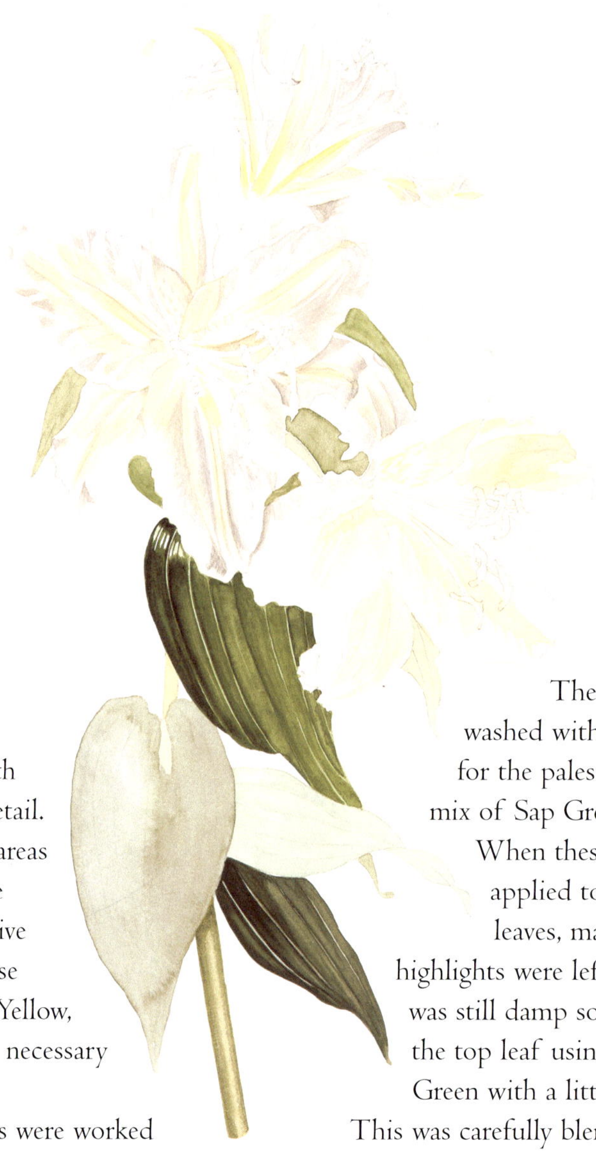

△ **Stage I**
I made a very light outline drawing with the minimum of detail. Then I looked for areas on each petal where there was a distinctive yellow tint. For these I used Transparent Yellow, strengthened where necessary with Aureolin.

The shaded areas were worked using a delicate mix of Light Red and French Ultramarine, which produced a transparent grey. Occasionally a tiny amount of Glowing Violet was added to the grey tint.

The four lower leaves were washed with Schmincke Olive Green for the palest leaf or a very diluted mix of Sap Green with Perylene Green. When these were dry Sap Green was applied to the top and lower right leaves, making sure the veins and highlights were left clear. While the paint was still damp some shading was added to the top leaf using a stronger mix of Sap Green with a little added Perylene Green. This was carefully blended using a damp brush. The same mix with more Perylene Green was used to start modelling the lower right leaf. The lower stem was glazed with pale Daler-Rowney Olive Green, shaded with Perylene Green.

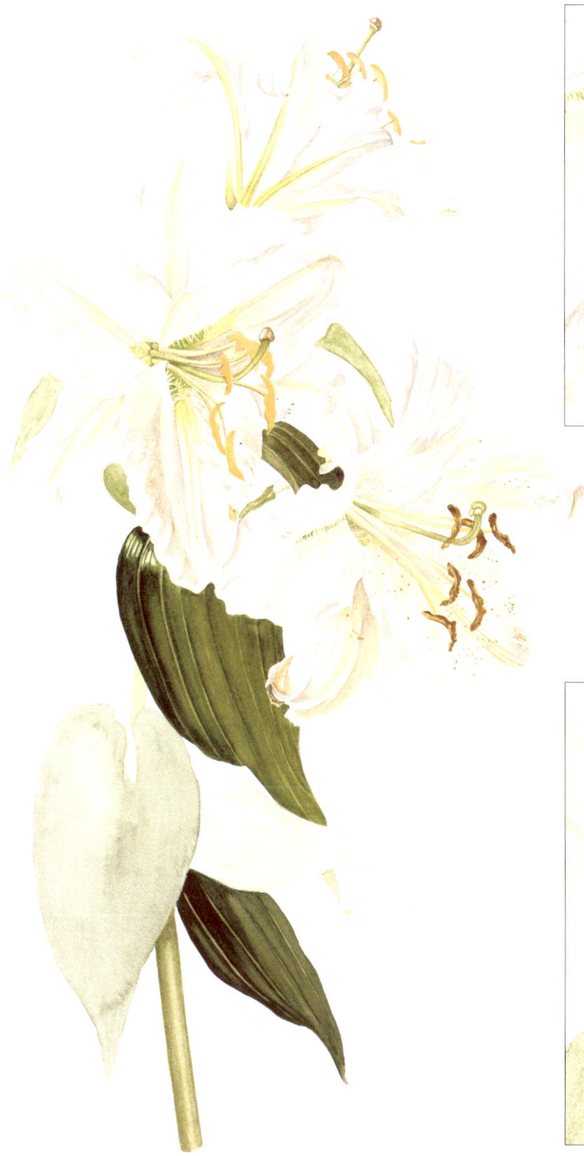

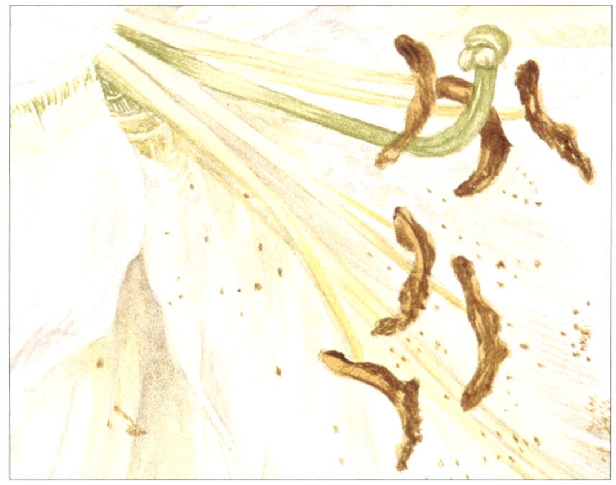

Detail of Stage 2: The anthers change as the flower ages, and the filaments become less robust as copious pollen falls from the anthers.

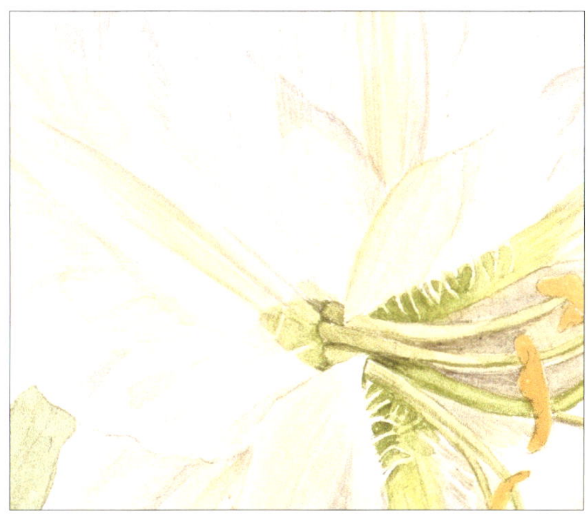

Detail of Stage 2: Negative spaces, painted with Sap Green, pick out the 'fringe' and give depth at the heart of the flower. The shape of the top petal gleams through from behind, showing up the raised textured area.

△ **Stage 2**

Concentrating on the flowers I started with the lowest one on the stem. This had been the first to open and showed signs of ageing. The petals were quite thick and very textured with fringed areas and little raised spots that demanded great care as they are an integral part of the mechanism for attracting pollinating insects.

I strengthened the shaded areas using the same grey mix, sometimes adding a little Sap Green or Transparent Yellow. You need to look very hard at this stage to pick up every nuance of colour, whether it be reflected or showing through from behind a petal.

Signs of decay were added using a little Burnt Sienna. For the stamens I used Transparent Yellow, shaded with Gold Brown on the filaments. The anthers were washed with Gold Brown, and detail added to them with Burnt Umber.

I used Sap Green to carefully paint the negative spaces on the fringed area. The style and stigma were washed over with Sap Green mixed with a trace of French Ultramarine, then shaded with a stronger mix of the same.

The little speckles were emphasized by shading on the lower side with the grey mix. Then I scattered pollen using Gold Brown and a touch of Transparent Yellow. The middle flower was treated similarly, but more time was spent on fine detail. I picked out the negative spaces using Sap Green with a size 3 brush.

Transparent Yellow mixed with Sap Green was shaded into the central veined areas of the right-hand and lower petals and the area around shaded with the pale grey mix over Transparent Yellow that had been applied at Stage 1. This was done with a fairly dry brush, which created texture. Speckles were lifted out and shaded on one side to throw them into relief.

A touch of Light Red added to the grey mix on the lowest petal was stroked on with a dry brush following the contours of the petal. The stigma was both sticky and shiny, at the peak of its life.

The top flower required more Transparent Yellow and Light Red in the grey shading mix. The stripes running up the back of the petals were painted with a mix of Sap Green and Transparent Yellow, then shaded with a touch of Daler-Rowney Olive added to the Sap Green.

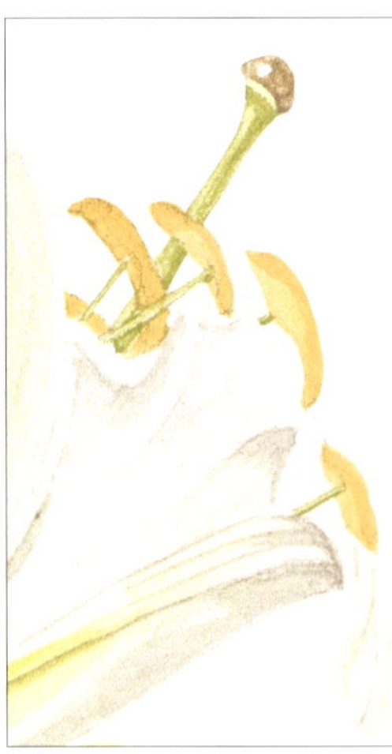

Detail from Stage 2: Particular care was taken to show the filaments joining the underside of the anthers. These are much smoother as they emerge from a newly opening bloom.

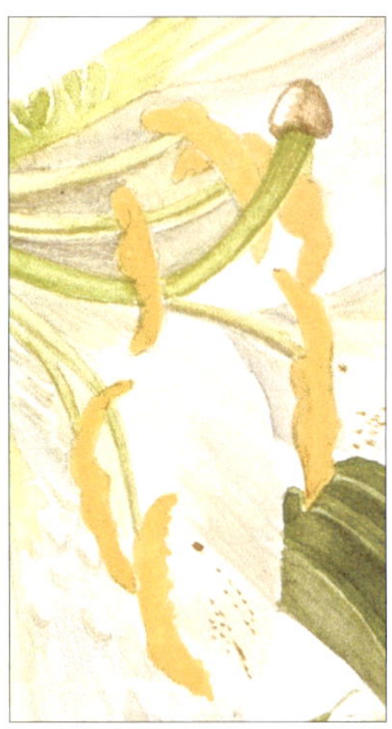

Detail from Stage 2: The stigma was painted with Light Red with a slight touch of French Ultramarine, for an accurate brownish-mauve. Care was taken over the highlights. For the style I used Sap Green shaded with Daler-Rowney Olive. The plump anthers were glazed with Gold Brown; the filaments with palest Daler-Rowney Olive, shaded with Sap Green.

The same colours were used for stamens and stigma as for the middle flower. A glaze of Sap Green with a little Light Red was applied over the two large bottom leaves and the same colours with added Perylene Green were used for the small central leaf.

▷ Final Stage

Concentrating on the leaves I darkened and tidied up the lowest leaf using the same Sap/Perylene Green/Light Red mix. When it was dry I applied a final glaze of Aureolin yellow to lift the colour while still keeping its dark tone, which its lower, far position decreed.

The right-hand leaf was worked up using a mix of Schmincke Olive with a touch of Burnt Sienna to warm it. Cast shadow was a mix of Schmincke Olive with a little Glowing Violet – remember there is purple in every shadow. When dry the veins beneath it were tidied up, using the tip of a size 2 brush. The other two large leaves were completed using Sap Green and Perylene Green, taking care to blend colour to the curve of the veins. Once again Light Red was applied to the mix or as a glaze. This warmed the three forward leaves, making the right-hand leaf cold and glossy by contrast.

Finally all leaf edges were tightened. Odd pencil lines were removed except for one or two places around the petals where the line was re-drawn using a 3H pencil. (This is essential where work is reproduced as white on white.)

▽ Detail from Final Stage: Particular care was taken to show the interesting vein twists in this furled leaf. The cast shadow adds interest and was brushed across wet-on-dry. This meant that the veins beneath needed tidying up a little when the shadow had dried.

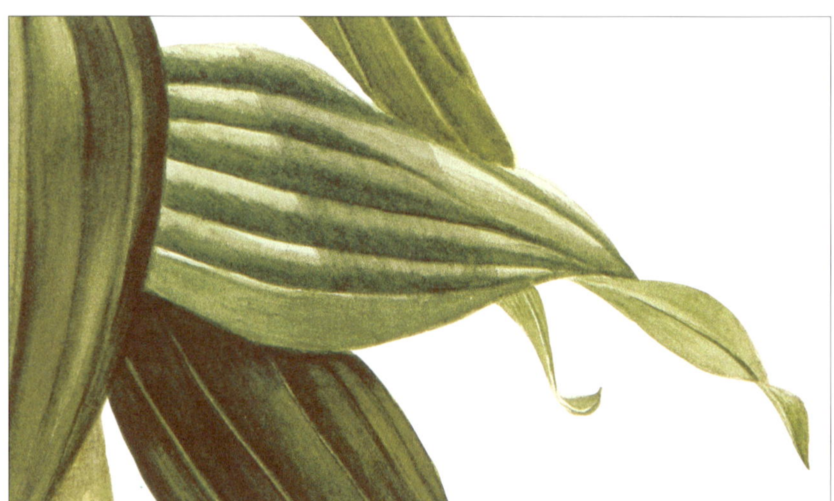

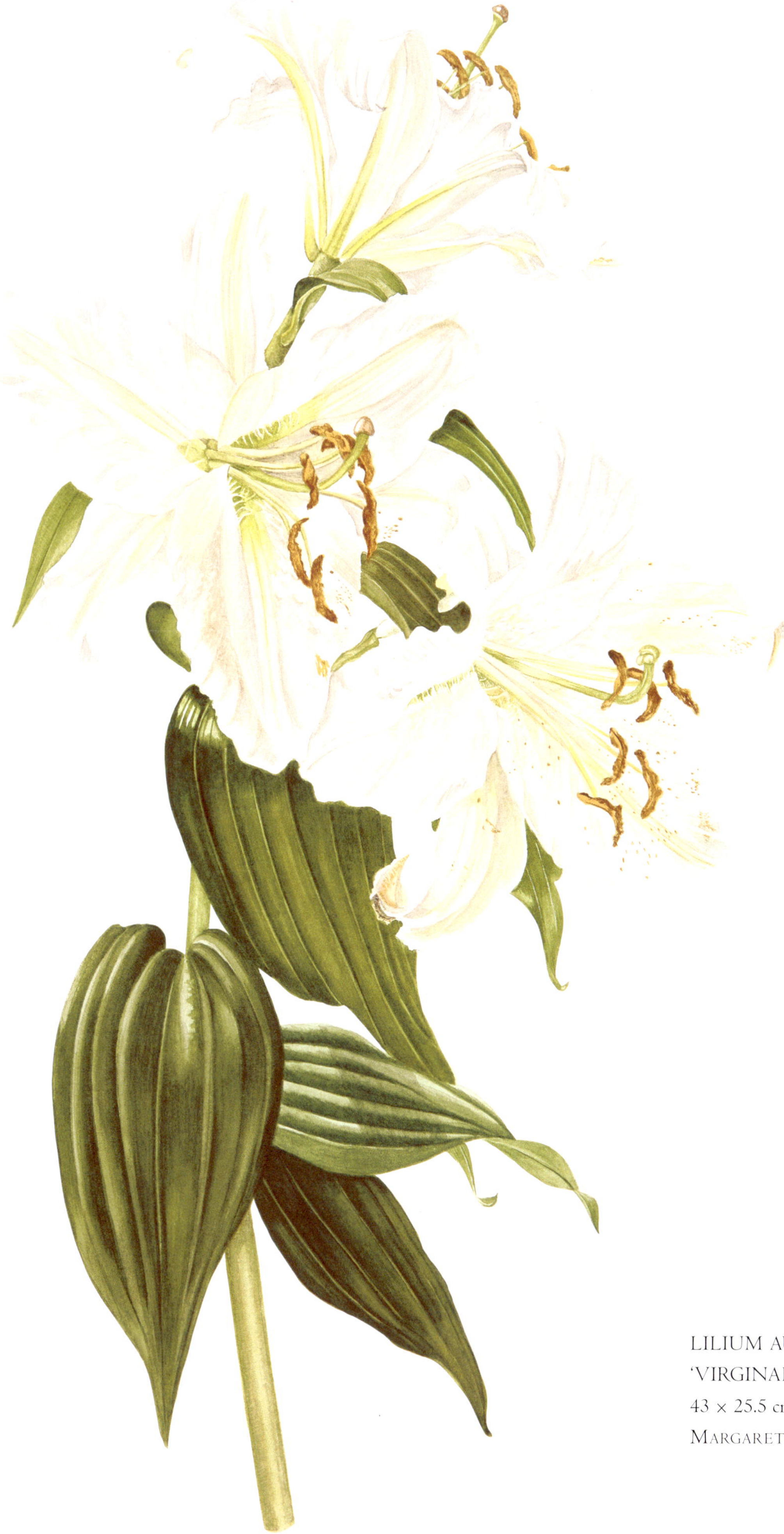

LILIUM AURATUM
'VIRGINALE'
43 × 25.5 cm (17 × 10 in)
MARGARET STEVENS PSBA

PROJECT *Lilium auratum* 'Virginale'

This version, with fewer leaves, enables you to try out what is considered by many a difficult subject. I think there is enough detailed information to guide you through and I hope you will try it as a way of building confidence and increasing observation.

When painting white or very pale flowers it is important to make the most of whatever detail is available to give impact. In the case of these lilies this means paying attention to the stamens.

MIXING GREYS

SBA Member Valerie Wright recommends an exercise that will help you experiment with mixing grey tones. Try working with three primary colours – in this case Aureolin, Cobalt Blue and Permanent Rose. Before you do so, however, you need to fully understand the relationship of one colour to another.

Each primary colour has a complementary, which is a mix of the other two. Therefore red is complemented by green, which is a mix of blue and yellow; blue by orange, a mix of red and yellow; and lastly, yellow by purple, a mix of blue and red. A complementary colour enhances the other when placed next to it, but when the two colours are mixed together in equal amounts they cancel each other out and produce a neutral grey. If you vary the amounts of the two you can produce an endless variety of beautiful tones, both warm (with more red) or cool (with more blue). Practise this using the colours mentioned above, starting with equal amounts of a primary and complementary to produce the neutral tint; then vary the ratio on either side to show the range of greys available.

COLOUR CHART

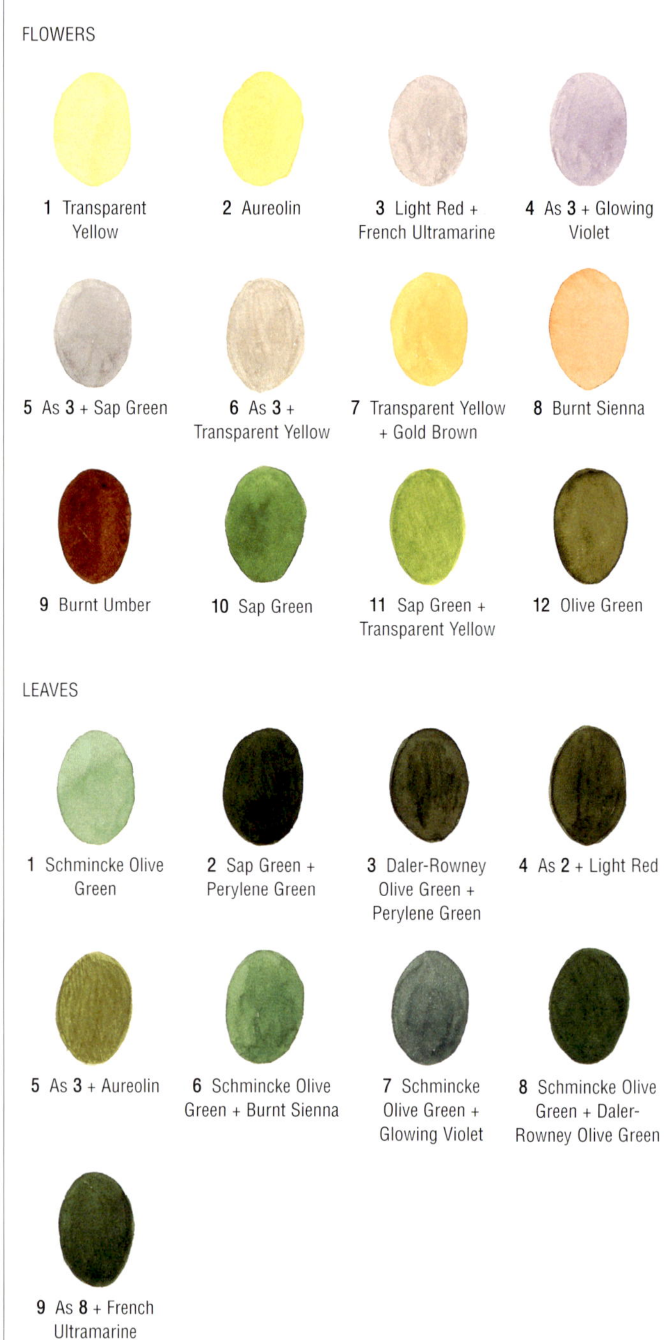

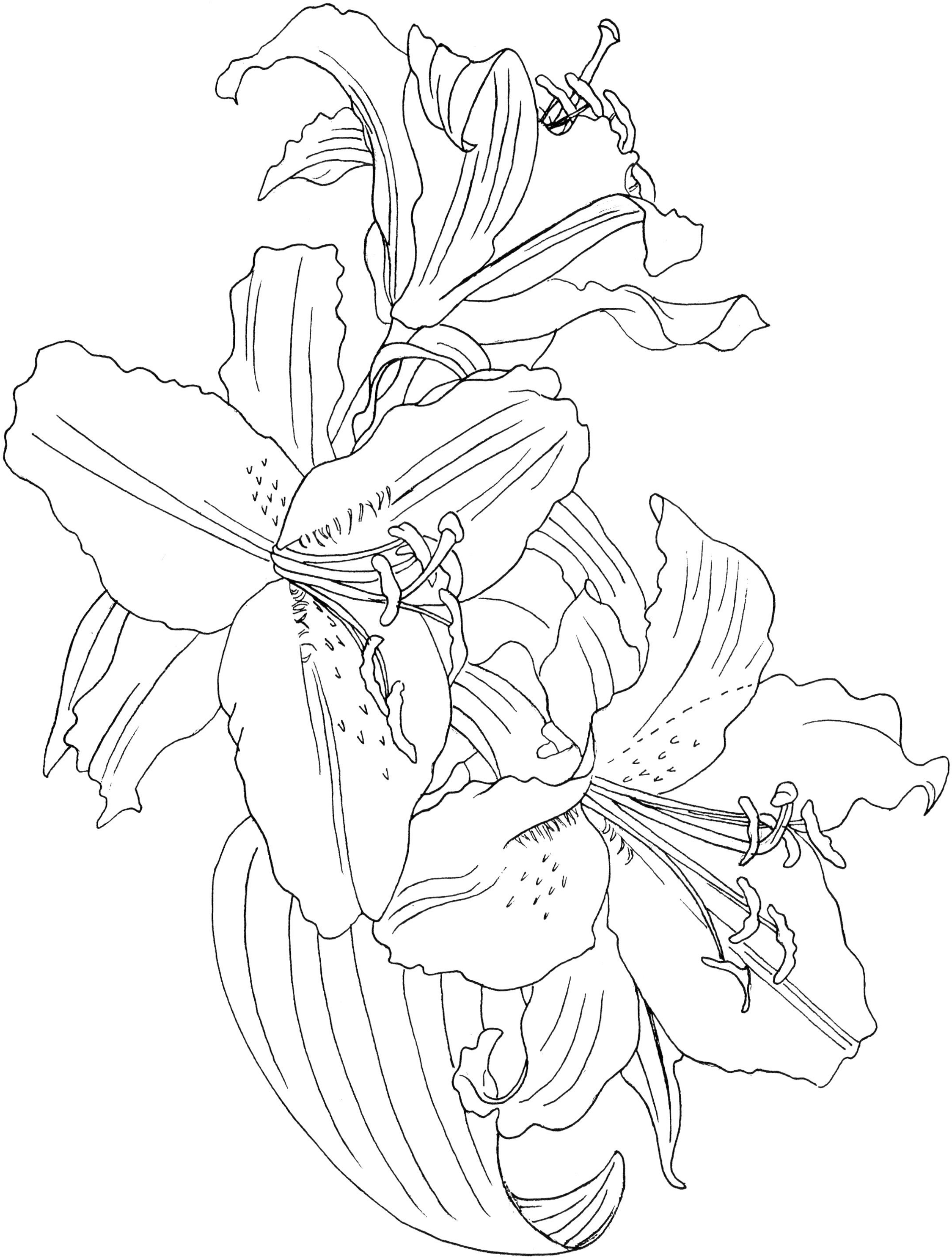

CHAPTER 2

YELLOW

THE BOTANICAL palette contains many yellows, from the body colour that is Naples Yellow, a lead pigment invaluable as an underlying wash for many subtle-hued flowers, including roses and some sweet peas and pansies, to the strong gold of Indian Yellow, thankfully no longer manufactured from cows' urine!

In order to do justice to the variety of wonderful shades of yellow flowers some pigments are particularly valuable. Rowney Aureolin, although expensive, is worth its weight in gold, a pure and transparent colour. Sennelier Yellow Light, also transparent, has a hint of acidity and Sennelier Naples Yellow is one of the best, not as dense or as murky as some, with a beautifully soft true yellow colour. To capture the glow of autumn a useful addition to the palette is Schmincke Translucent Orange; as its name suggests, it is a very effective glazing colour that adds a glow to the underlying colour.

Finding good shadow tones for yellow flowers is almost as challenging as for white ones. If there is too much blue in the grey mix the yellow will take on a greenish hue. On the other hand, too much red results in a muddy brown. I find that a VERY pale mix of Ultramarine and Light Red will do the trick, but remember that often the addition of a pigment such as Winsor Violet is sufficient to give all the shadow tone that is needed. Daler-Rowney produce a colour called Shadow, which is proving popular and effective. The following step-by-steps of *Rhododendron luteum* and Sunflower use each of these last two mentioned, so you can see how well they work and try them out for yourself by having a go at the Sunflower project. This is a bold subject, but not too intimidating even for the more inexperienced botanical painter.

▷ WATER LILY
40 × 31 cm
(15¾ × 12¼in)
ELISABETH DOWLE
SBA

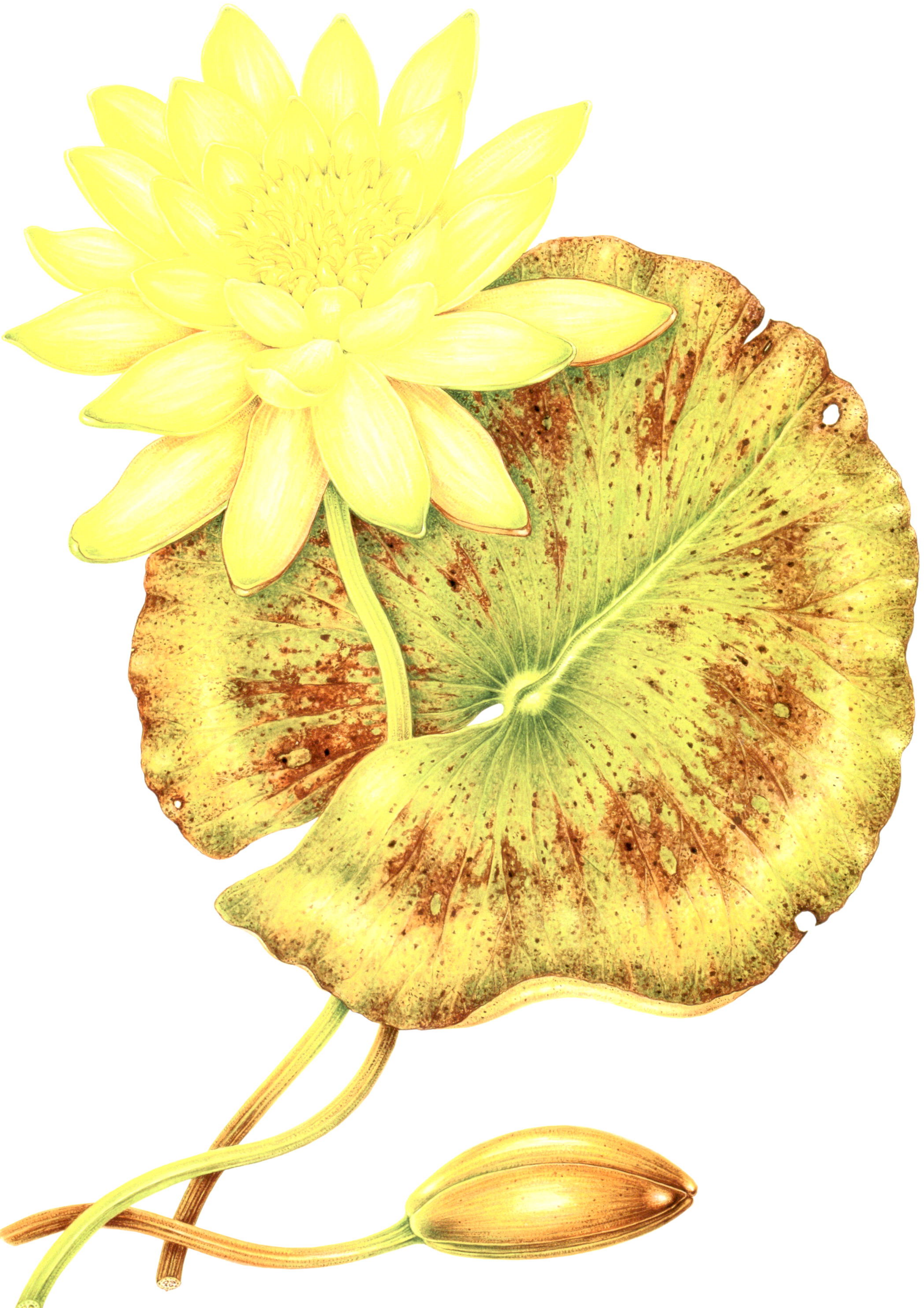

RHODODENDRON

Rhododendron luteum

Kay Rees-Davies SBA

A native of the Caucasus Mountains and Turkey, this highly scented shrub was introduced into Europe in 1792 and has since become a popular parent due to its hardiness and fragrance. Unfortunately, Kay could only paint the very attractive plant and you will have to imagine the perfume.

PAINTS

WINSOR & NEWTON
Indian Yellow
Transparent Yellow
Indanthrene Blue
Caput Mortuum Violet
Neutral Tint
Vandyke Brown

DALER-ROWNEY
Sap Green
Shadow

SCHMINCKE
Aureolin Modern
May Green
Midnight Green
Translucent Brown

BRUSHES

WINSOR & NEWTON
Series 7 sizes 1, 2, 3 and 5

DALER-ROWNEY

AF62 *Flat Shader*

SURFACE

PRINTMAKERS PAPER
HP 300 gsm (140 lb)

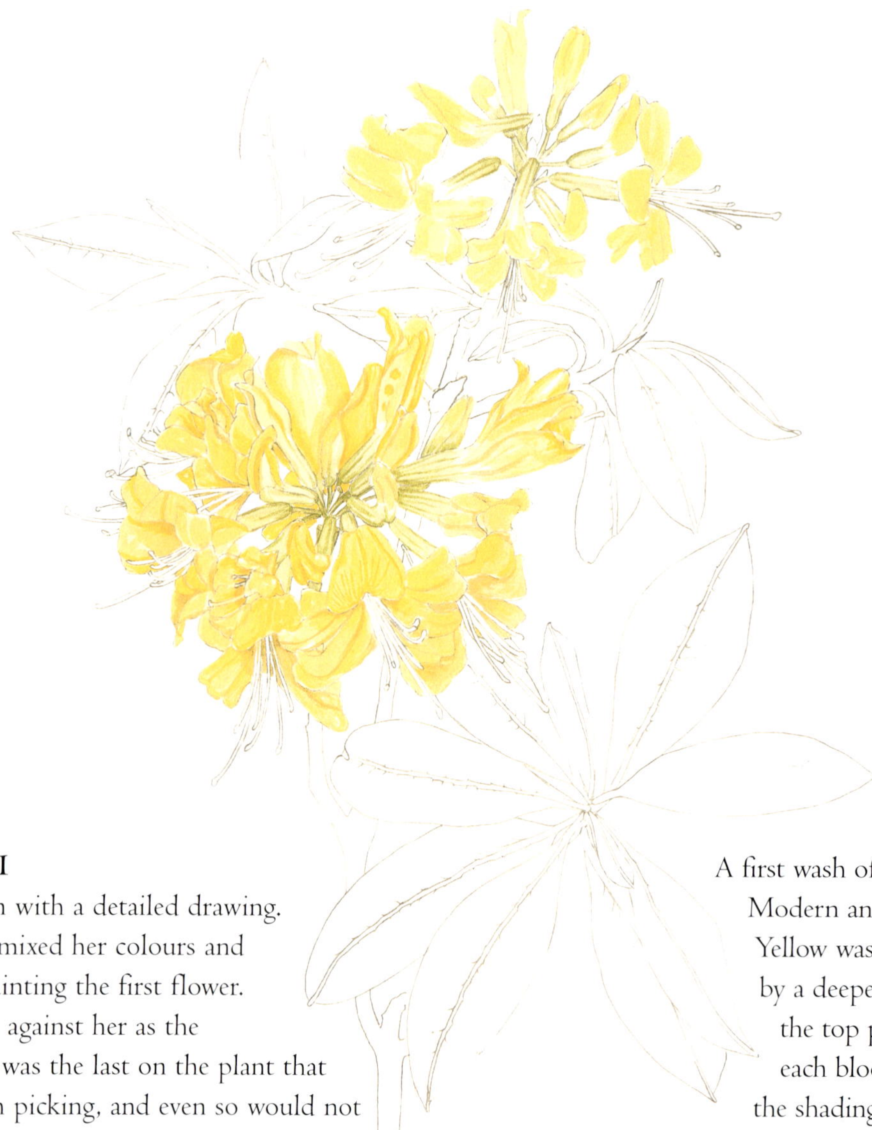

△ **Stage 1**
Kay began with a detailed drawing. She then mixed her colours and started painting the first flower. Time was against her as the specimen was the last on the plant that was worth picking, and even so would not last for long. It was one of those times when it was essential to concentrate on the flowers and not worry too much about the longer-lasting foliage. She wisely chose to start with the most obvious flowers facing her.

A first wash of Aureolin Modern and Indian Yellow was followed by a deeper tone to the top petal of each bloom. For the shading Kay used a mix of Aureolin Modern and Shadow, applied very gently. It is best to start off with light shading and deepen it as the tone of the subject becomes more established. Too dark too early usually gives disastrous results.

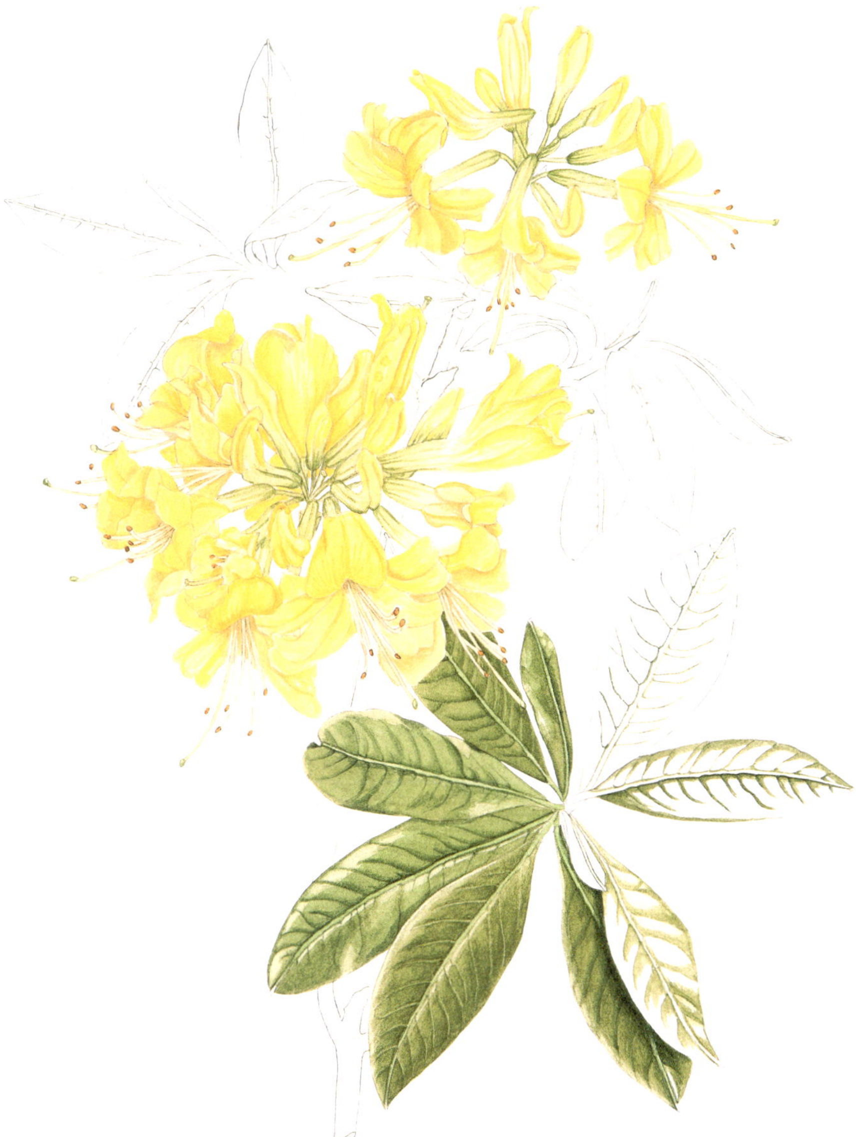

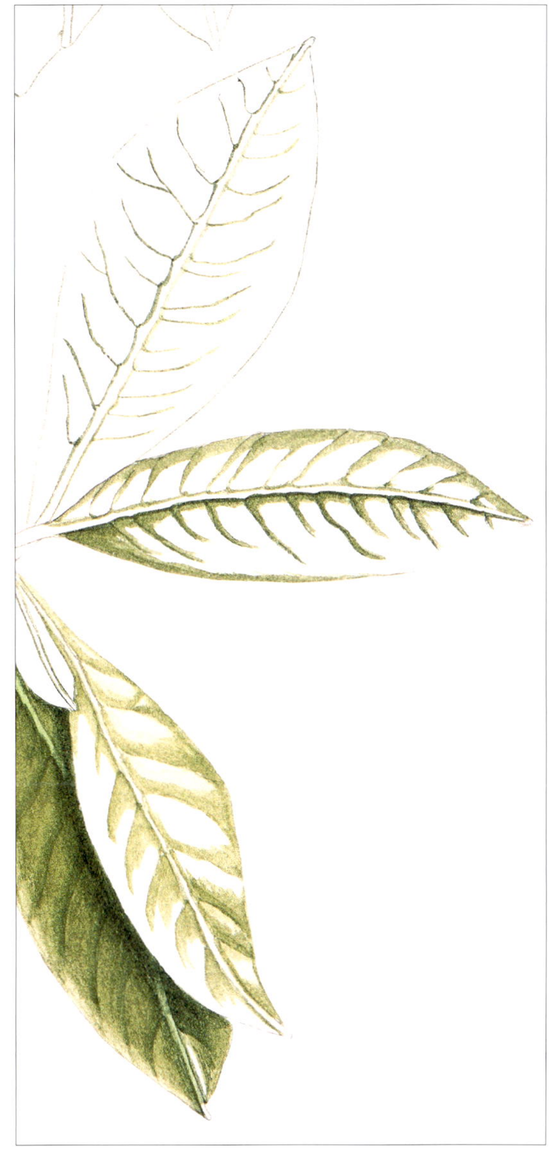

△ **Stage 2**
The green used for tubes and stems was a mix of May Green and Midnight Green. This was applied before the yellow was put on the blooms at the back of the cluster. Some of the stamens were painted with a pale green wash for the filaments, while Translucent Brown was applied to the anthers.

The second cluster was painted in the same way. The overall colour was deepened on both clusters with the same mix of Aureolin Modern and Indian Yellow, and shading was also intensified, while clarity was retained.

The paints used for the main colour on the leaves were Indanthrene Blue with Transparent Yellow and small touches of May Green and Aureolin Modern. Midnight Green was used for the veins and shadows.

The centre and secondary veins were drawn in pencil. They were then painted with a size 1 brush, using Midnight Green for the darker side of the leaf and the main blue and yellow mix for its lighter side.

Any pencil lines still visible were removed. Next the shadows were added using the same colours. Using an Aquafine 62 Flat Shader Kay softened the edges of the shadows. Leaving any shiny areas white, she then used a fairly dilute mix of the main colour and washed over the whole leaf. Any necessary deepening of colour could be done with a dry brush when the first wash was dry.

△ **Detail from Stage 2:** The stages in the process of building up a leaf from its basic structure are clearly shown here.

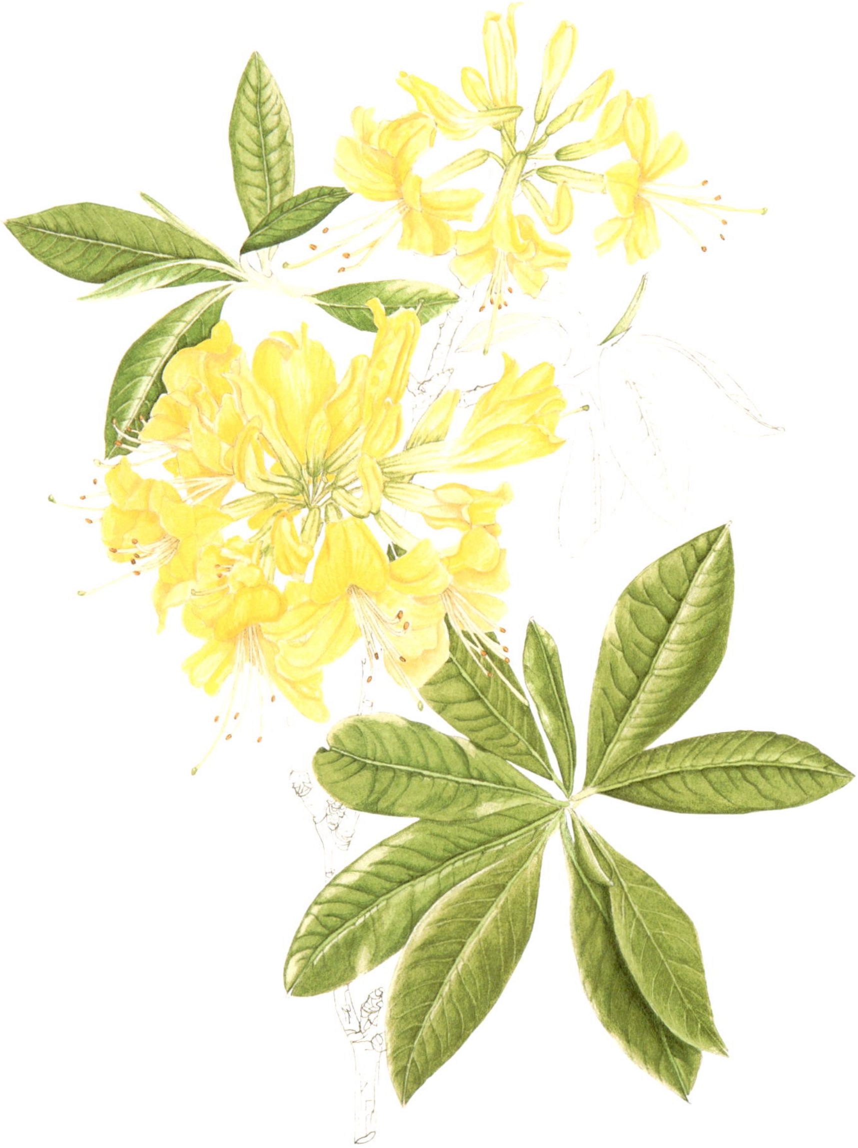

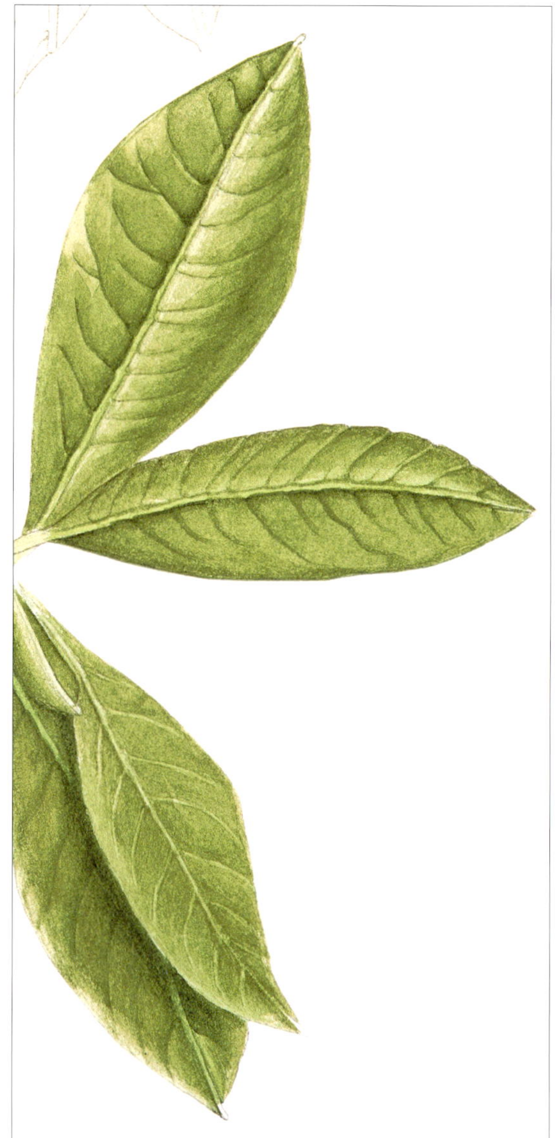

△ **Stage 3**
Further work was done on the leaves using the Flat Shader to merge the colour into the shine. When dry Kay dragged a large damp brush over the leaf, including the shine, to smooth out any tiny streaks that remained. Any parts of a leaf that came behind stamens she painted in very carefully using a size 1 brush. Next she drew all the markings in detail on the branch and twigs, deciding to finish the leaves later.

▷ **Final Stage**
Unfinished leaves were completed. Reddish markings were painted onto them with a dry brush using Caput Mortuum Violet with a touch of Translucent Brown.

The branch and twigs were painted over the pencil markings with a size 1 brush using Vandyke Brown. When this was completely dry Kay applied a dilute wash of Caput Mortuum Violet, Neutral Tint and Vandyke Brown to the whole branch. A deeper tone was used to darken the edges away from the light and areas of cast shadows. New stems were painted with a mix of May Green and Midnight Green.

Kay checked all the stamens and filaments, especially those crossing over leaves, stems or petals. She inspected all the edges through a magnifying glass and any slight errors were corrected. The colour of the flowers needed to be deepened, so a glaze of Aureolin Modern and Indian Yellow was applied.

Detail from Stage 3: Kay's method produced a totally realistic and accurate leaf, guaranteed to set off the painted flowers to perfection.

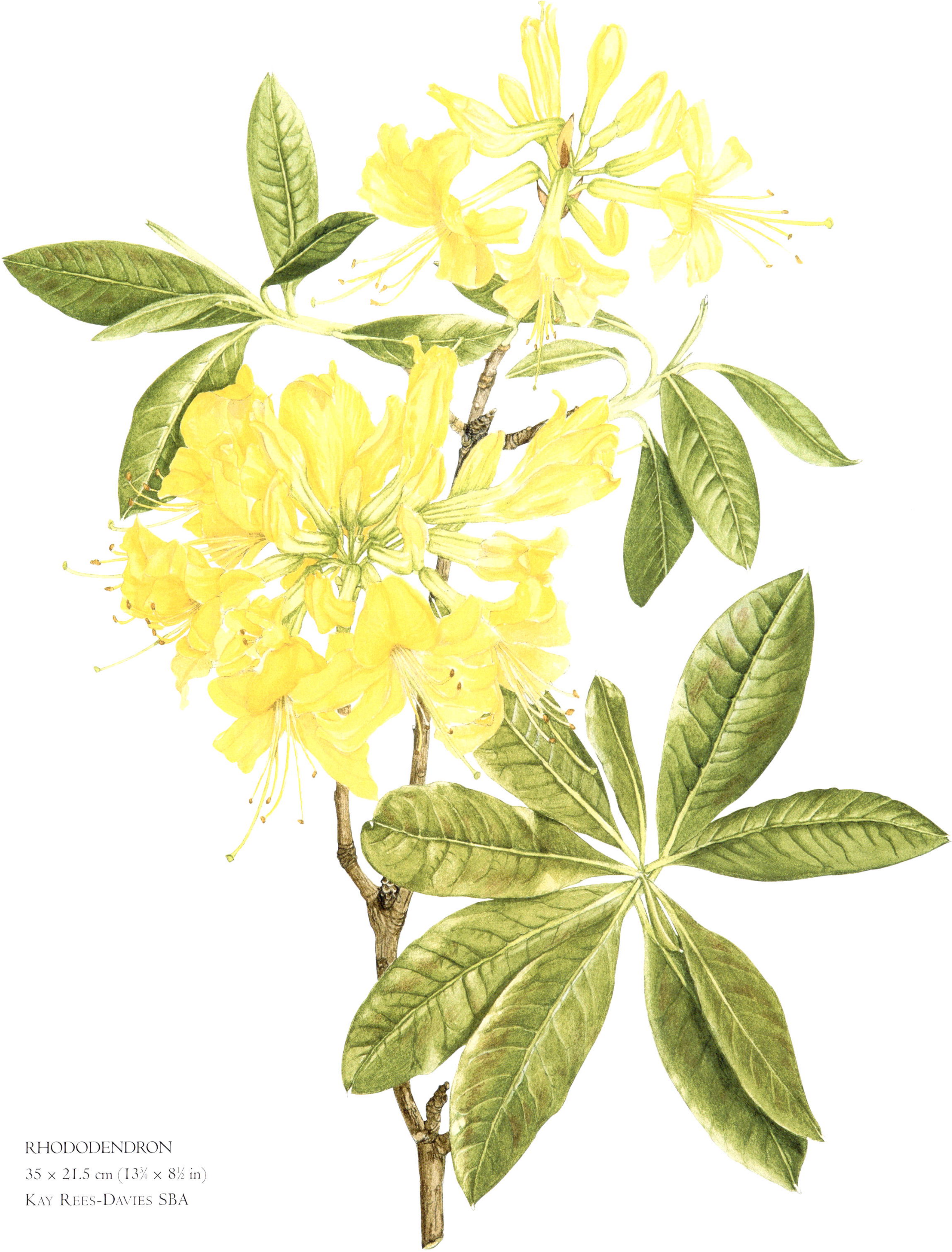

RHODODENDRON
35 × 21.5 cm (13¾ × 8½ in)
Kay Rees-Davies SBA

SUNFLOWER

Helianthus annuus

Paul Fennell SBA

Sunflowers are always popular as they evoke memories of holidays in the French countryside and their image brings warmth to a room at any time of year. Paul chose this bold subject because it allows the artist to exert freedom in the reproduction of curving petals and leaves, where the colours flow yet only a limited palette is required.

PAINTS

WINSOR & NEWTON
New Gamboge
Cadmium Scarlet
Indanthrene Blue
Winsor Violet
Cadmium Yellow

BRUSHES

ROSEMARY AND CO.
Kolinsky sable sizes 4 and 8

SURFACE

BOCKINGFORD
Not paper 300 gsm (140 lb)

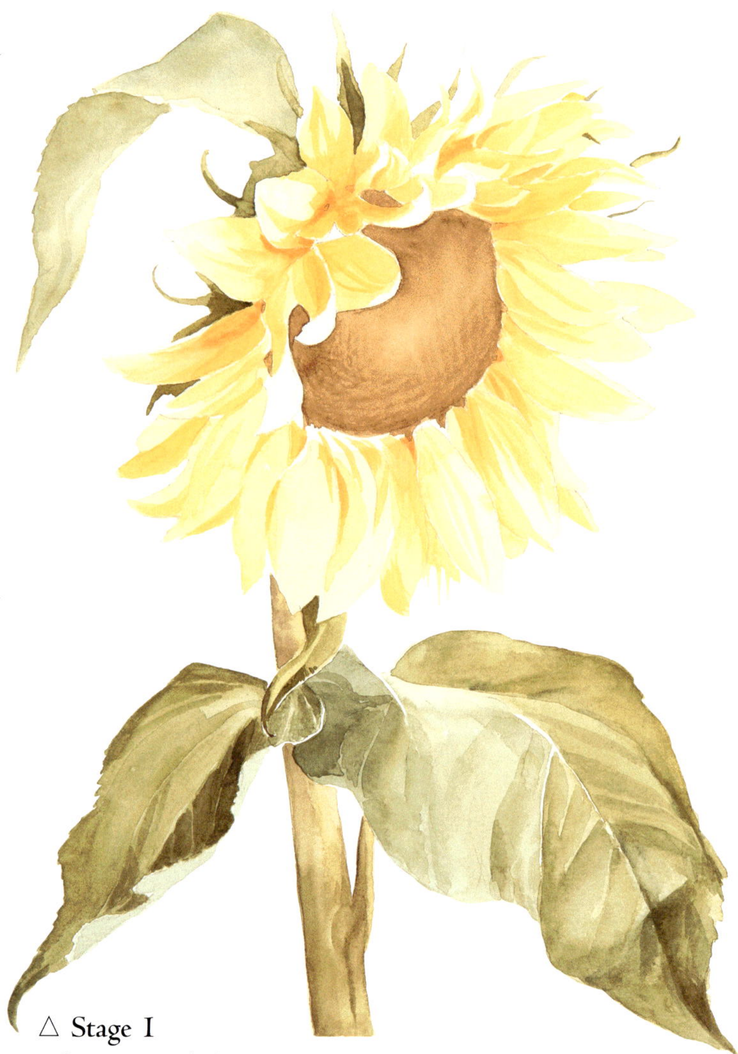

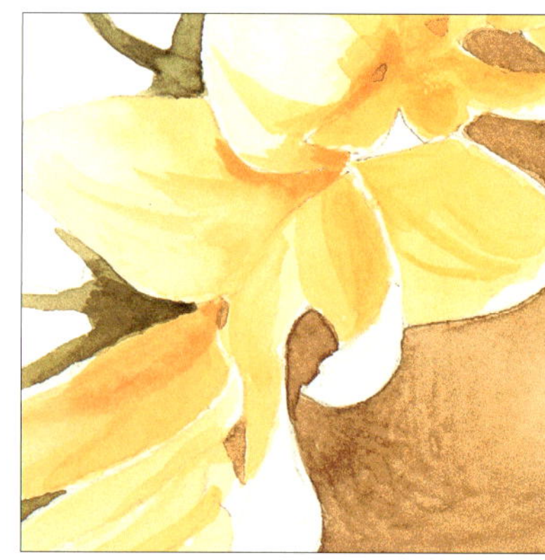

Detail from Stage 1:
The first colours and hints of tone were washed in varying strengths onto the petals.

△ **Stage 1**
After minimal drawing Paul applied thin washes of New Gamboge to the petals. When diluted, this colour takes on a cool hue and is ideal for the brilliant yellow petals of the sunflower. A very small amount of Cadmium Scarlet was added to indicate deeper shadows. A varying mixture of Indanthrene Blue and New Gamboge was used to wash over the leaves. The same mixture, but with slightly more Winsor Violet added, was used for the stem.

The centre of the flower, the capitulum, was painted with a mixture of New Gamboge and Winsor Violet (biased towards yellow) to indicate the colour beneath the surface.

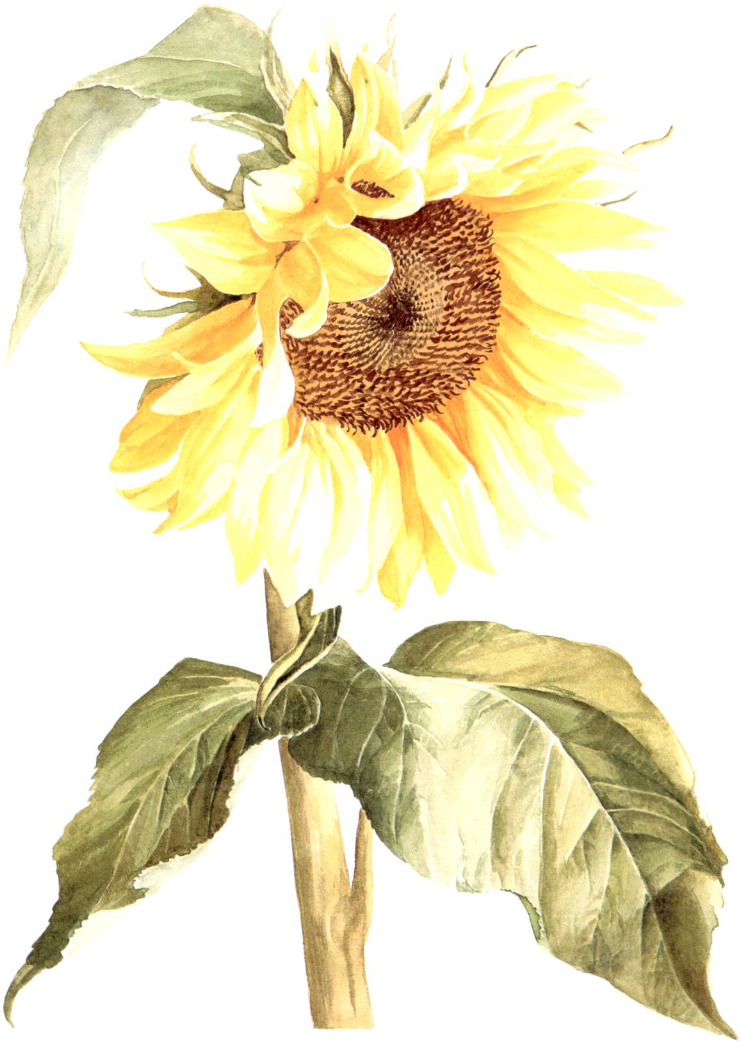

△ **Stage 2**

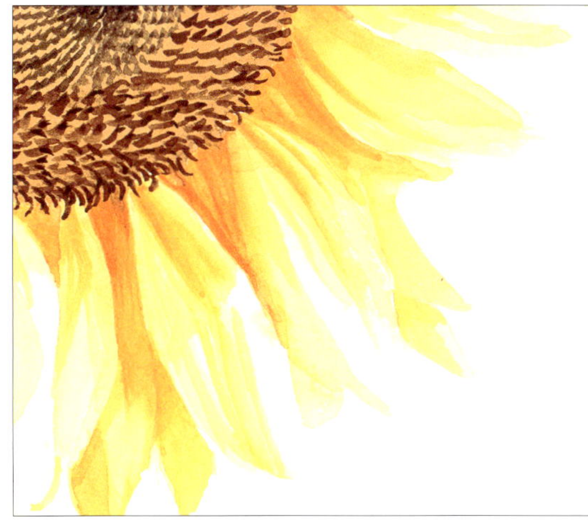

Detail from Stage 2:
Areas of white paper were left to allow for the highest, or lightest, tones on the petals.

Next Paul shaded the petals with either a mixture of New Gamboge and Cadmium Yellow, which is a warm orangey hue, or New Gamboge and Indanthrene Blue with Winsor Violet, giving a cooler greenish hue. The darker shades of yellow here were not the same at all and Paul needed to observe carefully whether the shadow colour was either warm or cool. It was important to differentiate one from the other so that the texture and translucency of the petals could be achieved. Areas where the light fell brightest were left as bare paper for now. Some might be darkened at a later stage but at this time Paul was comfortable knowing he had reserved these lights. Too often students put colour everywhere only to find they do not have anything left for their brightest tones later. By not holding back some whites they block their options and so cannot always achieve sufficient contrast and depth.

Indanthrene Blue and New Gamboge were mixed for the foliage, adding more blue and a touch of Winsor Violet for cooler shadow tones, and more yellow to suggest translucent parts. The tones were strengthened, taking care to leave light areas to suggest the veins.

Lastly, Winsor Violet was mixed with the basic green colour to create a very dark grey. The colour was used quite diluted to indicate the spiralling pattern of the inner capitulum. This would be darkened at a later stage.

For the outer part of the capitulum Winsor Violet was mixed with New Gamboge to create a warm brown. This was used to indicate the dense area of hundreds of tiny florets. This, too, would be darkened later.

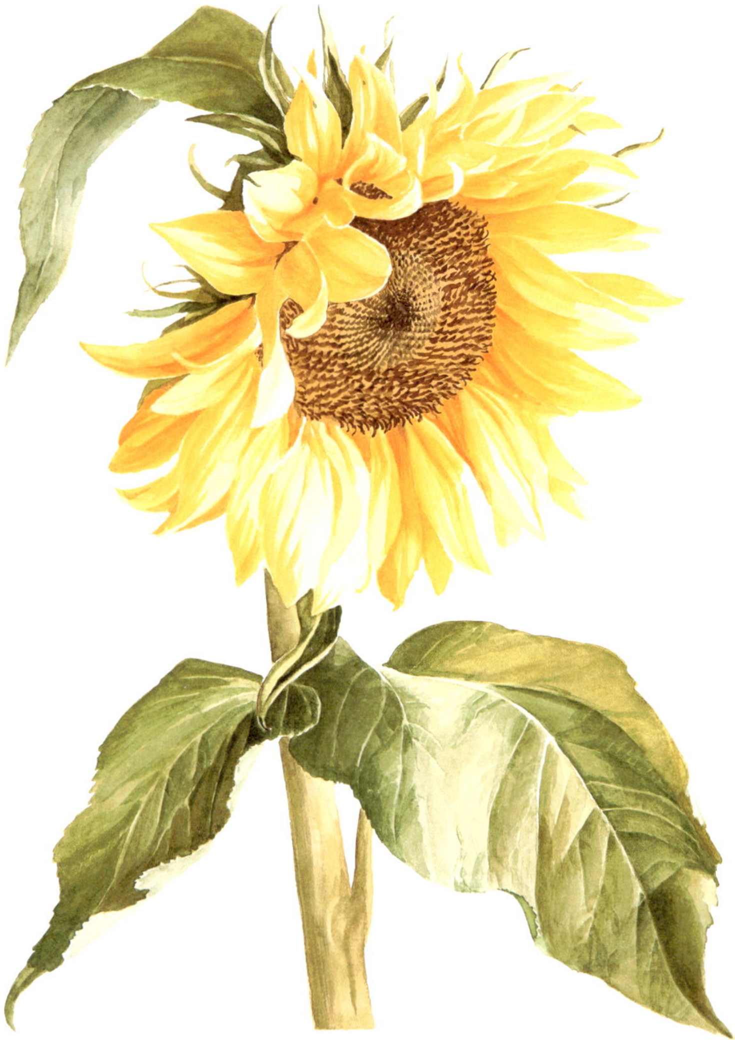

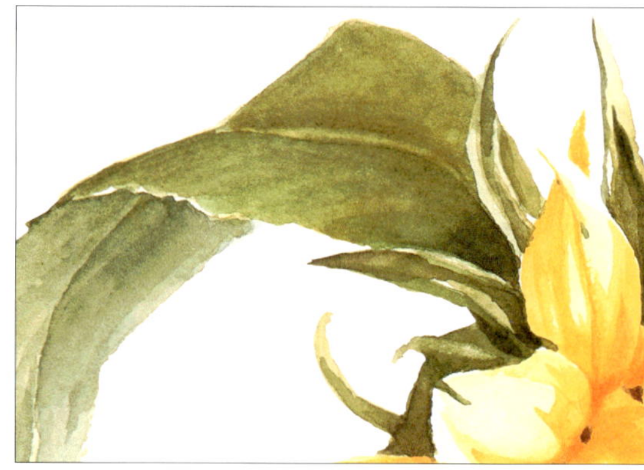

Detail from Stage 3:
More dark tones were applied to the top leaves, the perfect foil for the brilliant petals.

△ **Stage 3**

Now Paul concentrated mainly on the foliage, darkening and adding the detail of veins and folds in the floppy leaves. The colour mixes were the same, only varying according to the warmth or coolness of the tone. Shadows on leaves and petals were deepened. Where light reflected from other petals, inside the flower, the yellow was warmer, mixed from New Gamboge and Cadmium Scarlet. Where it was deeper still, a small amount of Winsor Violet was added. Further out, where the yellow was cooler, only New Gamboge was used, with Winsor Violet for a greater depth of tone if needed. The edges of the petals were refined.

Most of the work at this stage had gone into creating the texture that defined the leaves. Their slightly ragged appearance made a great foil for the neat, round flower. Sometimes a little Cadmium Scarlet was added to the green mix for a warmer tone; very small amounts of colour were sufficient to make a difference. The strongest mixes of Indanthrene Blue and New Gamboge had less water, and Winsor Violet was added to create the deepest tone.

Observing which side of the veins the minute shadows fell, Paul deftly applied tiny washes of the green mix, not disturbing the previous layers. These pale layered washes achieved subtle gradations of tone to define the leaf undulations. The edges were tidied up and even deeper tones were carefully added.

▷ **Final Stage**

Paul deepened the centre of the flower and created the texture that is so much a part of the sunflower; the perfect spirals of florets are a prelude for the large nutrient-rich seeds.

▷ SUNFLOWER
38 × 28 cm
(15 × 11 in)
PAUL FENNELL SBA

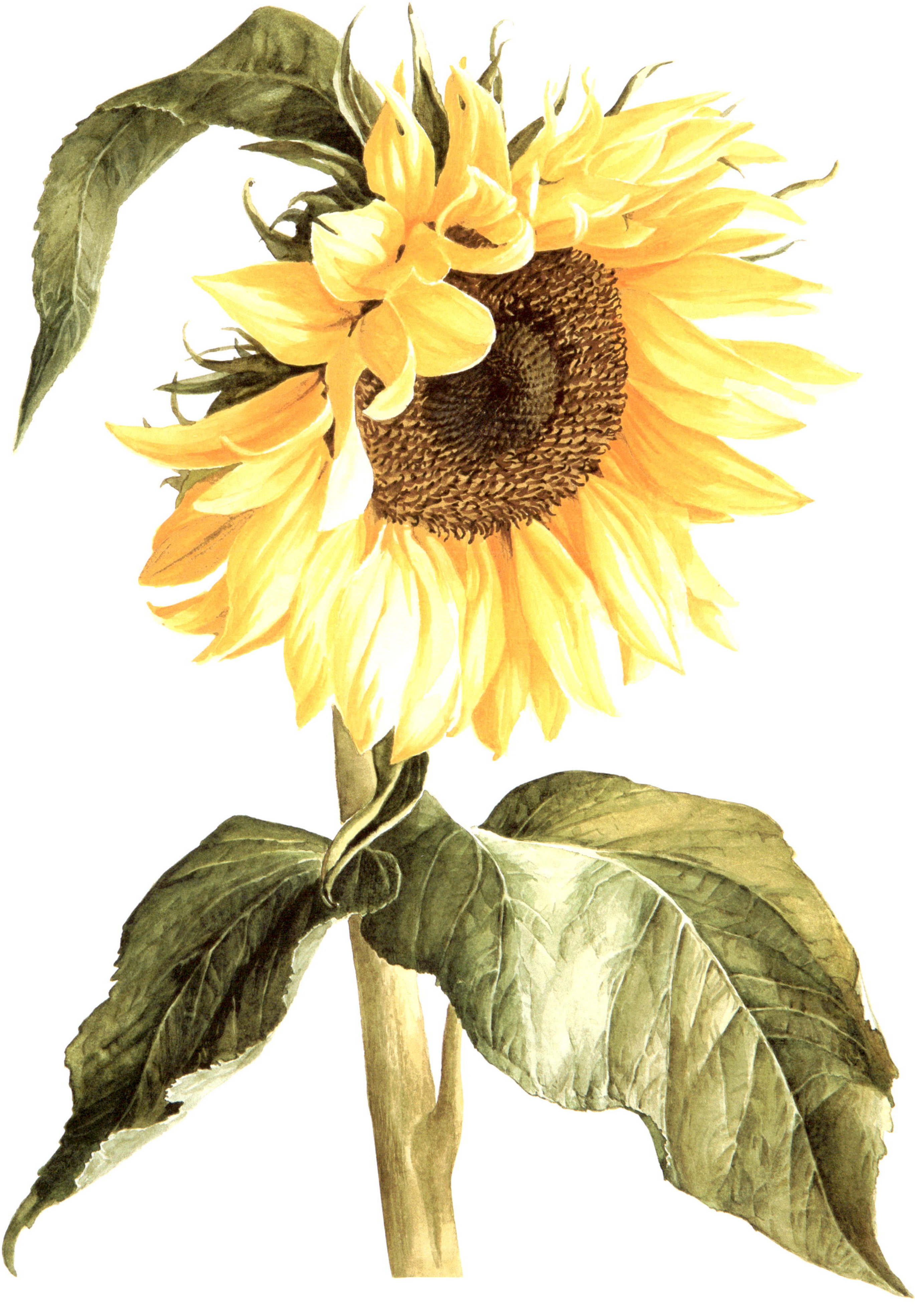

Project *Helianthus annuus*

This sunflower should appeal to anyone who wants to try their hand at quite a straightforward flower. It is a very direct 'in your face' specimen and it would also be good practice for working with a limited palette.

Just do not be deceived by its apparent simplicity, particularly when working on the centre, where care and a little extra time taken will pay dividends.

Colour Chart

FLOWERS

1 New Gamboge
2 Cadmium Scarlet
3 New Gamboge + Cadmium Scarlet
4 As 3 + Winsor Violet
5 New Gamboge + a little Winsor Violet
6 New Gamboge + more Winsor Violet
7 As 5 + Indanthrene Blue

LEAVES AND STEMS

1 New Gamboge + Indanthrene Blue
2 As 1 + more New Gamboge
3 As 2 + a little Winsor Violet

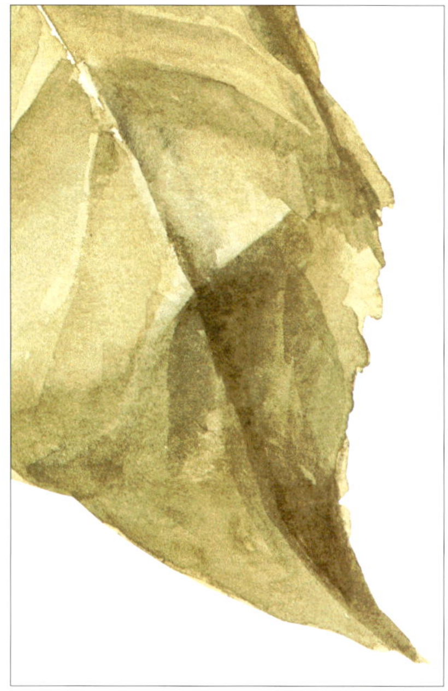

Detail from Stage 1: A green mix of Indanthrene Blue and New Gamboge was applied and the first details were added.

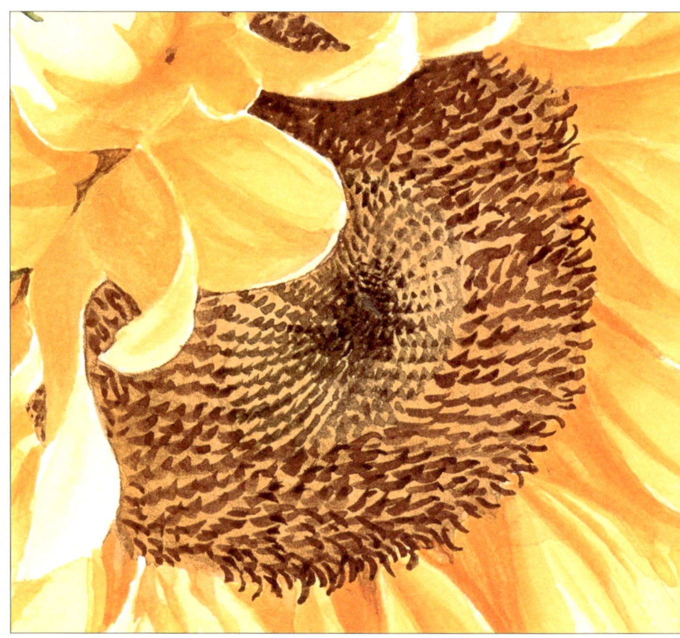

Detail from Stage 2:
Detailed florets were painted in the centre of the flower, working to the spiral pattern. This is not something that can be done quickly or haphazardly, as it is an important and characteristic feature of the flower's construction.

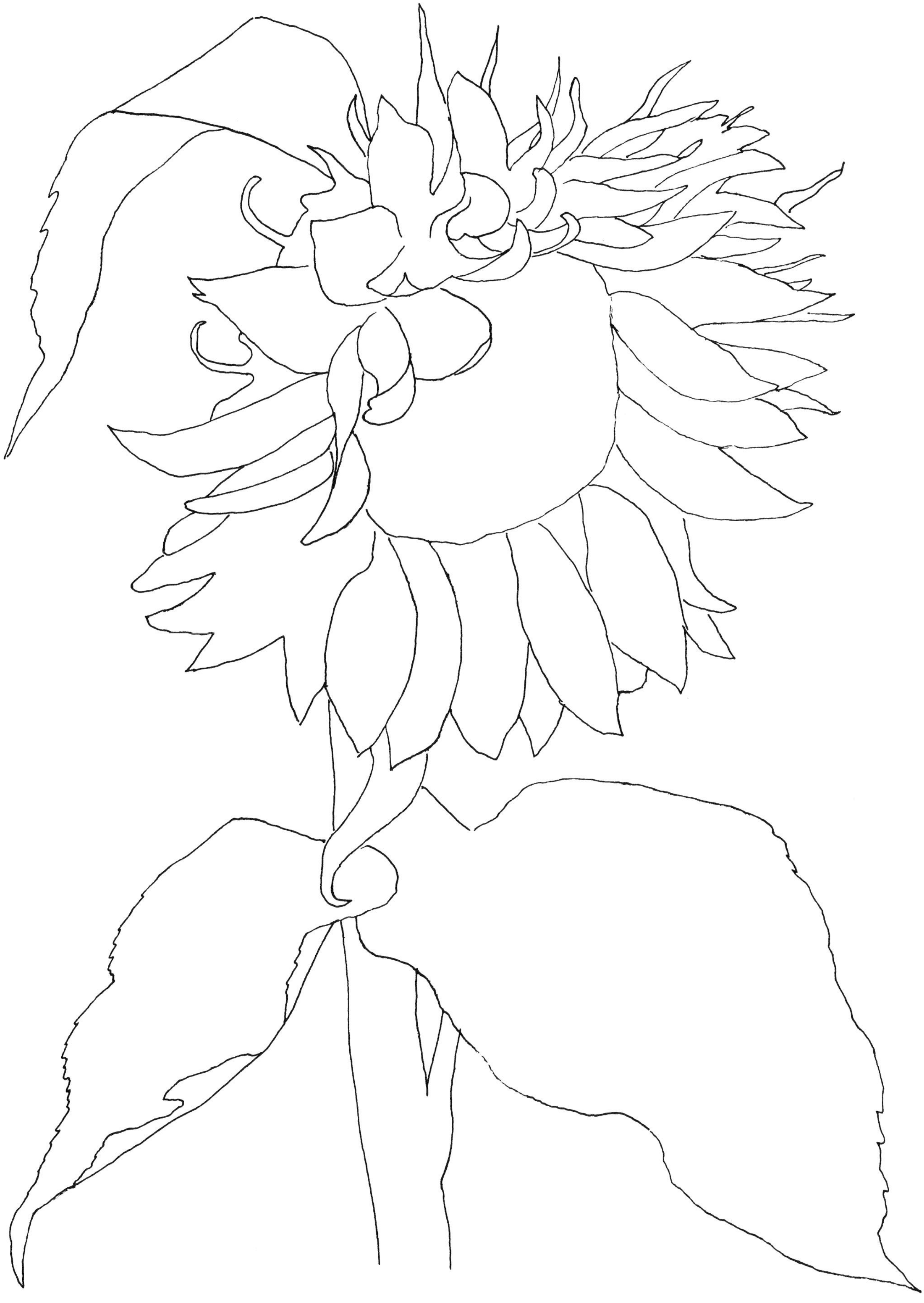

DAY LILY

Hemerocallis

Ann Swan SBA

Translated from the Greek, this flower is aptly named 'day beauty' since each bloom lives only for one day. Botanical artists get used to working quite quickly before their subject fades and in this case it is even more necessary. It is the first of the examples in the book of work in coloured pencil and should prove helpful to the many converts to this medium.

COLOUR CHART

Faber-Castell Polychromos

White 101	Ivory 103
Cream 102	Cadmium Yellow 107
Light Ochre 185	Light Yellow Ochre 183
Warm Grey II 271	Warm Grey III 272
Warm Grey IV 273	Caput Mortuum Violet 263
Grey Green 172	Chrome Green Opaque 174
Earth Green Yellowish 168	Apple Green 170
Soft Black 099	

Prismacolor/ Karisma

Goldenrod 1034	Limepeel 1005

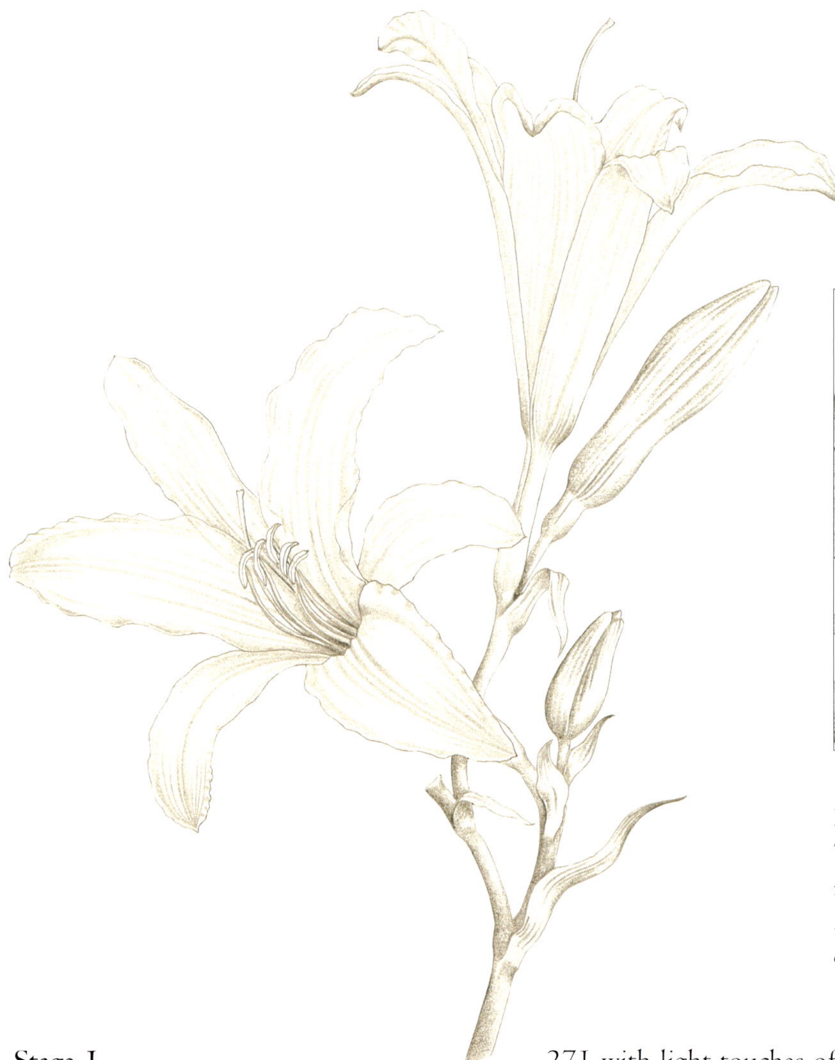

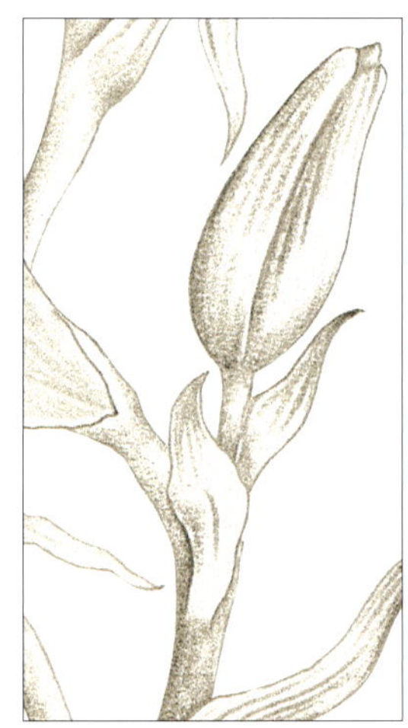

Detail of Stage I: The strongest tone required Warm Grey IV 273 for depth of shading on stems and buds.

△ Stage I
Ann drew the outline with a single fine pencil line on HP Fabriano Classico 300 gsm (140 lb) paper. She would have preferred to use a yellow the colour of the flower, but this would not have shown up in reproduction. She then shaded the flower using Warm Grey II 271 with light touches of Grey Green 172 on the tips of the opening flower and at the base in the centre of the main flower.

The darker sides of the stamens were indicated with Warm Grey III 272.

The stem, leaves and buds, being a darker green, were shaded with Warm Grey IV 273.

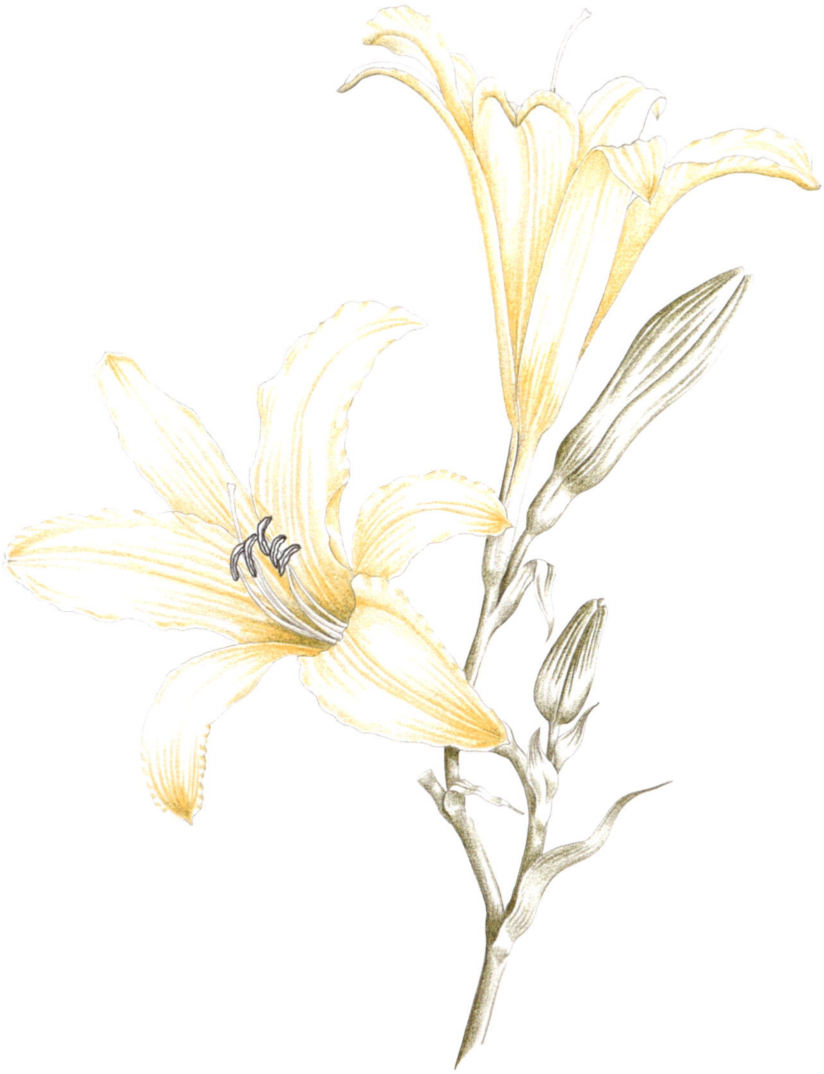

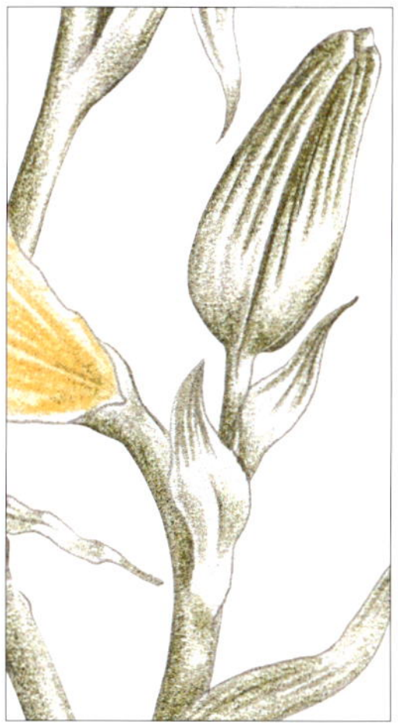

Detail from Stage 2: Chrome Green Opaque 174 absorbed the grey tones pencilled on leaves, buds and stems.

△ Stage 2

Overlaying the shading on the flowers with Light Yellow Ochre 183, Ann applied slightly more pressure in the darker areas and less in the lighter areas. The grey would all be absorbed by the Light Yellow Ochre.

Then she overlaid the Warm Grey IV 273 on the buds, leaves and stems with Chrome Green Opaque 174, again varying the pressure according to the density of tone.

The dorsifixed stamens were outlined in Soft Black 099. These will be the dramatic focal point of the finished flower.

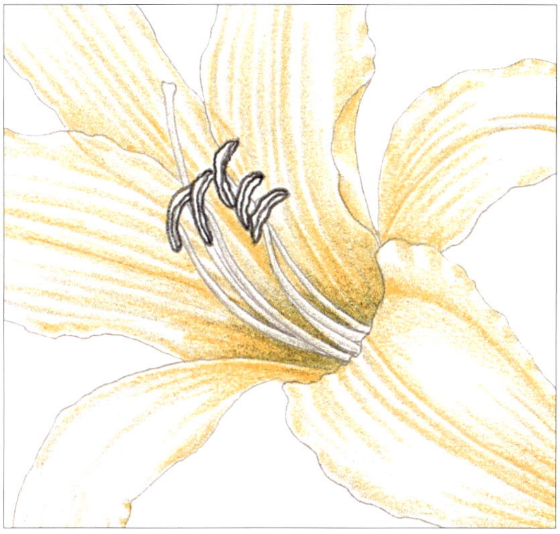

Detail from Stage 2: Light Yellow Ochre 183 now absorbed the grey tone on the petals. The stamens were outlined in Soft Black 099

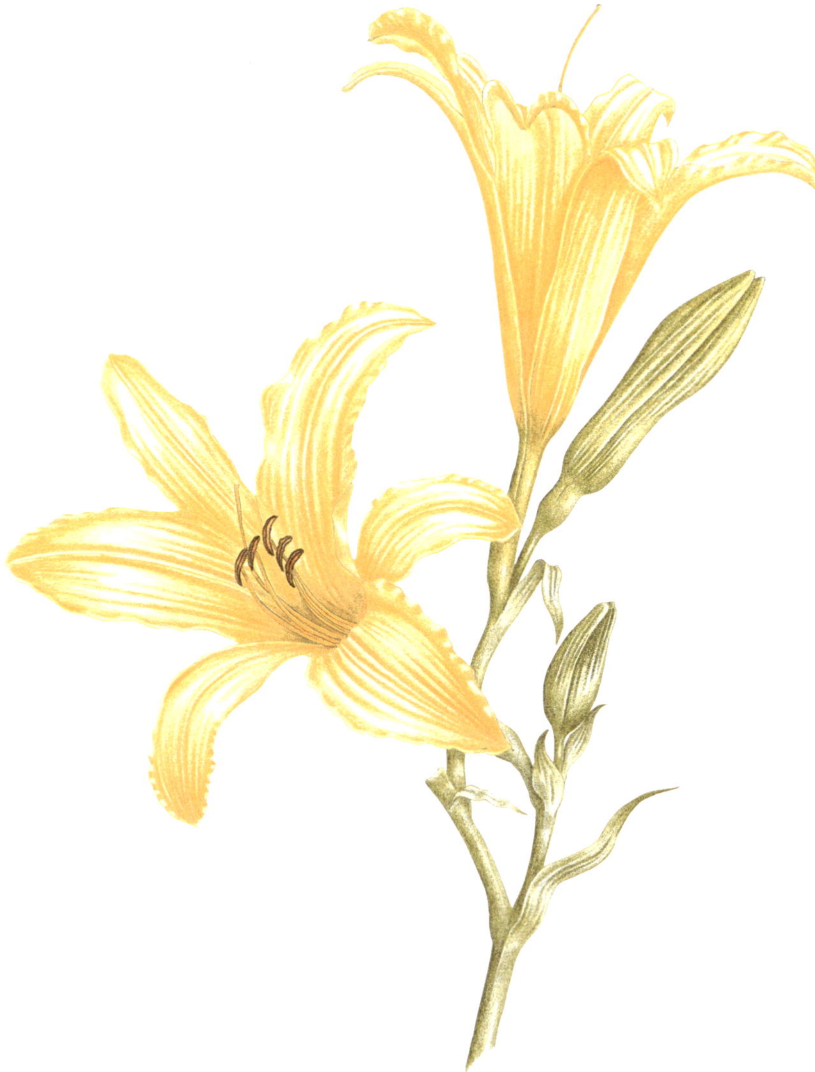

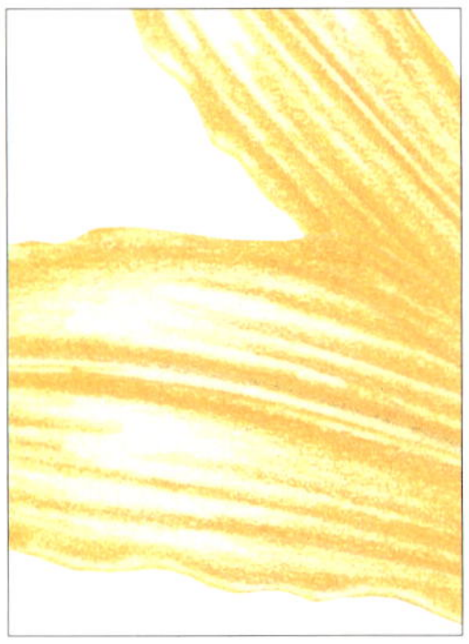

Detail from Stage 3: It was important to leave the white highlights on the petals when the colour was strengthened.

△ Stage 3

Ann continued working into the shaded areas of the flower with Light Ochre 185, again pressing more heavily into the darker areas, and then working into the unshaded areas, leaving the very lightest areas white.

The same procedure was followed for the leaves, stem and buds, using Earth Green Yellowish 168.

Caput Mortuum Violet 263 was used to overlay the black on the stamens. Ann then used Prismacolor/Karisma Goldenrod 1034 to fill in between the lines.

The flowers were overlaid with Cadmium Yellow 107, more heavily in darker areas and lightly in brighter areas, then burnished by pressing heavily over the lighter areas using Cream 102 and Ivory 103.

If the work still looked grainy at this stage it could be intensified and burnished with a blender pencil.

The leaves, stems and buds were overlaid with Apple Green 170, then a light touch of Light Ochre 185 was added onto the buds to yellow them slightly. This was followed by Prismacolor/Karisma Limepeel 1005. If necessary Ann would burnish the work again at this point, using a blender pencil.

▷ Final Stage

Ann checked the work over carefully to see if any areas needed extra depth, using additional Grey Green 172 on the flowers and Chrome Green Opaque 174 before being satisfied that the work was complete. Clarity and skilled shading combined to create a perfect flower.

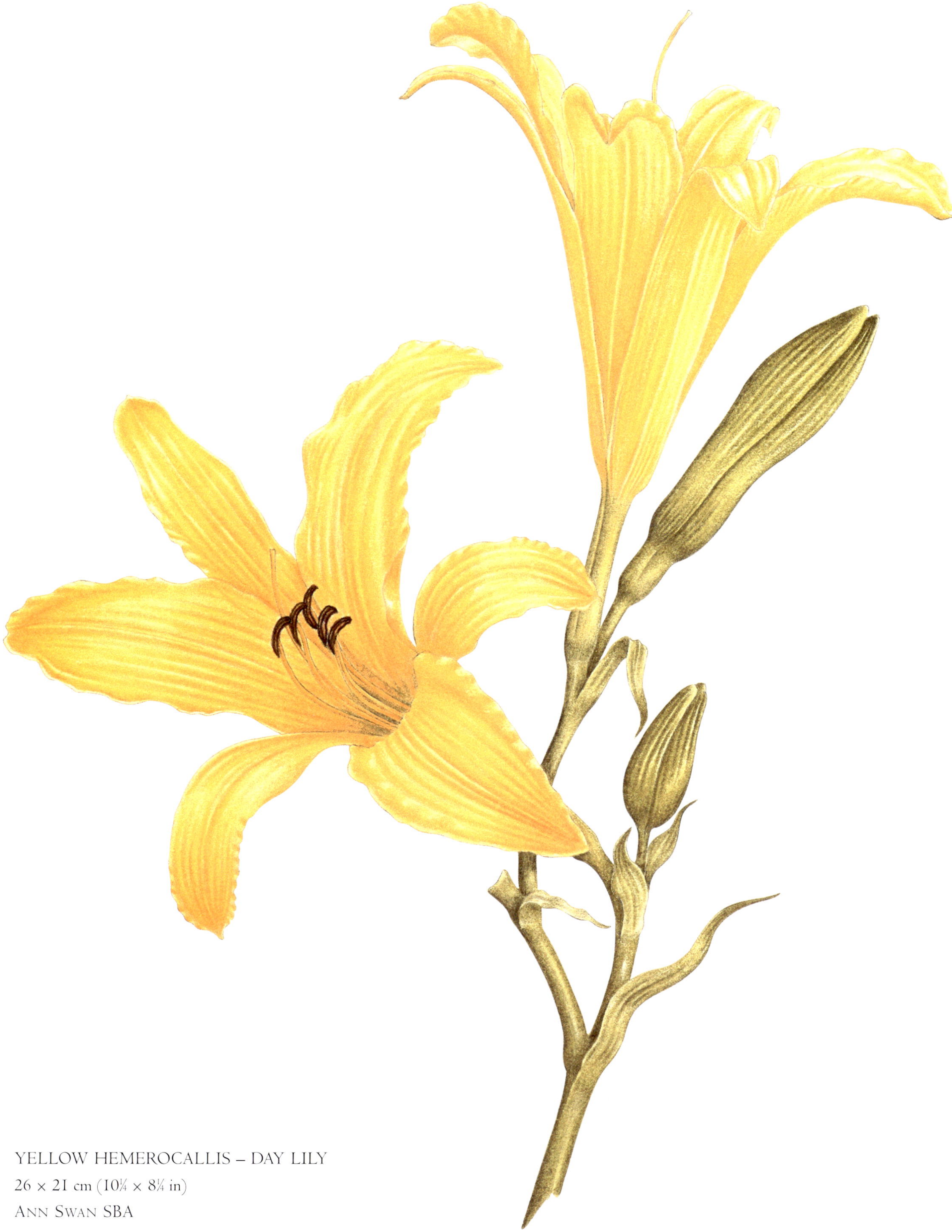

YELLOW HEMEROCALLIS – DAY LILY
26 × 21 cm (10¼ × 8¼ in)
ANN SWAN SBA

CHAPTER 3

GREEN

THE GREEN palette is vitally important to the botanical painter as it provides the harmonious and often calming link that pulls a picture together. However beautiful the blooms they invariably depend on their foliage to prevent a gaudy mishmash of colour. This is often aided by colour transference when a hint of the flower colour shows in the stems or leaves. A good example of this can be seen in the *Papaver orientalis* on page 89.

It often seems as if the student's interest wanes once the flowers are painted and it cannot be said too often how the same attention to detail, in colour and form, needs to be maintained throughout the work. From a botanical illustrator's point of view the leaves may hold the key to the identification of the plant. Perhaps one variety has hairs on the stem and leaves whereas another is smooth, or maybe the underside of the leaves show staining, as is commonly seen in some African violets or cyclamen. The latter may also have very different colouring on their elaborately marked leaves, sometimes a silvery-olive and sometimes a drab dark green, either of which you can be sure act as a perfect foil for the colourful flowers standing proudly above them (see page 83).

Whether you choose to mix your own greens or use those prepared by the manufacturers, with other pigments added as necessary, it will still make life a lot easier if you prepare a colour chart, which will always act as a point of reference and can be added to whenever you try out a new mix in response to unfamiliar foliage. It does not matter if you mix your own or use manufacturers' colours – there is no 'right' thing to do and it is a matter of personal choice. Usually you will modify tube colour by adding a small amount of another pigment.

▷ COELOGYNE PANDURATA
47 × 37 cm
(18½ × 14½ in)
SUE WICKISON SBA

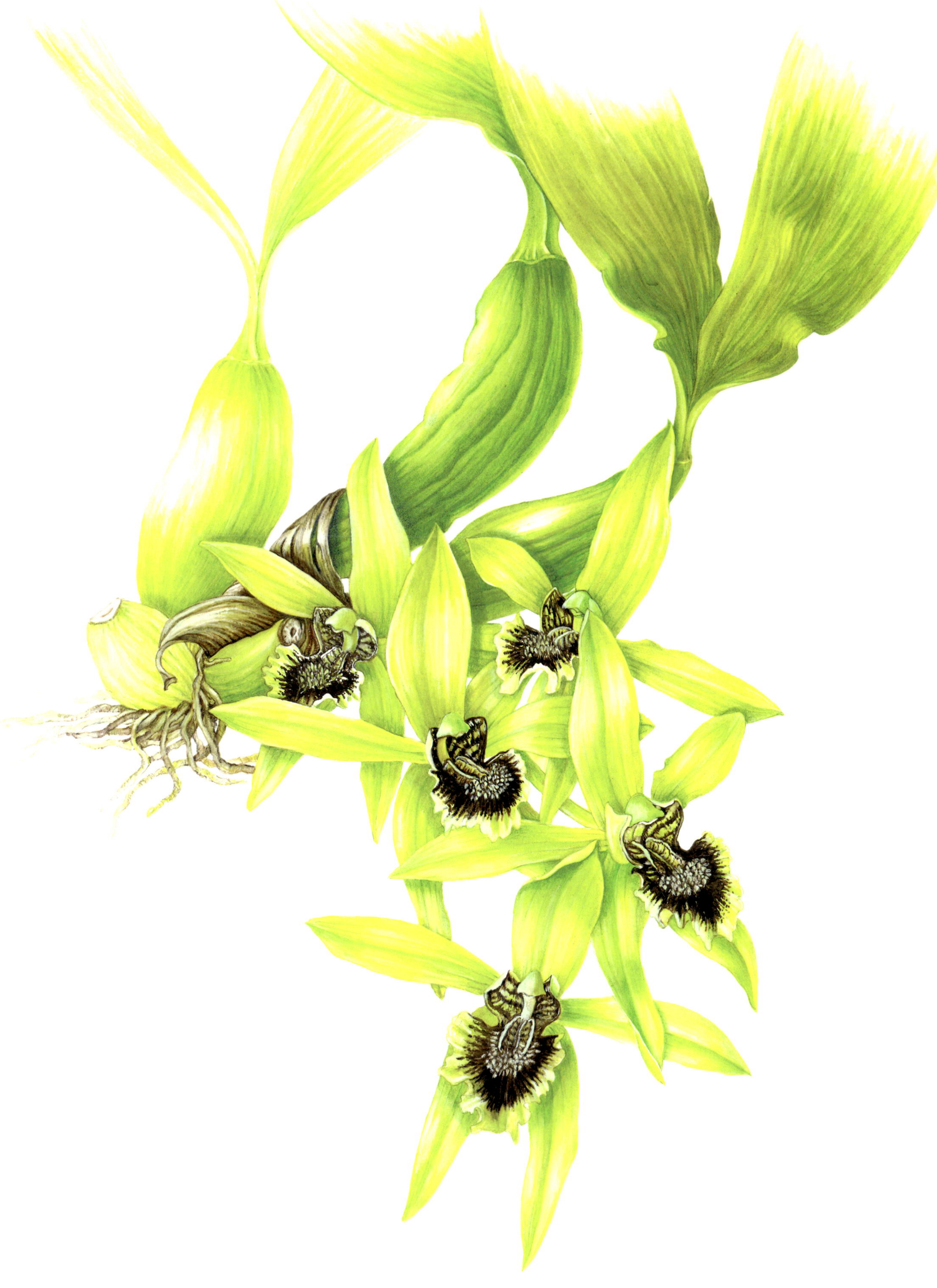

PLANTAIN LILY

Hosta

Janet Wood SBA

The combination of sculptural shapes, varied leaf textures and colours that range from Chartreuse to holly green, with some so glaucous that they are almost a true blue, ensure these plants are an asset in the summer garden. Their delightful symmetry and long-lasting quality make them an ideal subject for both artist and gardener.

PAINTS

WINSOR & NEWTON
Naples Yellow
Indanthrene Blue
New Gamboge
Payne's Grey
Winsor Lemon
Prussian Blue
Burnt Sienna
Cobalt Blue
Yellow Ochre
Neutral Tint

BRUSHES

DA VINCI
Maestro sizes 2 and 4

SURFACE

FABRIANO
Artistico HP paper 300 gsm (140 lb)

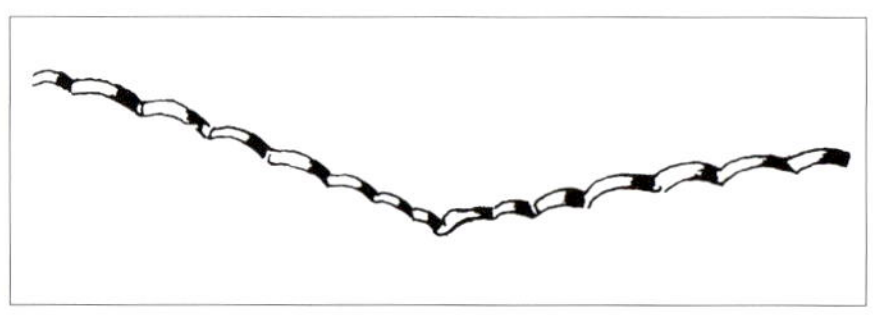

Cross-section of venation, giving leaf texture to be reproduced by shading.

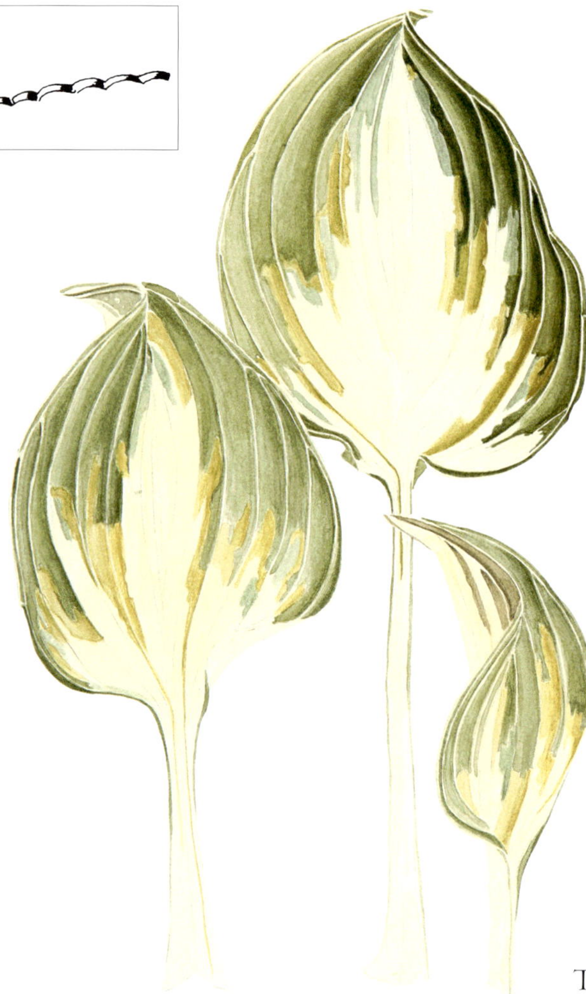

△ **Stage 1**
Janet drew the leaves first on tracing paper in order to carefully map out the paired veins. The cross-section detail (above) shows this coupled with the undulating character of the leaf surface.

The tracing was transferred, with the aid of a light box, onto watercolour paper and a thin wash of Naples Yellow was applied.

The leaves consisted mainly of three shades of green on a cream background. Janet mixed these and tested them on scraps of Fabriano paper before checking the colours against the leaves. The outer leaf edge was cream, then the outer part was widely and irregularly patterned in a dark green. This green was made with Indanthrene Blue and New Gamboge.

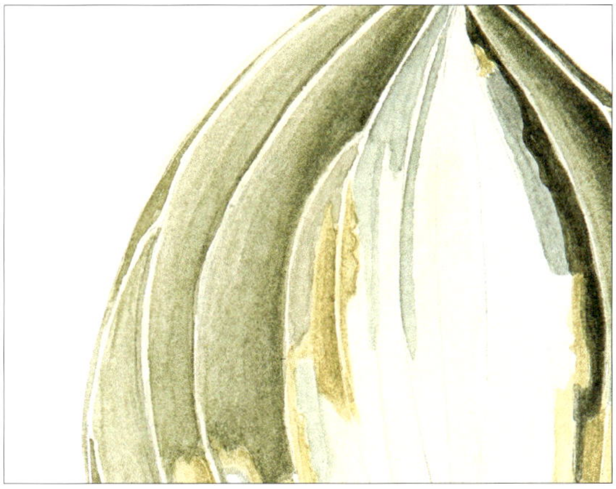

Detail from Stage 1:
First thin washes of the basic colours were applied to all the leaves.

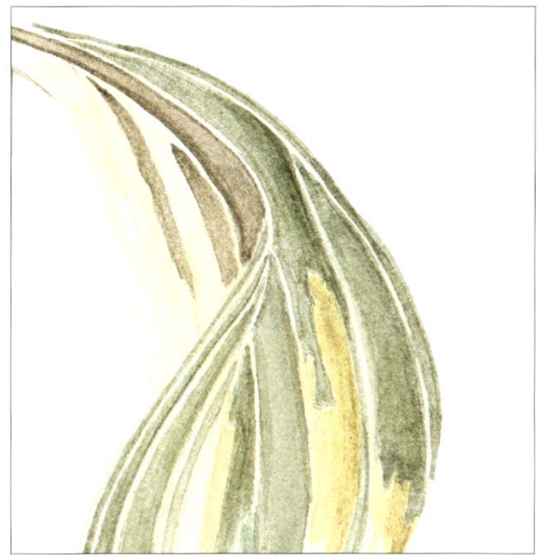

Detail from Stage 1:
The reverse side of the leaves required a slightly different mix of Cobalt Blue and Yellow Ochre.

A wash was put on carefully, following the gaps left between the veins and taking care to copy the pattern of the variegation. The veins were left untouched as these are essential in the appearance and form of the leaf. Janet also ensured that any leaf edge that was up against another leaf was left cream. It was time, too, to change the water in order to keep the integrity of the colours.

The second green was made of Payne's Grey and Winsor Lemon. A thin wash of this was put on, keeping to the pattern on each leaf; then another change of water.

The third green was made from Prussian Blue and Burnt Sienna and a thin wash was added again following the leaf pattern; then a third change of water.

Where the small section of the reverse of two leaves was visible another green was made using a mix of Cobalt Blue and Yellow Ochre.

To show the leaf form – curving between each vein – the tone needed to go from light to dark between one vein and the next. To do this Janet added a second wash of the darker green. She left a light area of the first wash untouched as this was to be the lightest tone, then added another wash of the other two greens, always ensuring the variegation remained true. (The cross-section diagram on page 40 relates to this.)

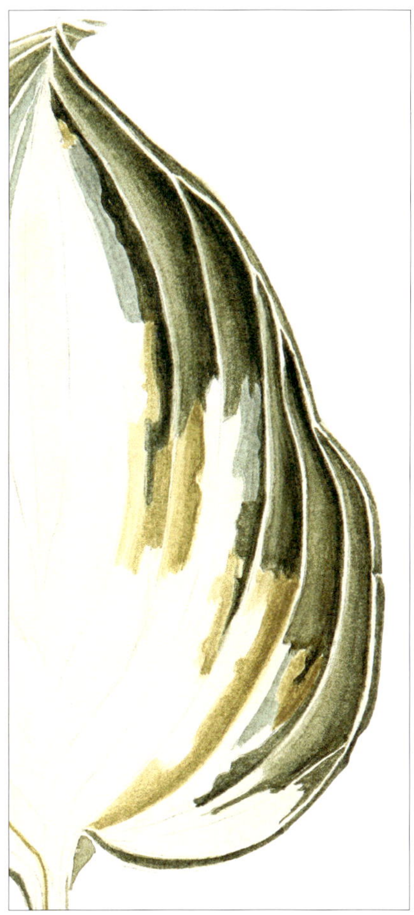

Detail from Stage 1:
It was important to keep the variegated pattern as washes of stronger colour were built up.

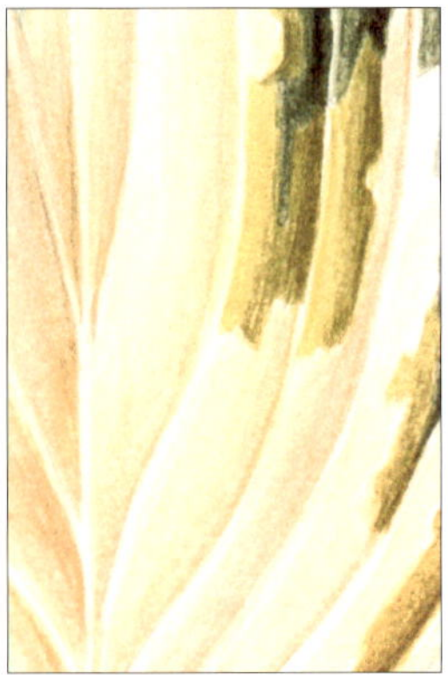

Detail from Stage 2: Neutral Tint with Naples Yellow deepened the cream leaf areas.

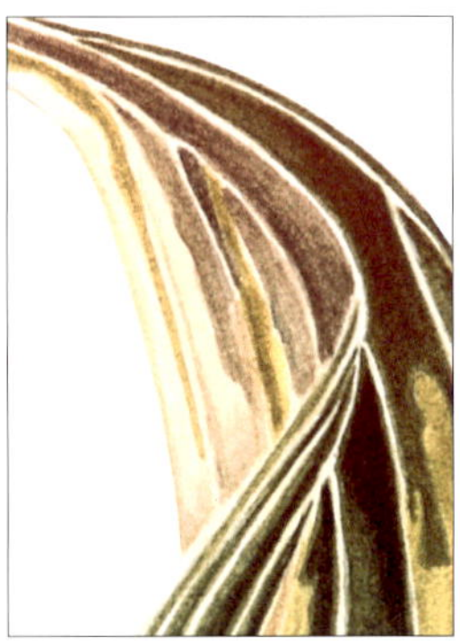

Detail from Stage 2: Hosta veins are seen in relief on the underside of the leaves.

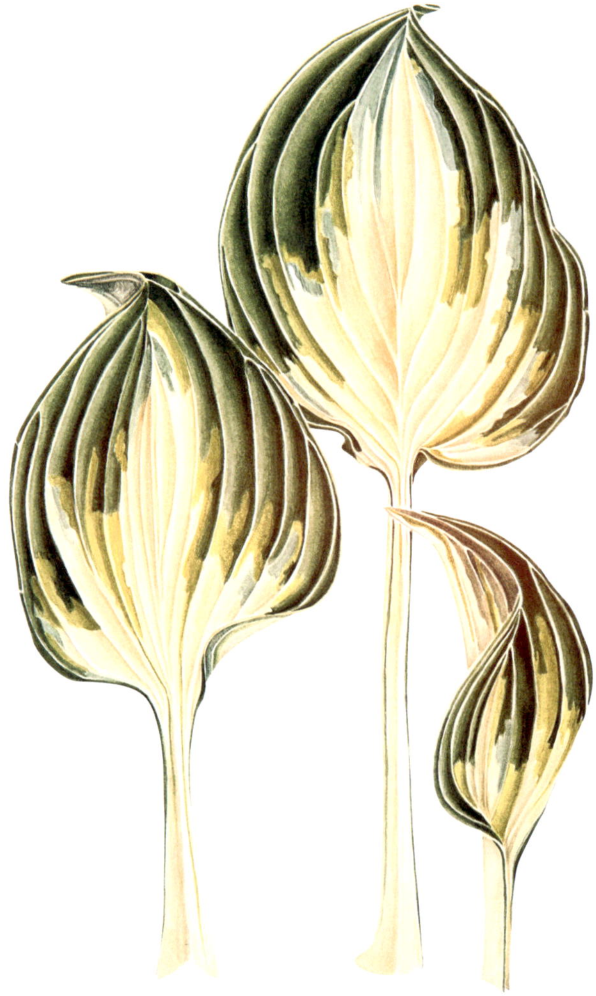

△ **Stage 2**

Janet added several further washes to ensure that the greens were built up to the correct depth of colour. She then blended the colours using a nearly dry brush so that no edges were visible. To show the darker tones in the creamy parts of the leaves Neutral Tint was added to the Naples Yellow and applied to each leaf.

Janet painted the reverse of the leaves, taking care to show the veins in relief; this is something that is sometimes easily overlooked by the student.

The veins were filled in with a thin wash in the appropriate green, narrowing them where necessary. In places the edges were slightly blurred, so Janet used a slightly damp brush, moving it along the light side of the vein to achieve this. She then strengthened the edge on the dark side to show up the dip of the undulation. This was repeated with the creamy sections of the leaves. She added darker tones to the centre of the leaves where they are slightly folded. The leaf stalks also folded in 'U' shapes, so darker tones were added along their length to show this. At the base of the stalk she added touches of weak Neutral Tint and Naples Yellow to show that some of the tissue structure was visible.

▷ **Final Stage**

Hosta leaves have very thin horizontal veins between the main veins, so these were added with little fine lines of varying length. This work needed to be very delicately done as these veins are barely visible, but it did add to the appearance of the leaf.

Any overlaps were strengthened with darker tones and finally a light wash of Winsor Lemon was put over the lightest tones of the dark green to give it a lift.

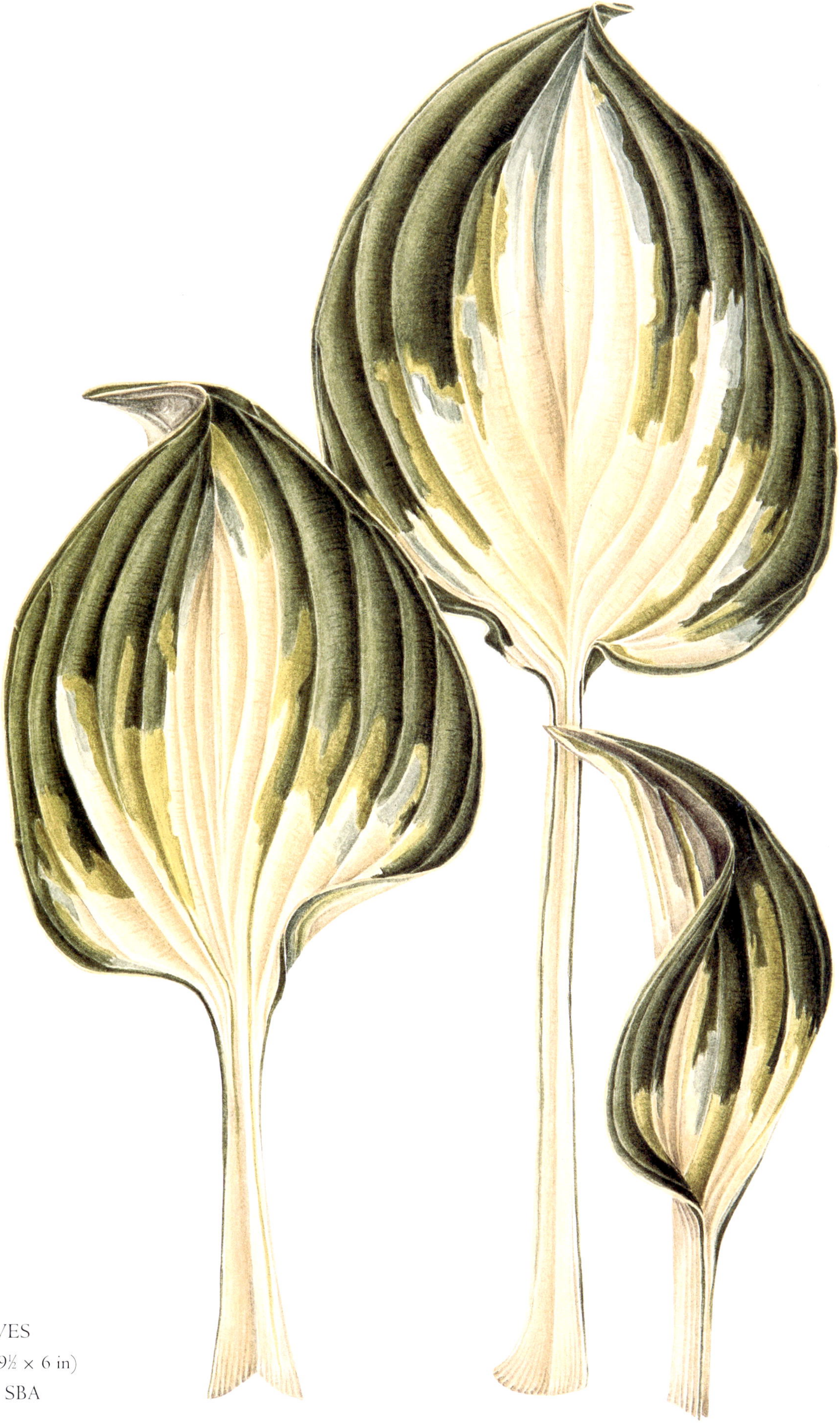

HOSTA LEAVES
24.5 × 15 cm (9½ × 6 in)
Janet Wood SBA

Project *Hosta*

Attempting this project will give valuable practice in mixing greens and working on variegated leaves, as well as demonstrating the need for shading veins in order to create form. The symmetry of the hosta veins makes this an ideal subject before moving on to more complicated patterns of venation.

In order not to become confused by the patterns of variegation do not try to take in everything at once. Concentrate on smaller sections; for example, paint half a leaf from the mid-rib before moving on to consider the next area. Work your way through the study carefully in this manner, stopping at intervals to look at your work and sum up the overall picture. By doing this you are far less likely to make one area too dark at the expense of another, for instance. Above all, take your time to complete the painting.

Colour Chart

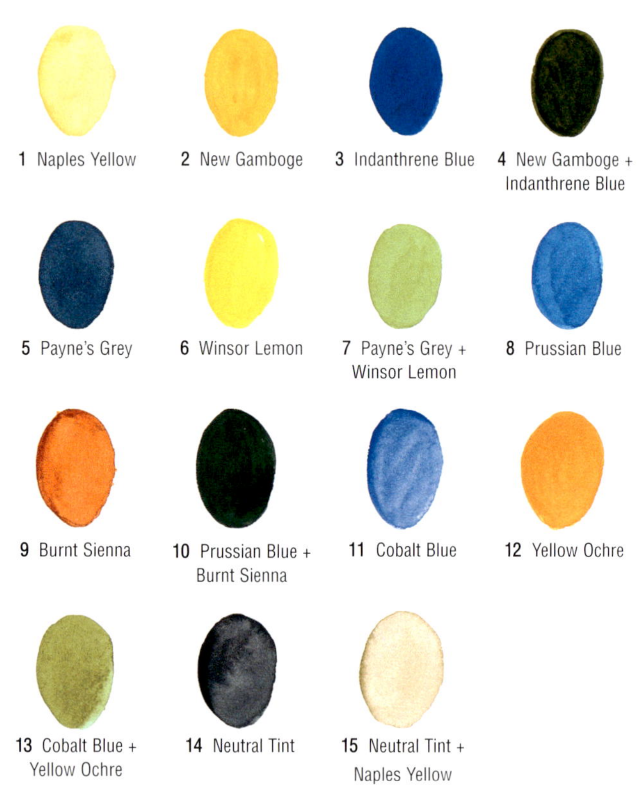

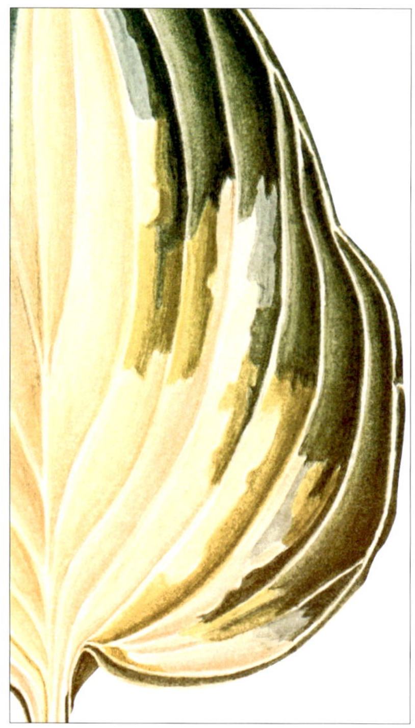

Detail from Stage 2: Strengthening the tones helped to show the undulation between veins on the leaf surface.

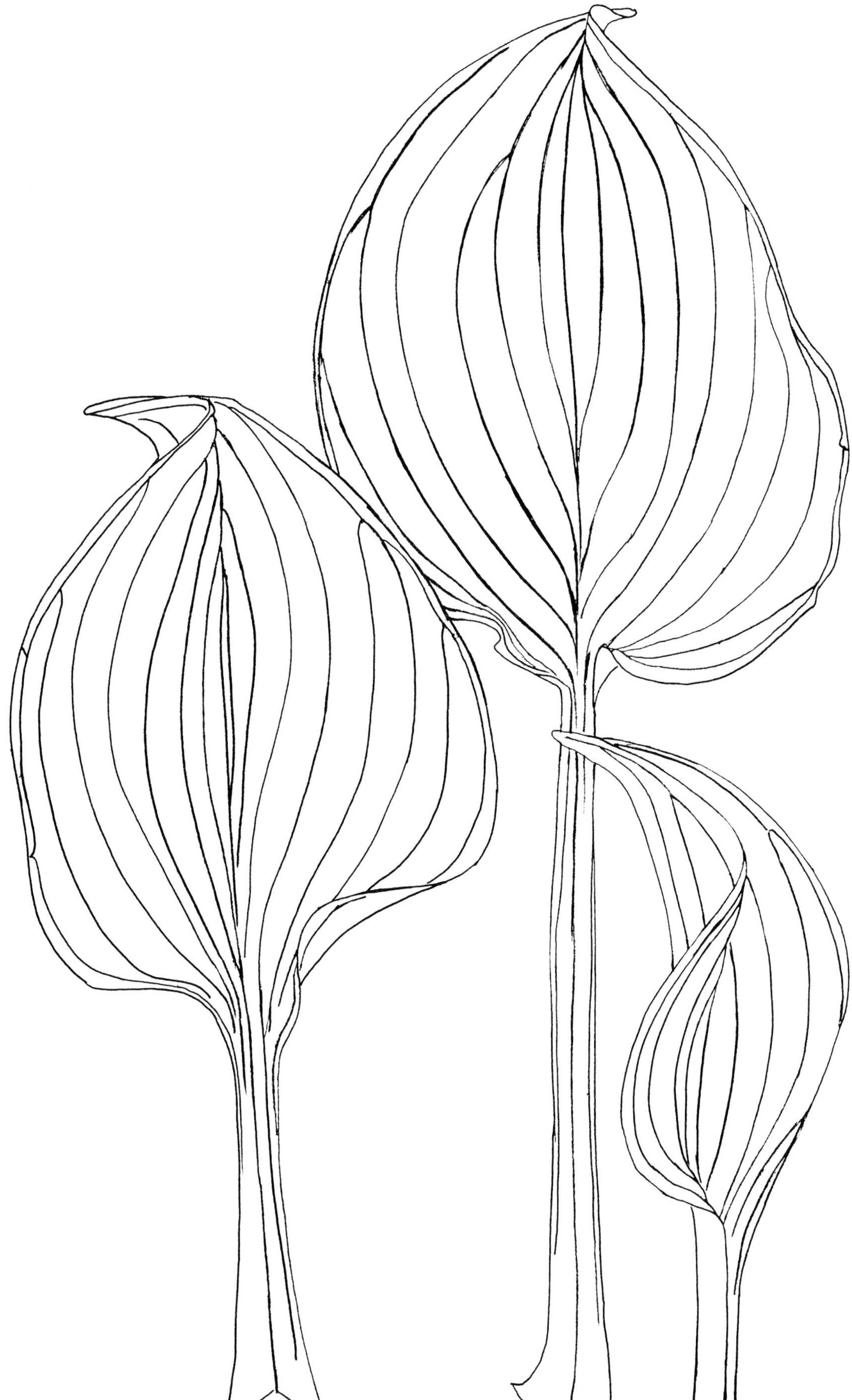

MADAGASCAR JASMINE

Stephanotis

Ann Swan SBA

We are all familiar with the highly scented white flowers of the stephanotis, a favourite for bridal bouquets and as a pot plant. Most of us are less familiar with these dramatic seed pods, so not surprisingly Ann took the opportunity to capture them in coloured pencil. This demonstration is a simplified version of her original larger work.

COLOUR CHART

Faber-Castell Polychromos

- Ivory 103
- Warm Grey V 274
- Warm Grey IV 273
- Warm Grey III 272
- Chrome Oxide Green 278
- Chrome Green Opaque 174
- Earth Green Yellowish 168
- Apple Green 170
- Grey Green 172

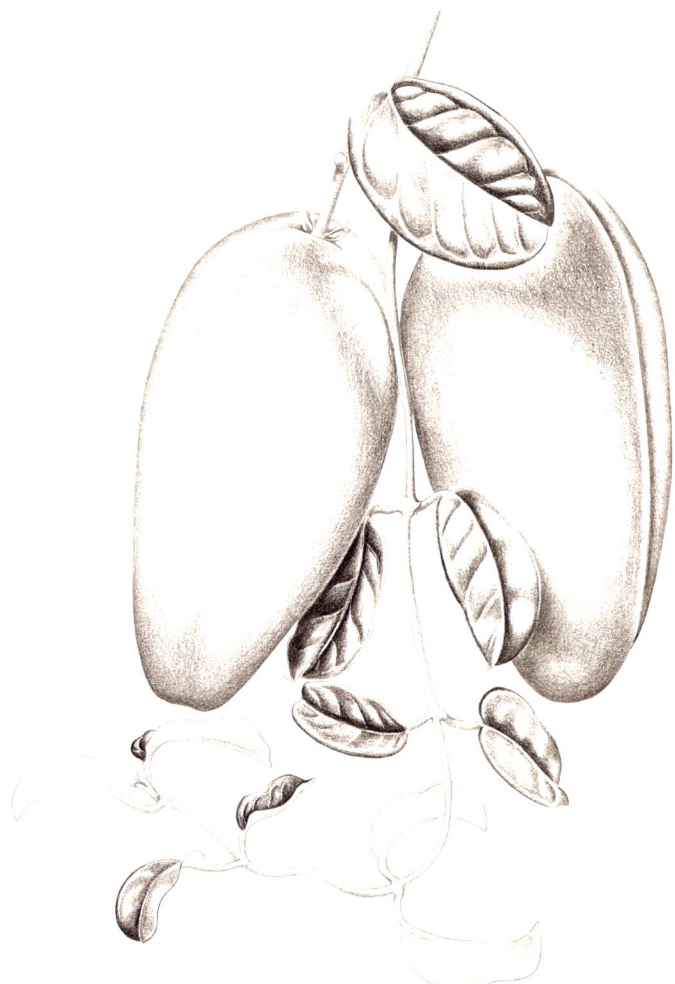

△ **Stage I**
Ann started by drawing a single clean pencil outline of the work. She then stippled the seedpods using Ivory 103 and indented the veins in the same Ivory. She went on to shade the front of the leaves using Warm Grey V 274. Next Ann shaded the backs of the leaves using Warm Grey III 272.

▽ Detail from Stage I: A light 'disappearing' edge was left between the leaf and carefully graded stippling on the pod.

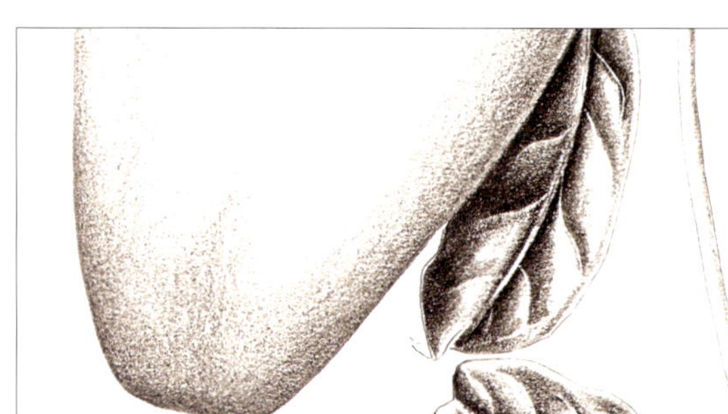

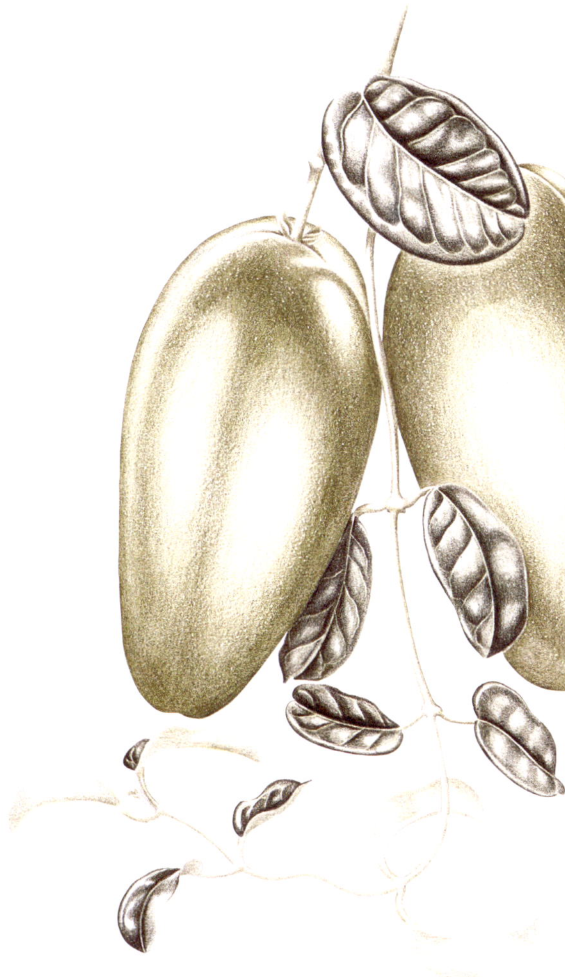

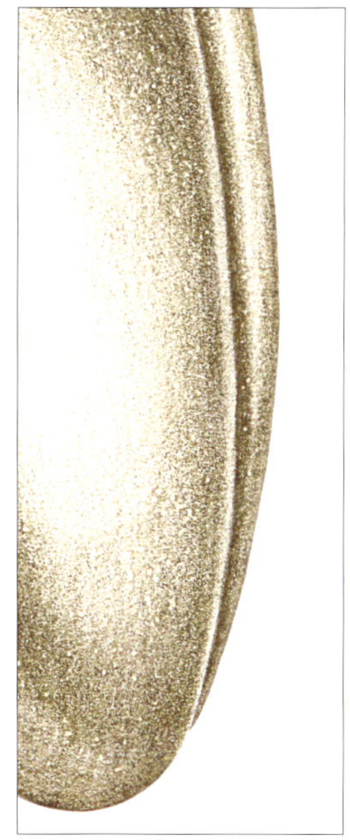

Detail from Stage 2:
Colour and tone changes gave the seed pod an interesting cleft.

△ **Stage 2**

The dark fronts of the leaves were overlaid with Chrome Oxide Green 278, using more pressure on the darker areas and less in the lighter areas. The highlights were left white.

The seed pods were overlaid with Chrome Green Opaque 174.

The backs of the leaves were lightly overlaid with Grey Green 172.

Ann overlaid the fronts of the leaves with Chrome Green Opaque 174 to modify the level of blueness. She continued to build up the colour of the seed pods with an overlay of Earth Green Yellowish 168. The backs of the leaves were overlaid with Apple Green 170. The 'disappearing' edge on the left-hand pod received some colour, but remained pale.

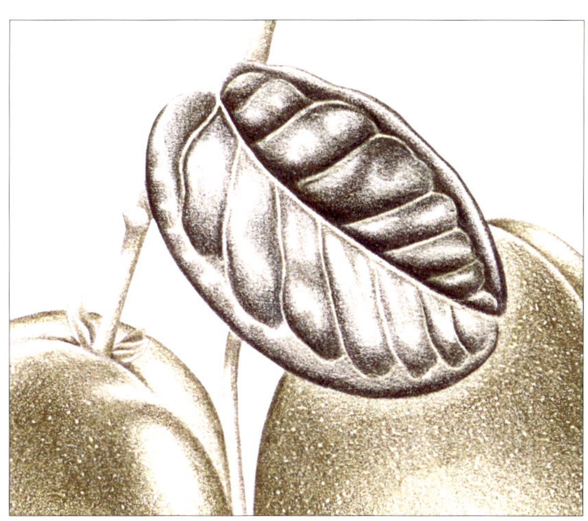

Detail from Stage 2:
Confidence allowed Ann to apply varying pressure to create the required darker tones.

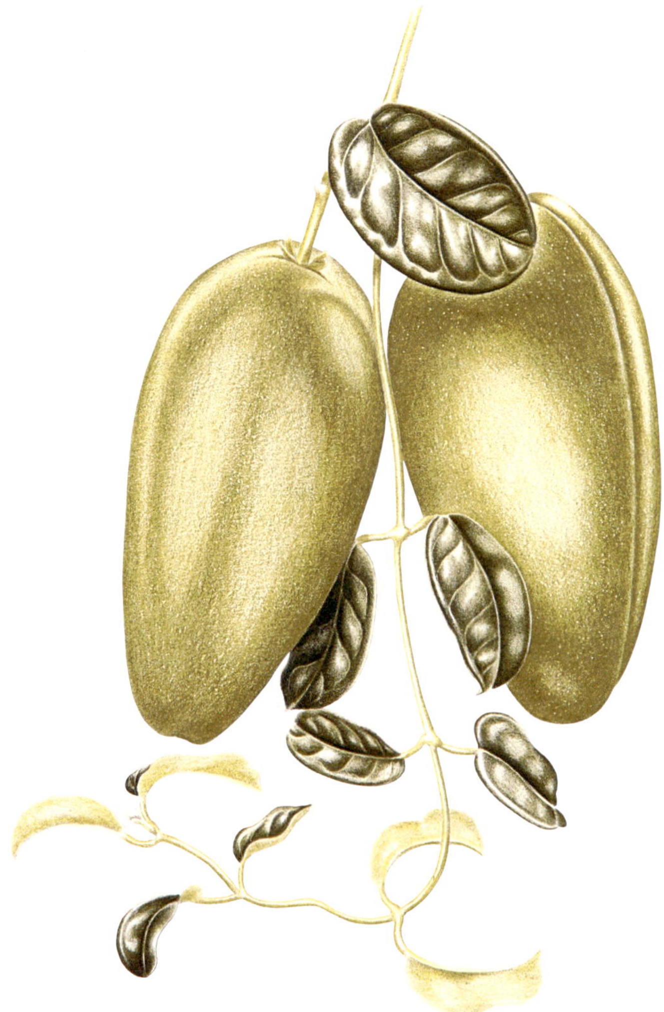

△ **Stage 3**

The fronts of the leaves were burnished with a colourless blender pencil, pressing heavily and taking colour into the highlights to soften them slightly. The seed pods were also burnished with the colourless blender. The backs of the leaves were burnished with Ivory 103 and the veins were lightly drawn in with Chrome Green Opaque 174.

▷ **Final Stage**

Where the shadows needed deepening, or any veins needed narrowing, Ann went back in with the greys and then overlaid the appropriate colour on top. Finally, she checked the work over with a magnifying glass, which helped to achieve really clean lines. The edges were crisped up as necessary, again using the appropriate colour.

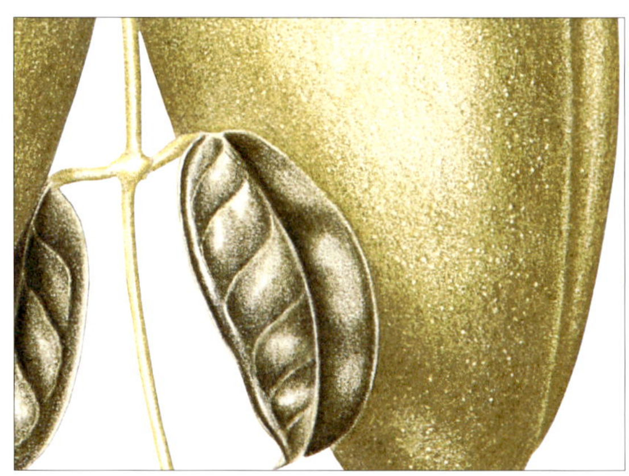

Detail from Stage 3:
The colour was softened into the highlights using a colourless blender.

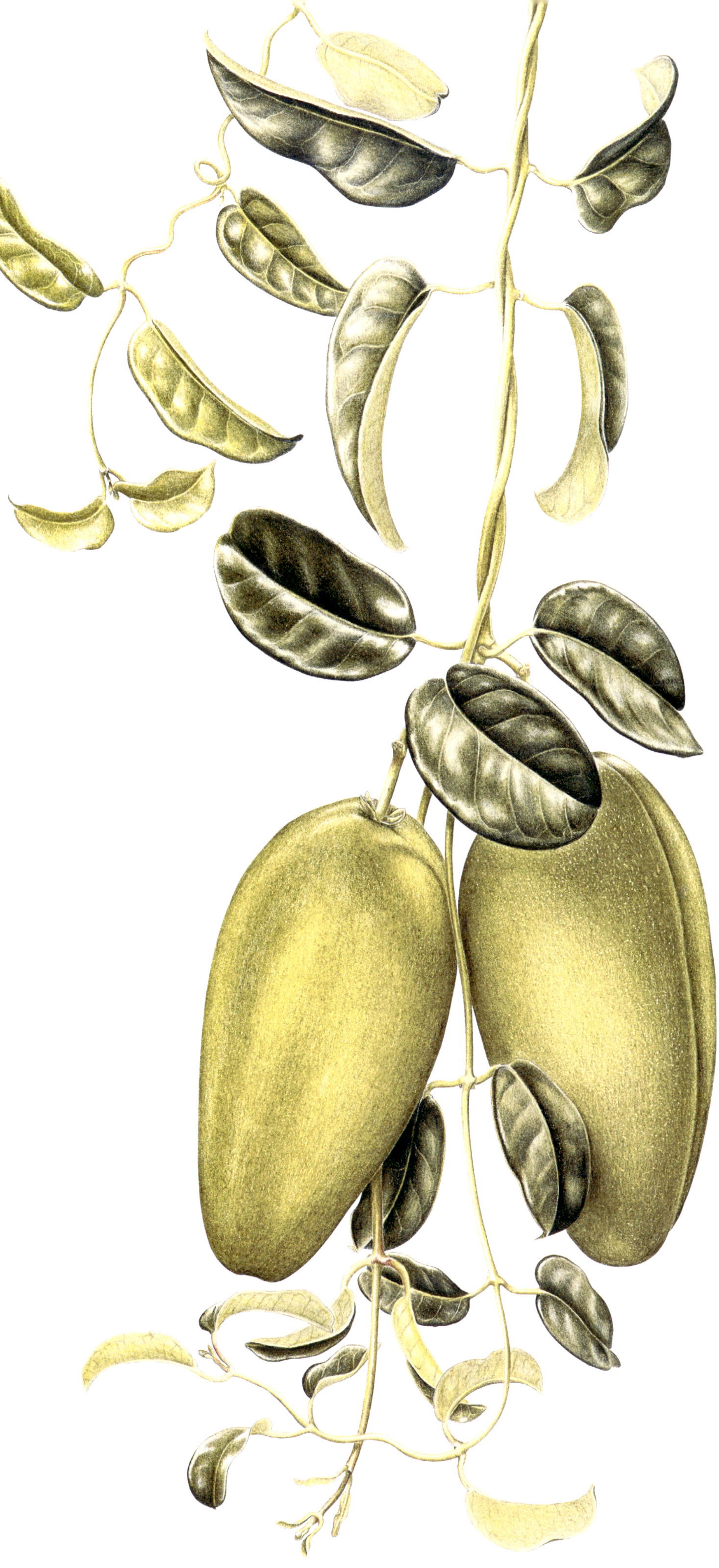

STEPHANOTIS
SEED PODS
27 × 20 cm (10¾ × 8 in)
Ann Swan SBA

CHAPTER 4
BLUE

BLUE IS a colour that does not push itself forward in a crowd. In a painting of mixed flowers the blue ones will always take the eye back and they are therefore invaluable for giving depth to a painting, never more so than when the profile or back view is shown. This will add enormously to the three-dimensional effect in any painting whether it is a mixed display or a single species.

The magnificent painting of *Meconopsis* × *sheldonii* on page 55 shows iridescent blue to great effect. It takes a very experienced painter to master such a complex flower and attempting such a task could well result in tears before bedtime. For that reason alone I decided not to include this splendid flower amongst the projects and my advice to any student would be to start small with a bluebell!

Today we are lucky to have a range of blue pigments at our disposal. When the artist had to rely on ground lapis lazuli – the 'Colour of Heaven' according to the writer James Runcie – it was prohibitively expensive and the sitter had to pay more for a portrait if it was used in the painting. Found in the mountains of Afghanistan, supplies of this rare mineral have always been unreliable, particularly in the troubled times of the modern world, although a new source has been found in Chile. Mined by hand and with a very complex labour-intensive method of extracting the pigment it is still a luxurious commodity and we should give thanks to the French chemist who created a synthetic version in the 1830s. French Ultramarine is essential to our palette, along with Cobalt and Cerulean. Many might prefer Indanthrene to Prussian Blue as it is less intense, but it is a valuable colour for darkest tones and as a mixer for greens.

▷ BLUE HYDRANGEA
44.5 × 36.5 cm
(17½ × 14½ in)
ANNIE MORRIS SBA

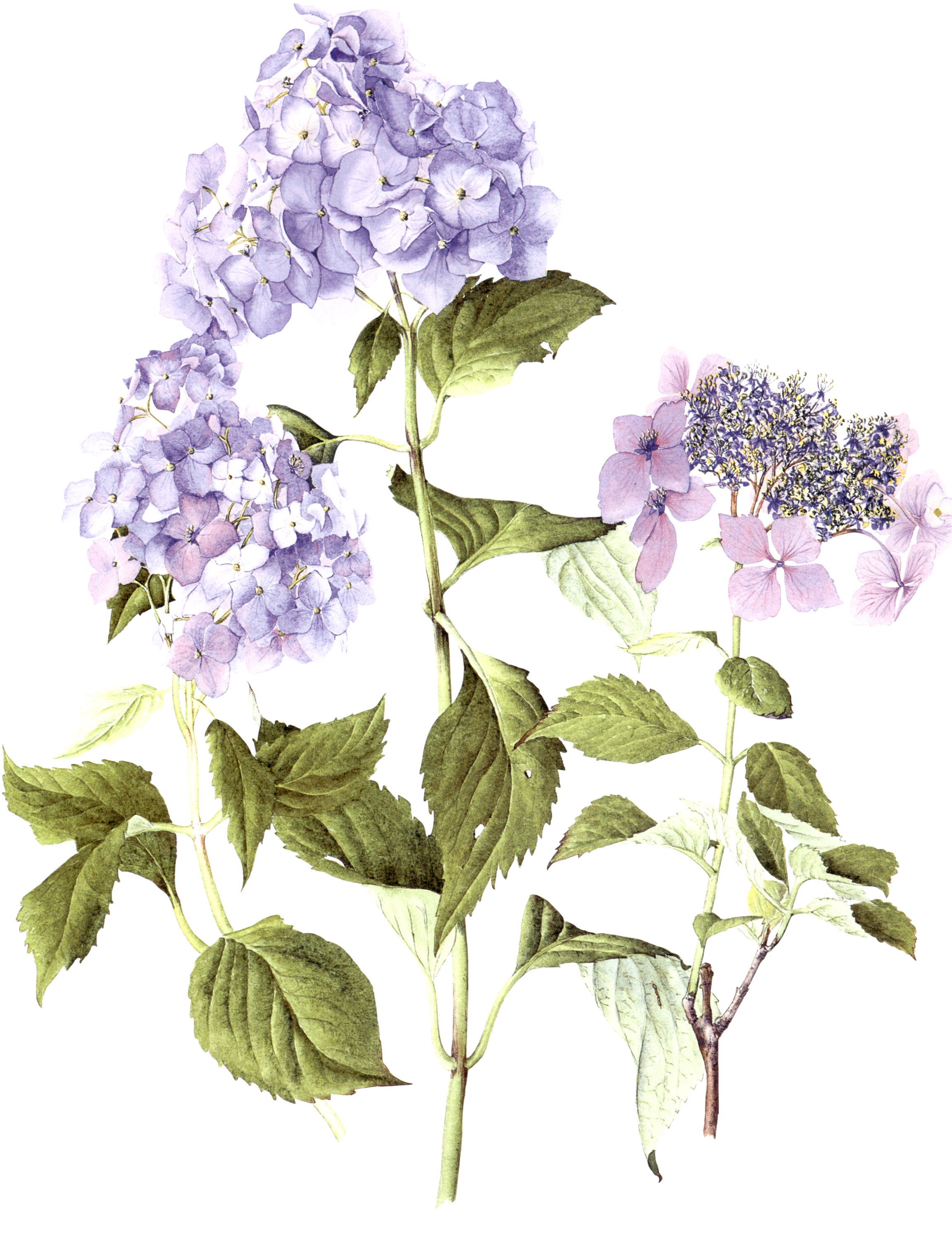

HIMALAYAN POPPY

Meconopsis × sheldonii 'Branklyn'

Brigitte E M Daniel SBA

These stunning flowers shimmer with all the iridescence of a butterfly's wings, an effect that Brigitte has captured perfectly. Combined with the complexity of the centres and the densely hirsute leaves and stems, this is a subject for the very experienced painter. The student is best advised to try out small sections to practise the techniques involved.

PAINTS

WINSOR & NEWTON
Cobalt Blue
Winsor Violet
Rose Madder Genuine
Cadmium Yellow Deep
Cadmium Orange
Prussian Green
Permanent Sap Green
Payne's Grey
Alizarin Crimson
Chinese White

SCHMINCKE
Helio Cerulean

GRUMBACHER
French Ultramarine

DALER-ROWNEY
Permanent Rose
Nickel Titanate Yellow

BRUSHES

RAPHAEL
Kolinsky sable sizes 0, 1, 2 and 3

DA VINCI
Maestro size 3

SURFACE

SCHOELLERSHAMMER
6R HP 300 gsm (140 lb)

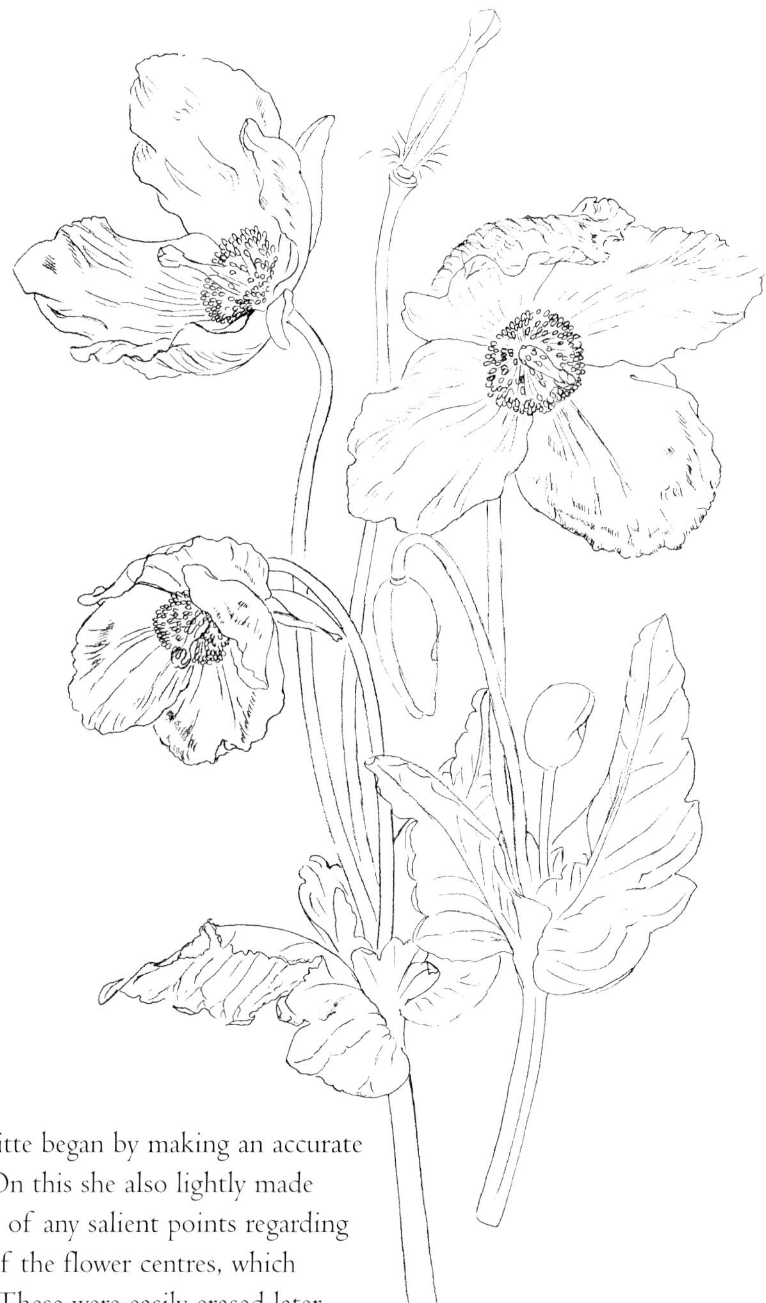

△ **Stage 1**
As always Brigitte began by making an accurate line drawing. On this she also lightly made notes in pencil of any salient points regarding the structure of the flower centres, which might change. These were easily erased later.

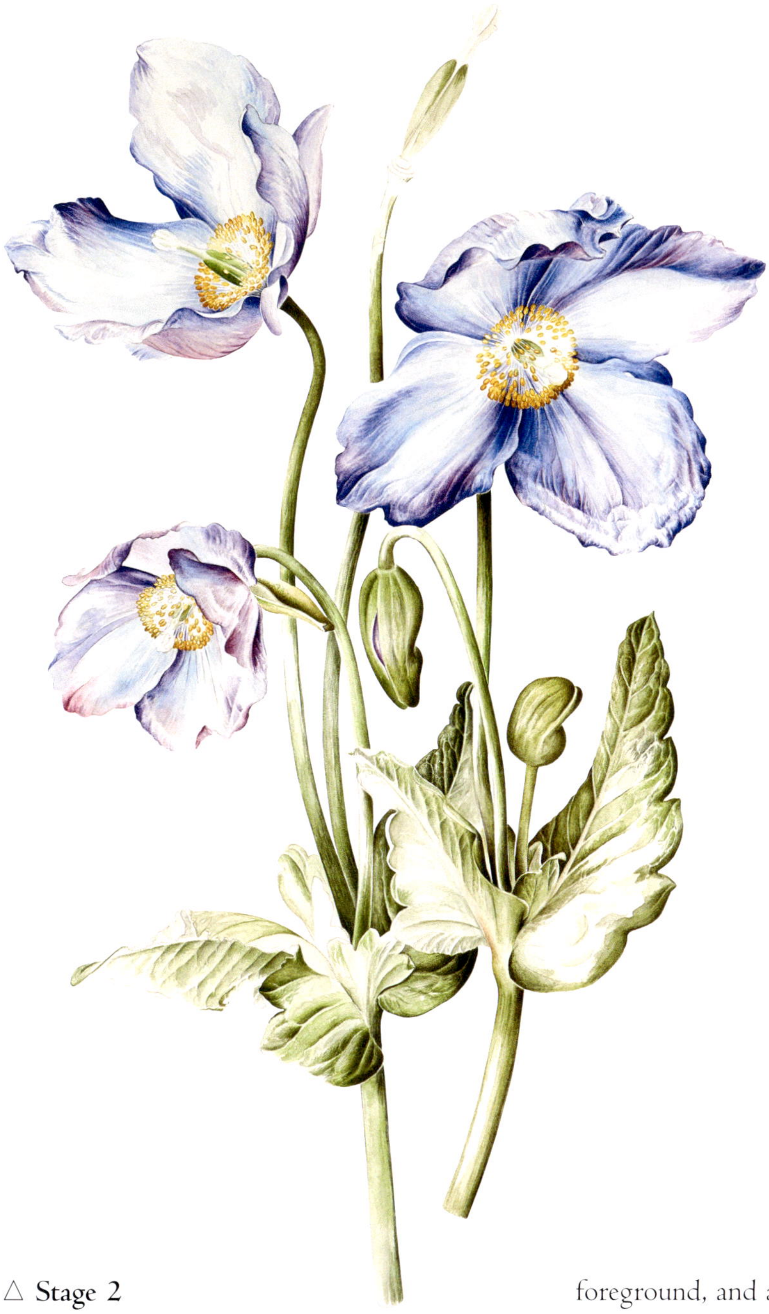

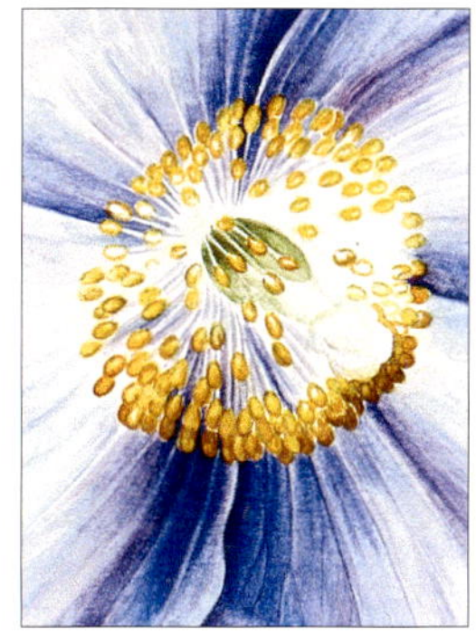

Detail of Stage 2: The brilliant golden anthers and the white filaments required great care to preserve them while the painting was being worked upon.

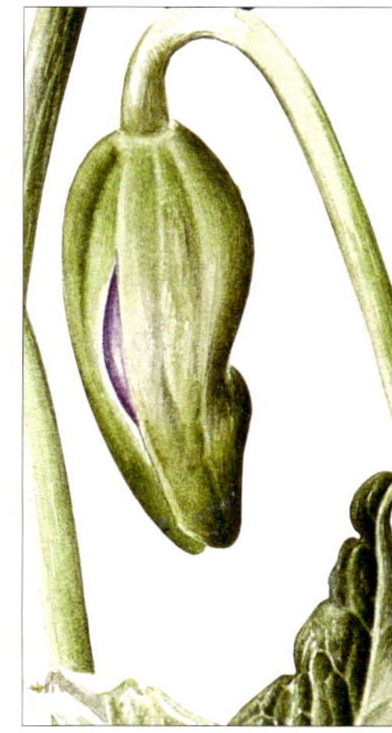

Detail of Stage 2: Deep petal colour just showed through the opening bud and needed to be noted at the start as the petals would fade on opening.

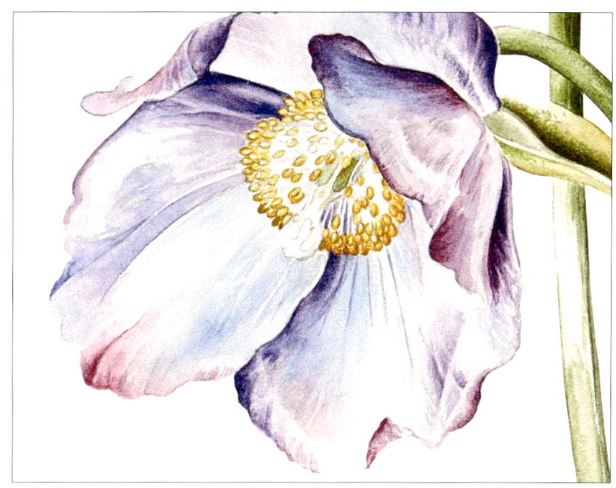

Detail from Stage 2: The delicate venation showed up against the iridescence of the petal.

△ **Stage 2**

A watery mix of Permanent Sap Green was then used to wash the leaf areas in the foreground and to define the edges away from the light source. Brigitte also picked out the anthers at this early stage to establish them and to ensure that they stayed clean and bright. For these she used Cadmium Yellow Deep and Cadmium Orange.

It was important to capture the flower colour that was just visible in the opening bud. This would become paler as the flower faded. The same colour was used immediately on the opening flower and petal edges in the foreground, and also on the shaded areas of the petals. The colours used were a combination of Winsor Violet, Rose Madder Genuine, French Ultramarine and Cobalt Blue, applied in glazes and taking care to leave the well-defined veins unsullied.

Brigitte moved on to further develop the leaves. She used French Ultramarine, Winsor Violet and Permanent Sap Green, with a touch of Payne's Grey, as a mix to add depth to leaves and stems. This was softened with Nickel Titanate Yellow for the leaf undersides. A tiny amount of Cadmium Yellow Deep was used to wash the junction of leaf and stem.

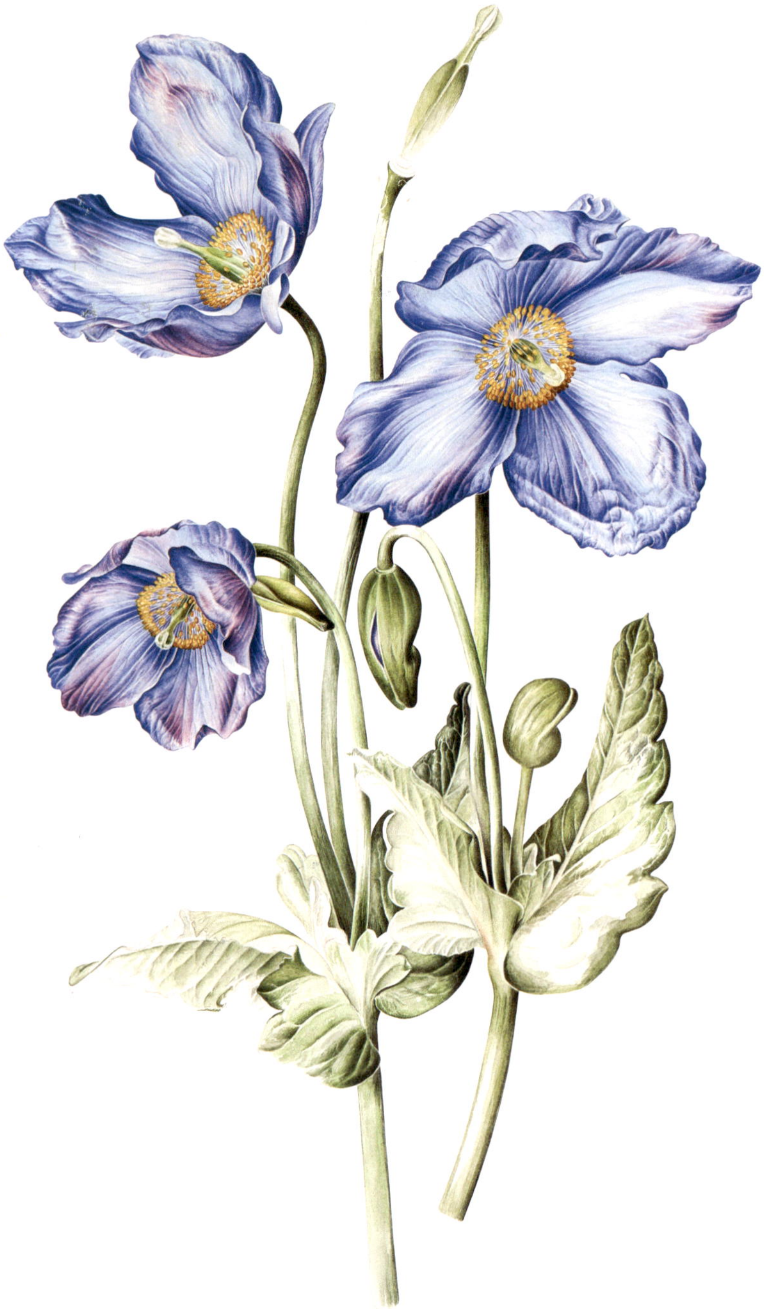

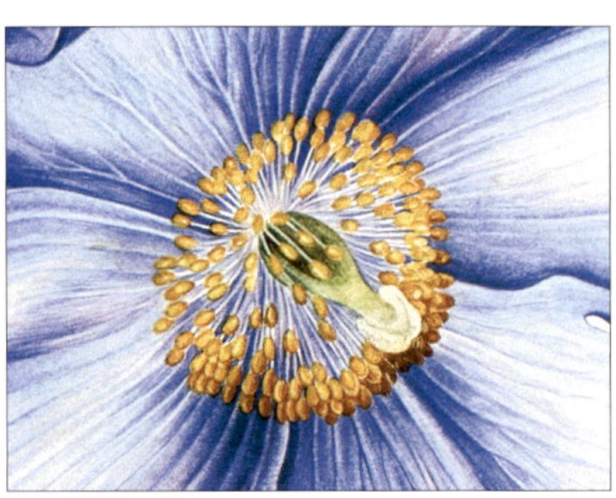

Detail from Stage 3:
Care and patience were needed for the fine painting around the filaments.

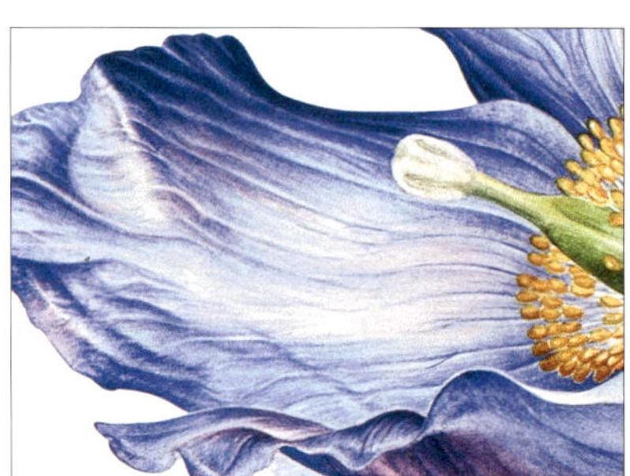

Detail from Stage 3:
Stronger colours in the petals were created using the original pigments.

◁ Stage 3

Brigitte now started work on the larger areas of petal using Cobalt Blue and Helio Cerulean, first of all picking out the areas behind the filaments at the flower centres. A small brush with an excellent point was essential for delicate work of this type. Note that the filaments were left white throughout. The colours of the petals were strengthened using the original pigments named above. The stigmas were painted with a pale Permanent Sap Green with a little Winsor Violet added for shading purposes.

▷ Final Stage

At this stage more work was done on the leaves as Brigitte developed and deepened the tonal range, again using the same French Ultramarine, Winsor Violet, Permanent Sap Green and when necessary a little Payne's Grey for the darkest areas. All leaves and flowers required tidying up, especially between the filaments and around the developing fruit capsule. Hairs were 'pulled out' finely using a fairly dry mix of Chinese White, particularly where these showed up against dark leaves and stems, using a very fine brush. Brigitte paid great attention to the difference between the hairs on the light side and those on the dark side of the plant and leaves.

Note: The red hairs were a mix of Alizarin Crimson and Rose Madder Genuine, with Payne's Grey in the shadow. This mix was also used on the torn left-hand leaf edge and on the ageing tissue of the pollinated stigma. A wash of the mix was also used on the leaf ribs of the right-hand flower spike.

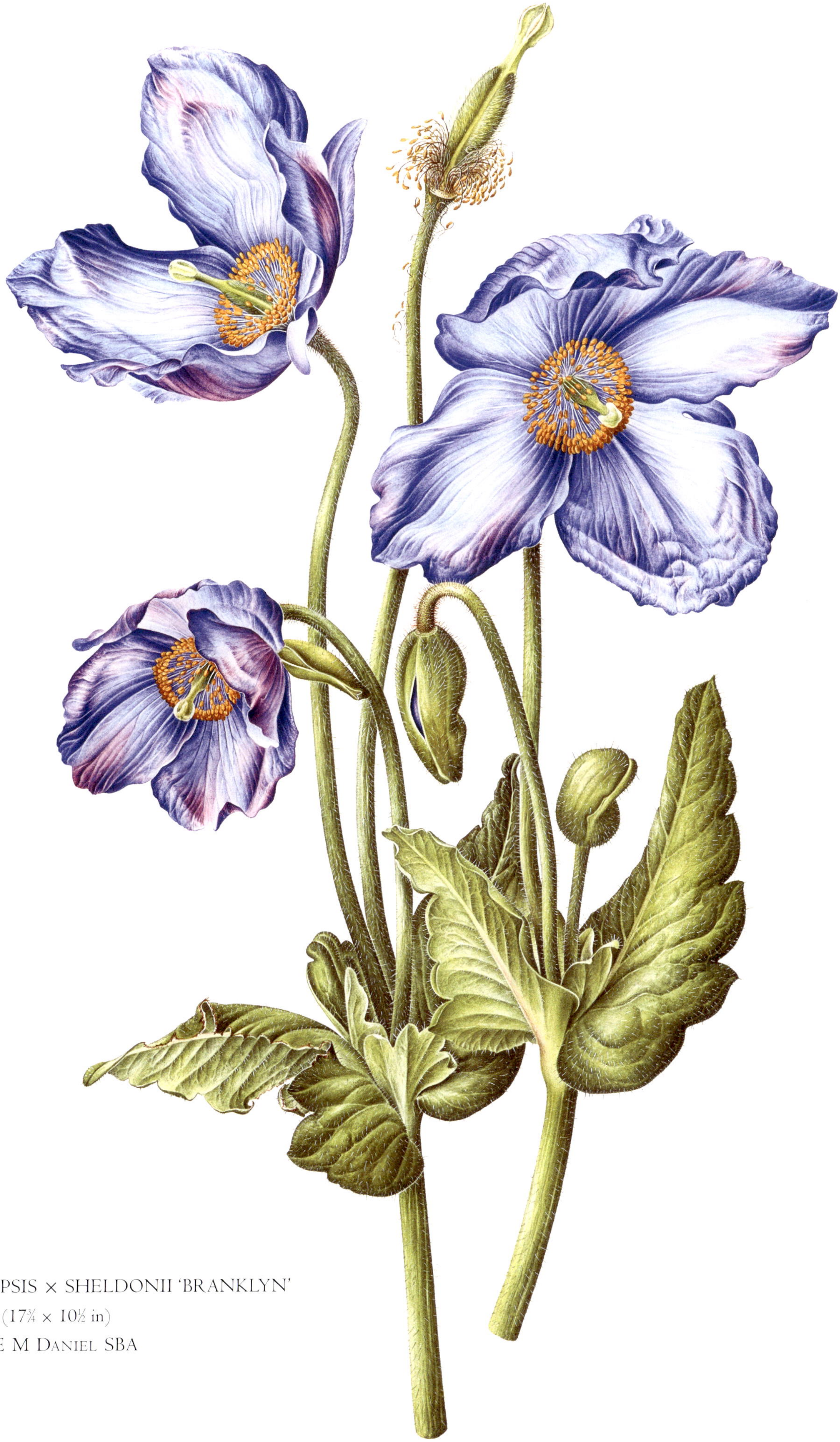

MECONOPSIS × SHELDONII 'BRANKLYN'
45 × 27 cm (17¾ × 10½ in)
BRIGITTE E M DANIEL SBA

DELPHINIUM

Delphinium

Vicky Mappin SBA

Vicky was attracted by the brilliant blue of the spire, the delicate flower spikes, each of which was different, and the elegant leaves. With a single variety of this type it is possible to appreciate the individual beauty of the flowers, which seem to mimic the flight of an ascending spiral of butterflies.

PAINTS

WINSOR & NEWTON
Winsor Violet
Cadmium Yellow
Alizarin Crimson

DALER-ROWNEY
Sap Green

SENNELIER
Light Ultramarine

BRUSHES

WINSOR & NEWTON
Series 7 sizes 1, 3 and 4

SURFACE

FABRIANO
Artistico HP 300 gsm (140 lb)

▷ Stage 1
Vicky started by drawing the outline, using a Pentel 0.3mm pencil. This had to be done quickly before all the flowers opened. She drew the tapering stem first, making sure that she captured the curve. The spire was quite complicated with so many petals at the back and front of the stem.

A first wash using Winsor Violet and Light Ultramarine in varying strengths helped to sort this out. Sizes 1 and 4 brushes were used.

Note: Vicky did not mix any colours – all were applied in glazes to take full advantage of the transparency of watercolours.

The flower spike seemed to be lighter in the centre, darkening nearer the petal margins, which was a help when removing pencil lines. Spurs at the top of the spike were painted using Winsor Violet and Sap Green whereas the more mature ones lower down were painted with just Winsor Violet.

The central 'bees' of the flowers were painted with Cadmium Yellow and Winsor Violet. A light wash of Sap Green was applied to the leaves and stems. The buds on the right-hand side were painted with pale Alizarin Crimson. All washes were kept pale throughout.

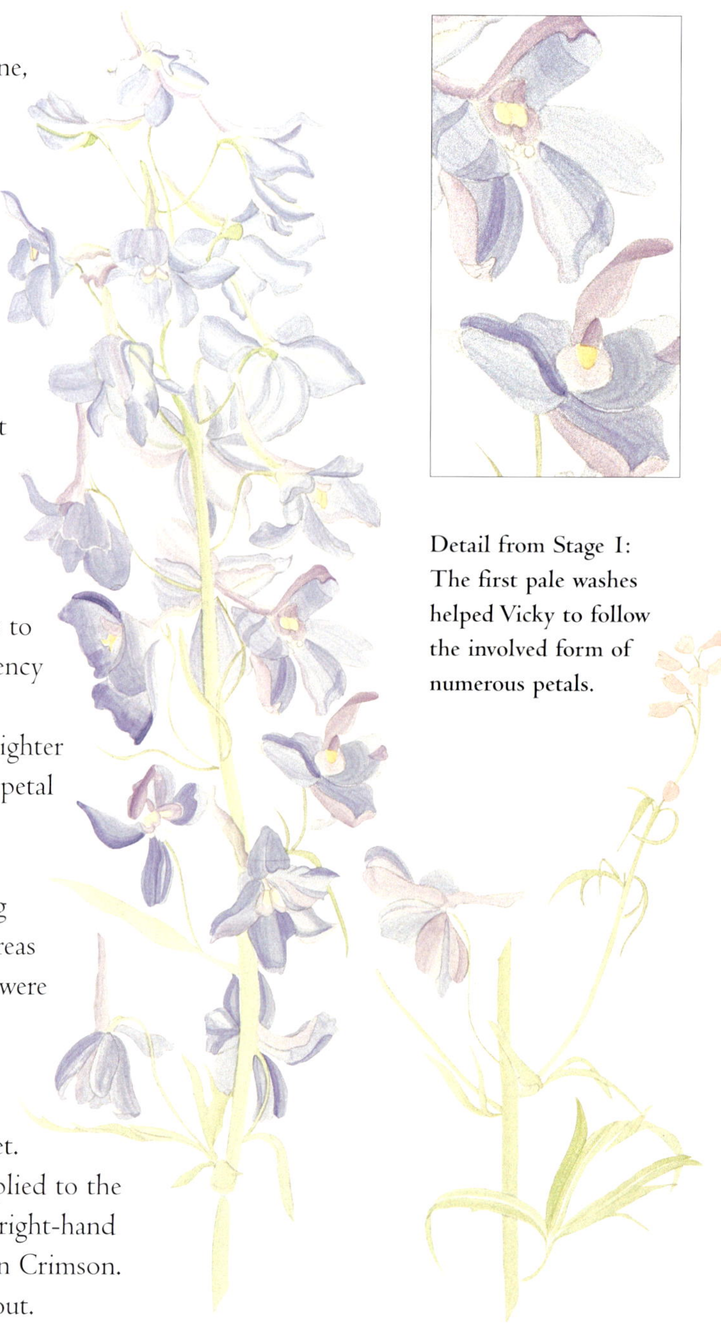

Detail from Stage 1: The first pale washes helped Vicky to follow the involved form of numerous petals.

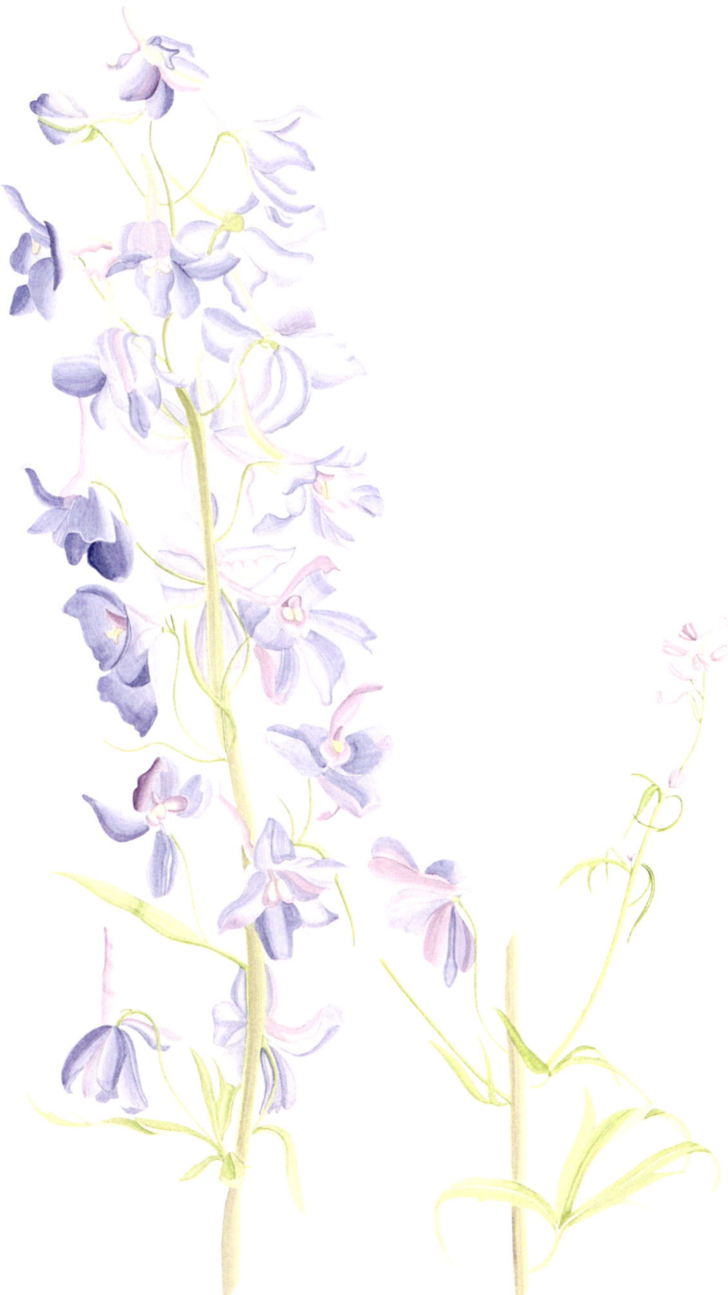

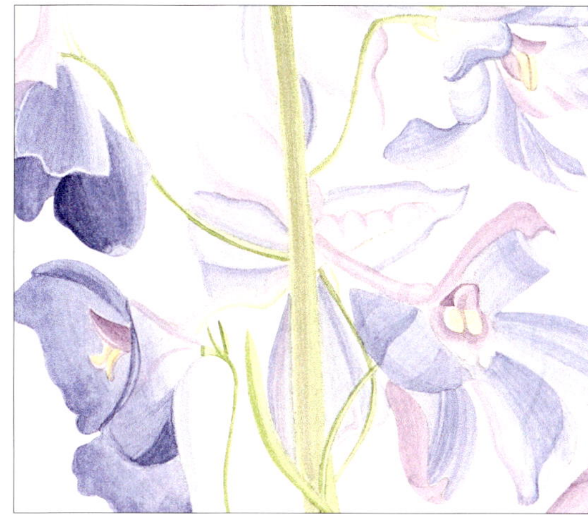

Detail from Stage 2:
Varying tone suggested the play of light on the flowers.

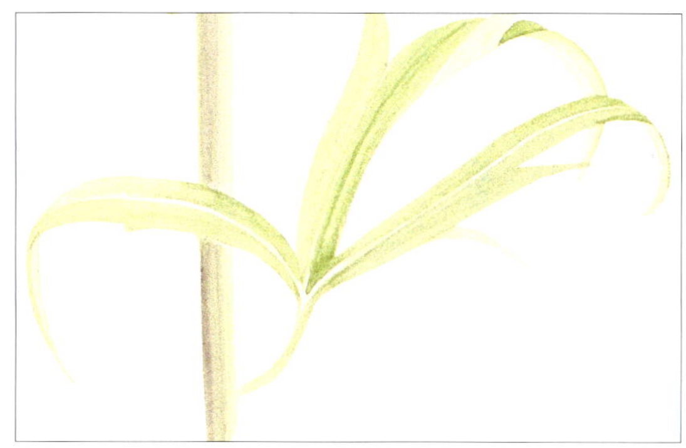

Detail from Stage 2:
Additional Sap Green started to give form to the leaves.

△ **Stage 2**

Using the size 1 brush Vicky started to build up the Light Ultramarine and Winsor Violet on each flower. This was quite a difficult task as the sepals were fairly small, with frequent colour changes. As always, two of the character traits required by the botanical artist came to her rescue – patience and perseverance.

Next the colour on the left-hand side was strengthened considerably, in relation to the light source from the right. Vicky also wanted to keep the flowers behind the stem quite pale. This gave an attractive impression of light shining through the flower spike.

Once again all colours were glazed, not mixed in the palette.

Sap Green was added to the leaves, leaving the midribs as the first wash. Winsor Violet was introduced to the main stem, and this was followed by another Sap Green wash using a size 3 brush. Winsor Violet was also added to the delicate young side shoot. Although a seemingly simple study, the painting required numerous layers of colour in its build-up.

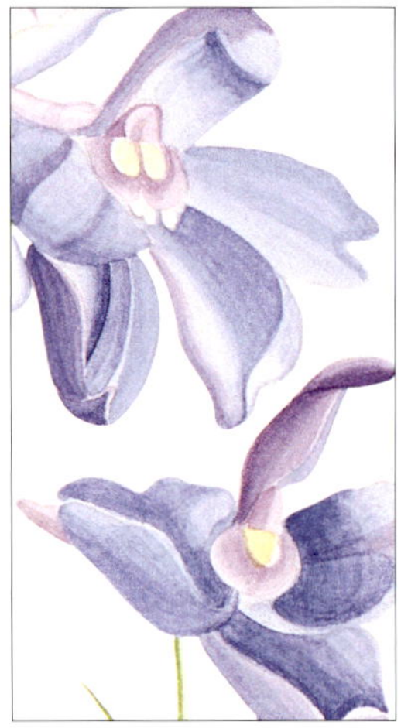

Detail from Stage 3:
Work on the 'bees' added interest to the flowers.

◁ Stage 3

Using a size 1 brush Vicky continued to build the colour with light washes. Where she wanted the blue to be darker she painted Winsor Violet washes on top of the Light Ultramarine. Detail was added to the central 'bees' on each flower.

Using alternate washes of Sap Green and Winsor Violet Vicky strengthened the main stem with a size 3 brush. She also added Sap Green to the leaves and deepened the side shoot with Winsor Violet as appropriate.

▷ Final Stage

Vicky glazed the flowers with Light Ultramarine and a touch of Winsor Violet, although the intense colour on the left-hand side required glazes of Winsor Violet. The main stem was built up with alternate washes of Sap Green and Light Ultramarine, ending with a final glaze of Winsor Violet. The spurs were strengthened using the colours as before. Delicate flower stems were painted with Sap Green and shaded with Winsor Violet.

Leaves were glazed with Winsor Violet and Light Ultramarine over the Sap Green, using the brush to shape them.

Alternate Sap Green and Winsor Violet were used to give form to the buds, which were finished with a wash of Alizarin Crimson.

Vicky finished off by painting fine lines on each petal and then completed the 'bees' with Cadmium Yellow and Winsor Violet.

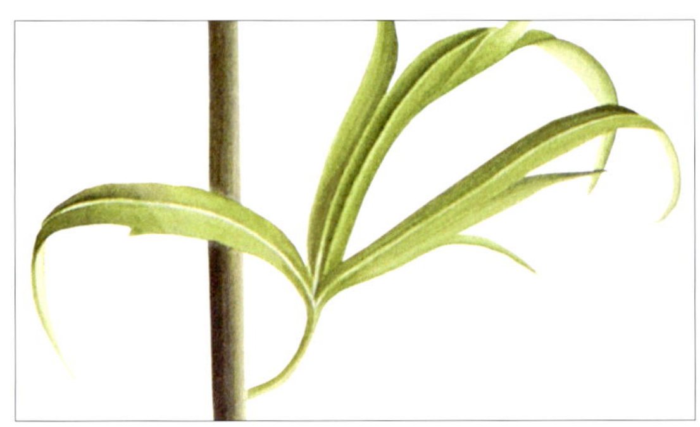

Detail from Final Stage:
A well-loaded brush gave form to the carefully sculpted leaves.

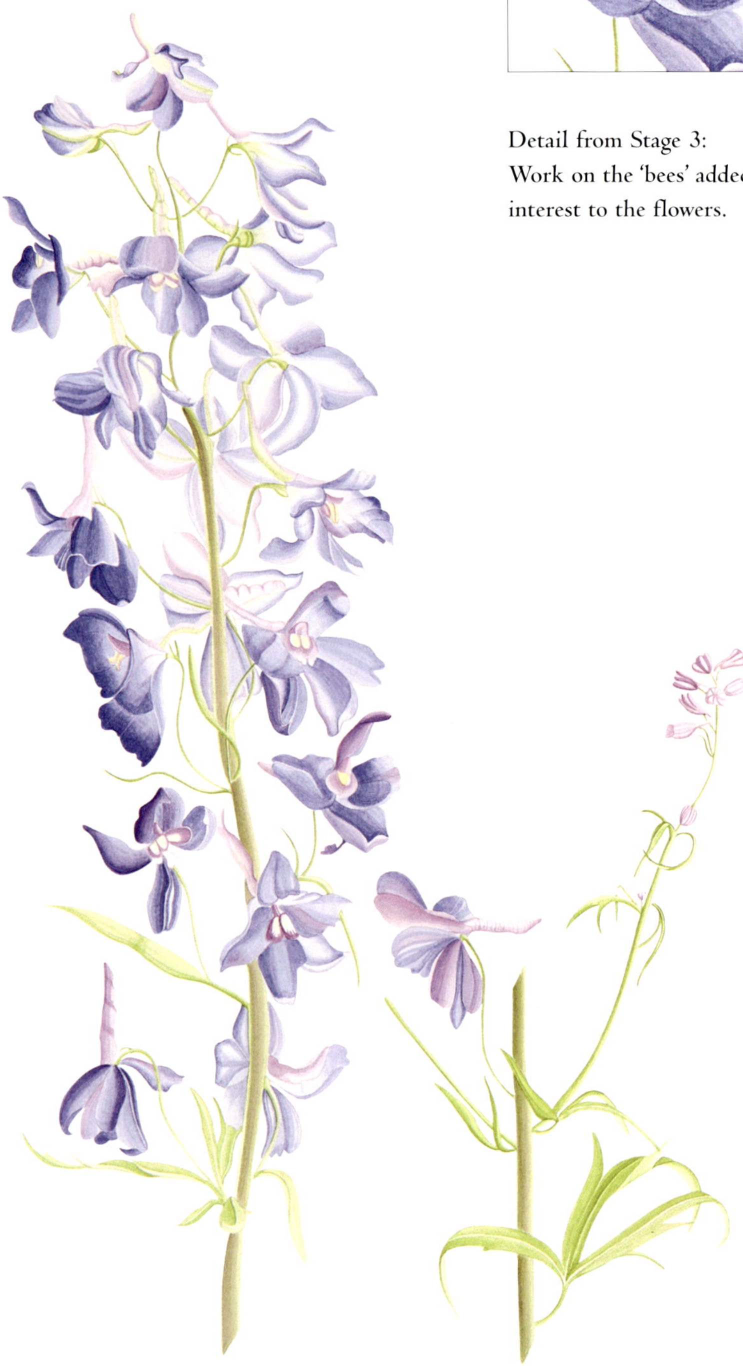

△ Stage 3

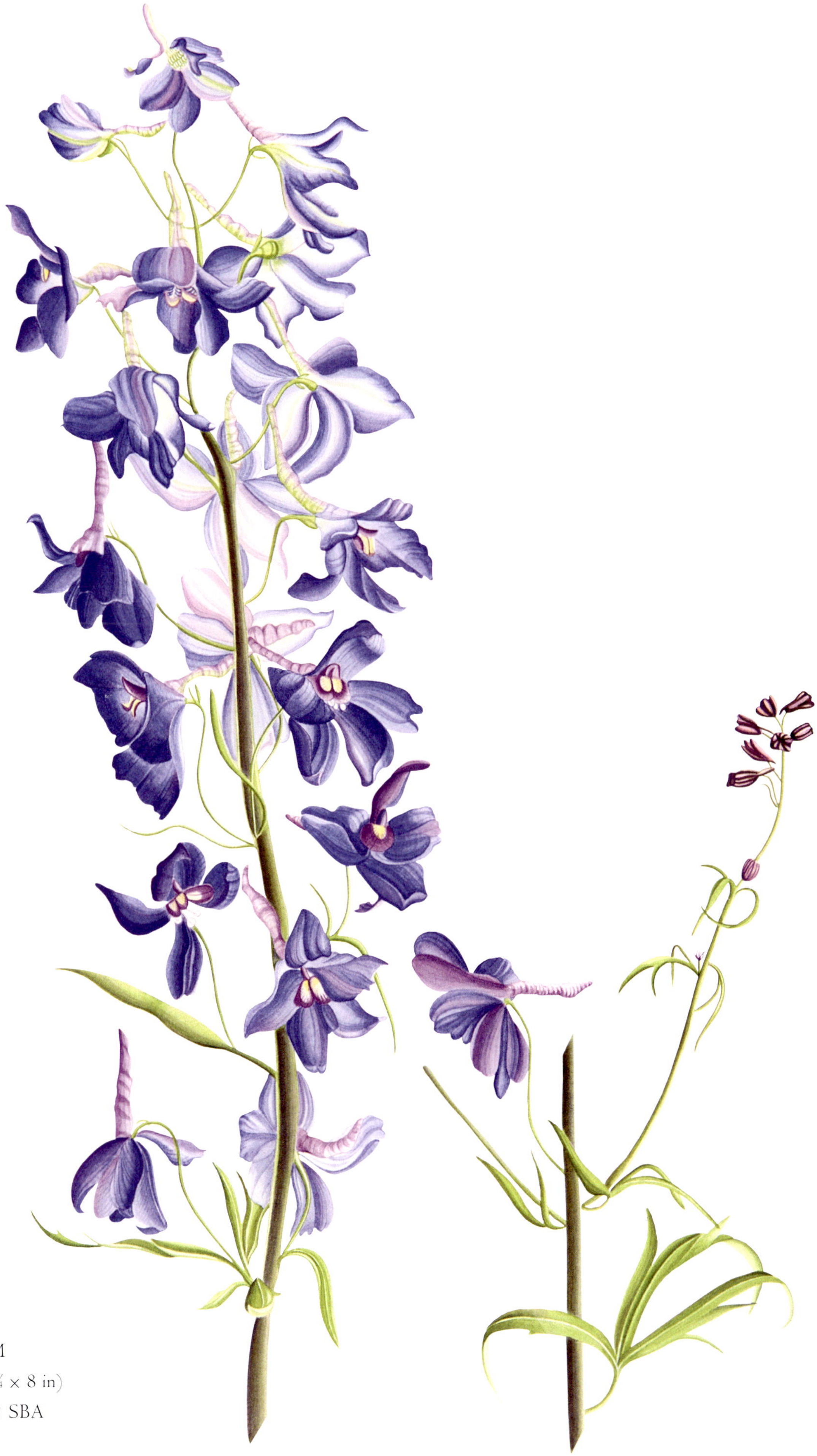

DELPHINIUM
36 × 20 cm (14¼ × 8 in)
Vicky Mappin SBA

PROJECT *Delphinium*

The drawing has been adjusted for this project, but this does not affect the working method described.

It may seem repetitive working with quite a limited palette, but you can see that they are beautifully clear colours and it gives very good practice in glazing rather than mixing colours. Trying this on a small scale, albeit sometimes a fiddly one, as the petals and sepals are quite tiny, will actually be easier than trying to cope with large areas of single washes. Take your time and allow the individual colours to dry before applying the next glaze. This simple larkspur-like flower may encourage you to try a double delphinium of the shorter Pacific hybrids range. There is a superb variety of blue shades, often with contrasting white petaloids in the centre. Sometimes a side shoot will be sufficient to add depth of colour and recession to a mixed flower study.

A NOTE ON USING BLUE

Blue can be a challenging colour, especially in a mass, such as with bluebells. From a distance they appear – what can one say – blue. Seen individually and close up they are often anything but blue, with a lot of pink in their make-up. In fact, more often than not, a pale wash of Permanent Rose or Quinacridone Magenta is needed before any blue is applied. Bluebells are not the quickest flowers to paint as each bell needs careful analysis.

COLOUR CHART

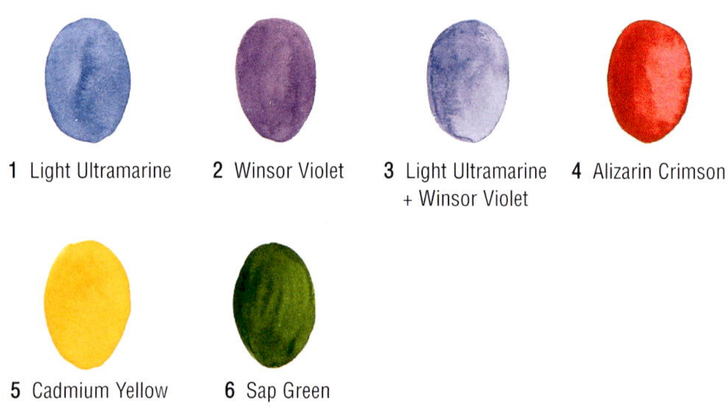

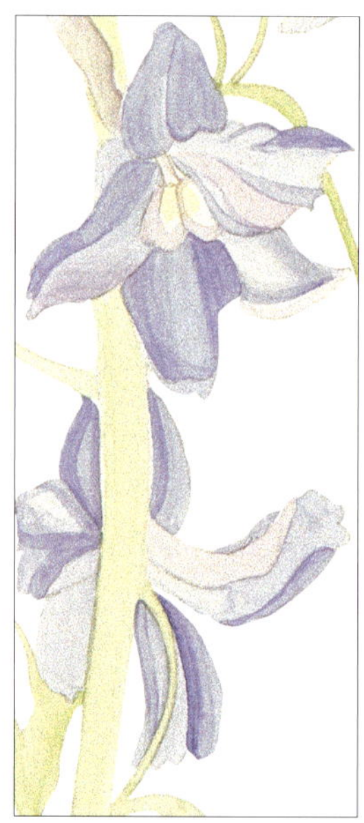

Detail from Stage I: Darkened petal margins helped to obliterate pencil lines.

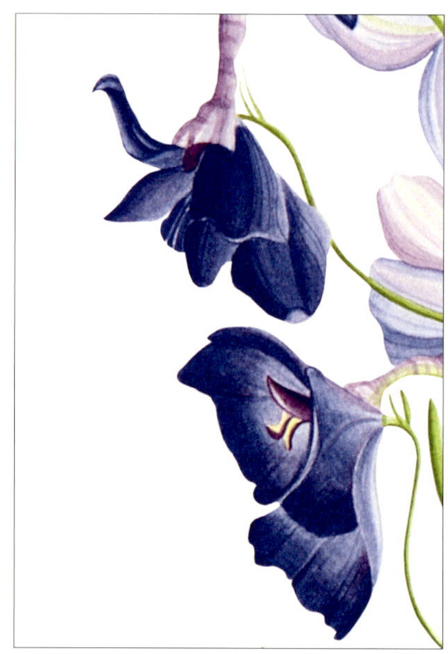

Detail from Final Stage: Strong glazes of colour were needed to give contrast to the side of the spike that was away from the light source.

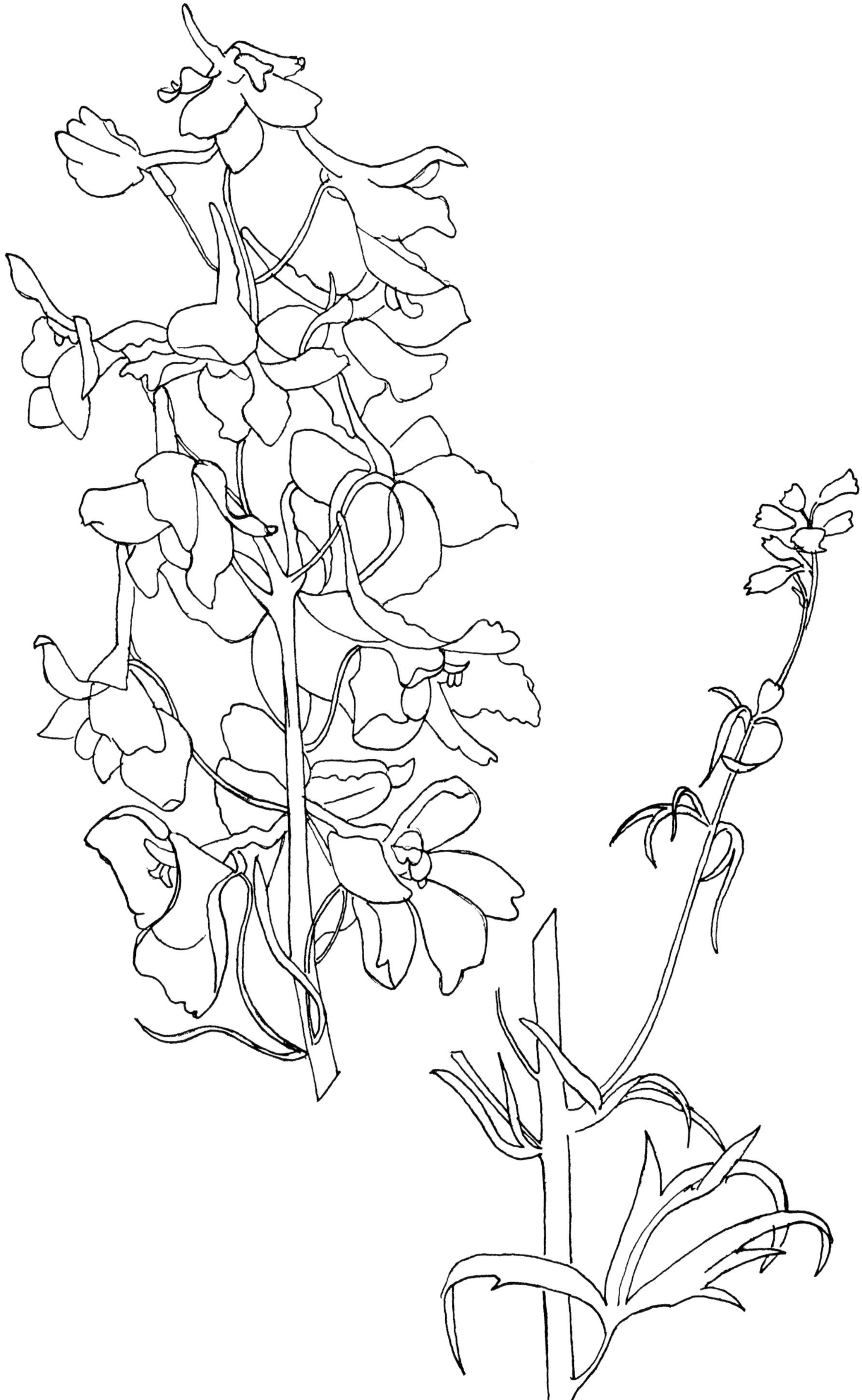

IRIS

Iris siberica

Susan Christopher-Coulson SBA

This iris, with its many cultivars, is often called the 'Butterfly Iris', which is apt in view of the apparent delicacy of the flower and its venation. When called upon to produce a coloured-pencil demonstration piece representing the colour blue Susan was lucky to find this last specimen still flourishing in her garden at the end of their flowering season.

COLOUR CHART

DERWENT ARTISTS UNLESS OTHERWISE INDICATED

Blue Grey 6800
Sunset Gold 6410
Venetian Red 6300
Sap Green 4900
Royal Blue 2810
Cedar Green 5000
Prismacolor Verithin: Purple
Light Violet 2600
Teal Blue 2830
Moss Green 5110
Chartreuse 5130
Chocolate Brown 6600
Caran d'Ache Supracolor: Violet 120
Felt Grey 5310
Caran d'Ache Supracolor: Lime Green 231

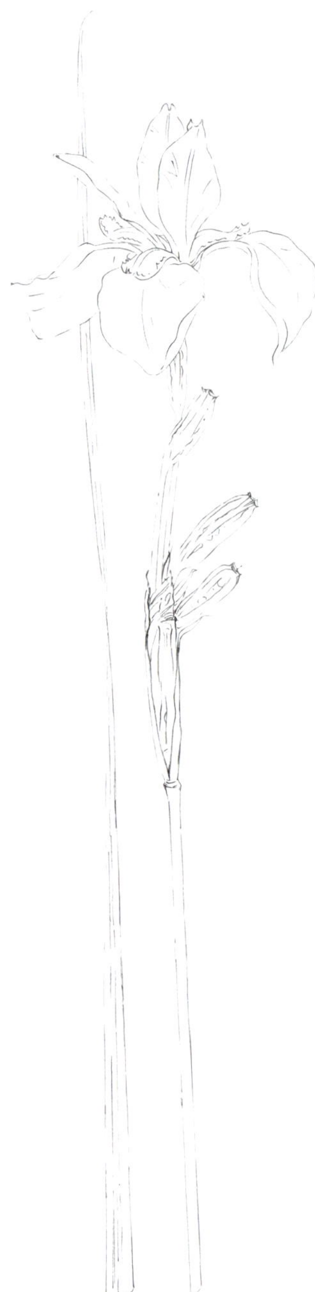

◁ **Stage 1**

Words of wisdom from Susan: 'Make sure you are comfortable with the aspect you have chosen to depict, particularly with any foreshortened views.'

Having satisfied herself on these points Susan began by making a faint line drawing using a well-sharpened B pencil (2B would also be suitable) on Bristol board. She cautions that minimal pressure should be exerted so as not to damage the paper surface.

Note: For the purposes of reproduction the line shown here is heavier than would normally be used. It is not advisable to draw the initial outlines in coloured pencil as it is very difficult, if not impossible, to completely remove any mistakes.

▷ **Stage 2**

This stage formed the base coat and used Blue Grey, Sap Green, Sunset Gold and Venetian Red. Susan removed all graphite marks before using any colour as graphite left under colour would be impossible to remove afterwards. She erased as much of the outline to the faintest of marks as she felt confident to work with (this could be only the small area you are working on at a time) and took care that her working hand did not inadvertently press any as yet unresolved pencil marks into the paper.

Using quick close-hatching strokes with only very delicate pressure, Susan applied a light layer of Blue Grey to the standard petals

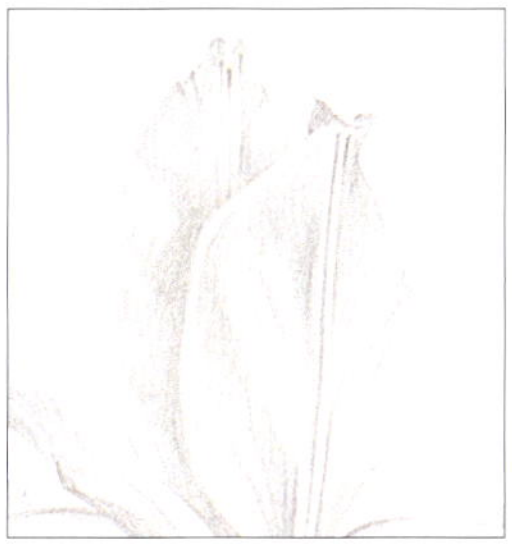

Detail from Stage 2: Darker shading and a light edge defined the front and back standards.

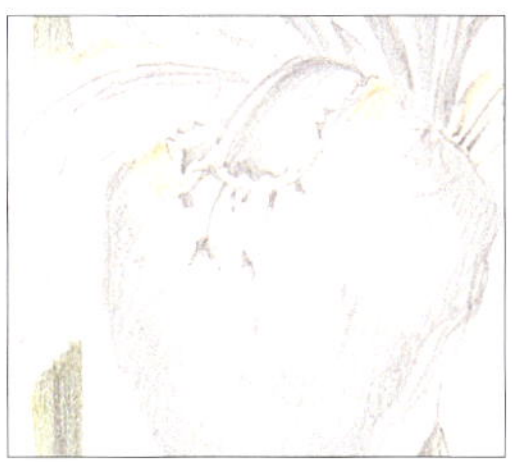

Detail from Stage 2: White areas were left in the fall petal and vein markings carefully added.

◁ Stage 2

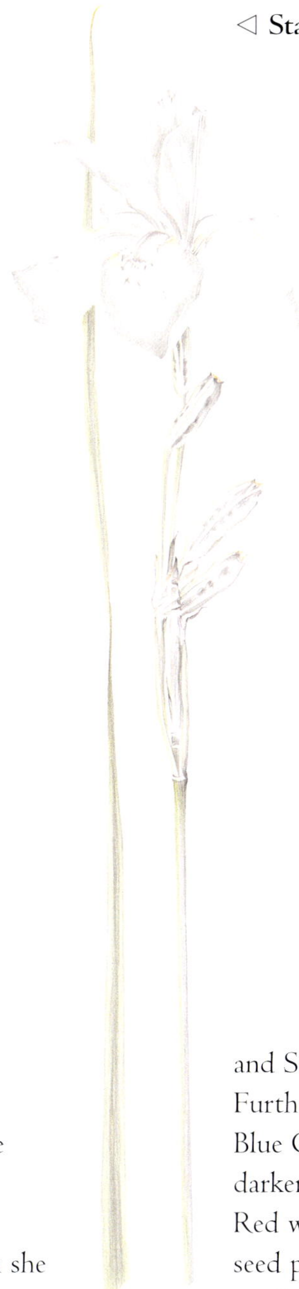

◁ Stage 3

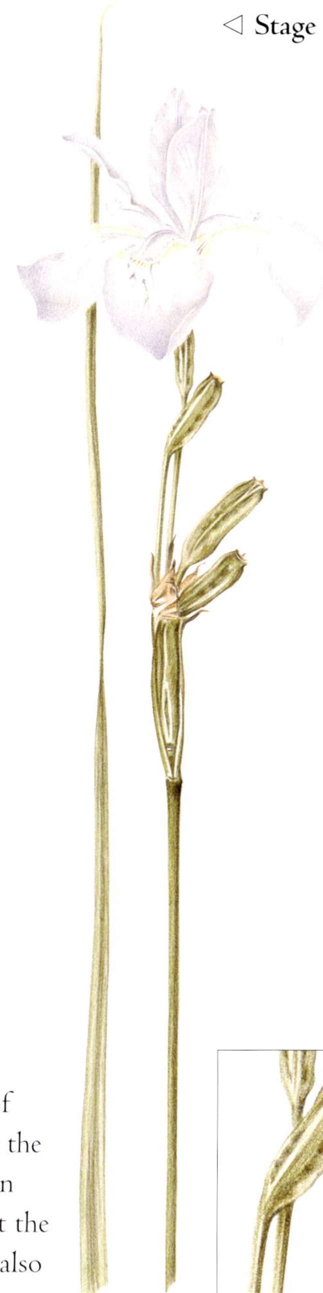

(uprights) to 'map in' the shadow areas, leaving the highlights blank, especially the fine edge of the back-view standard petal where it is seen against the petal behind. Then she mapped in the rib of the style crest and the darker serrated edges, followed by the blue areas of the fall petals, leaving the white areas under the vein markings blank. The rolled edge of the right-hand petal was also left blank. One or two of the vein markings were lightly suggested, which could act as 'landmarks'. A second slightly darker layer could also be added to areas of cast shadow or in dark folds. A light tint of Sunset Gold was used to indicate the position of then-yellow areas on the fall petals.

For the stem, leaf and seed pods a light layer of Blue Grey was applied to shadow areas and Sap Green to lighter areas. Further slightly heavier layers of Blue Grey would be needed for the darker shadows. Finally Venetian Red was applied to the detail at the seed pod tips. This colour was also applied to the drying tips of the calyx and to the leaf tip, which could also have a fine line of Sunset Gold.

△ Stage 3

This stage intensified the colour overall.

The Blue Grey base coat on the petals was intensified with light layers of Royal Blue to reinforce the blue colour, adding a little more depth of colour in cast shadows and creases.

A layer of Cedar Green was applied over the areas of Blue Grey and most of the green areas of the stem, leaf and seed pods, leaving any highlights or lighter areas blank.

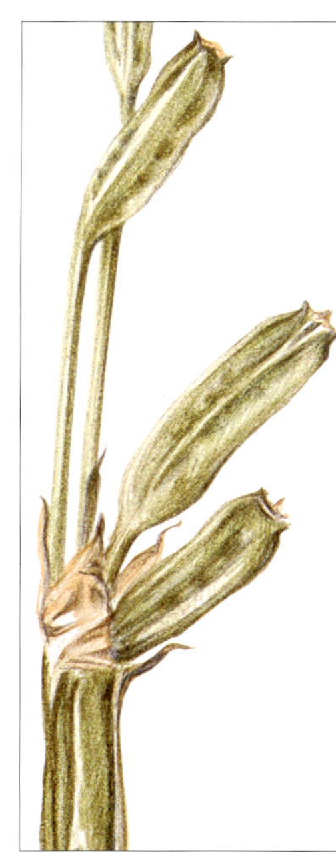

Detail from Stage 3: Limited greens were used to model the seed pods.

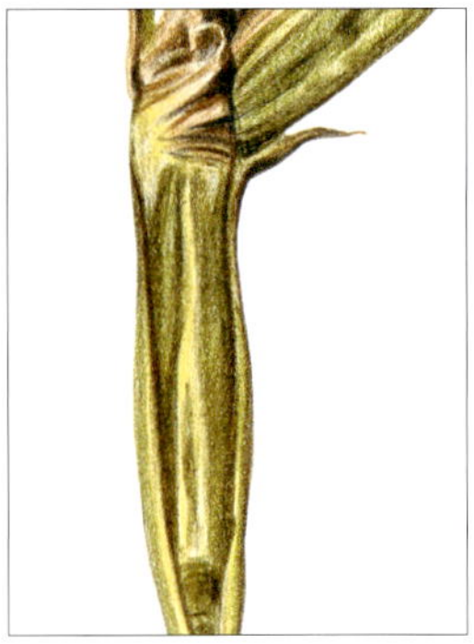

Detail from Stage 4: Venetian Red and Chocolate Brown added depth to the calyx.

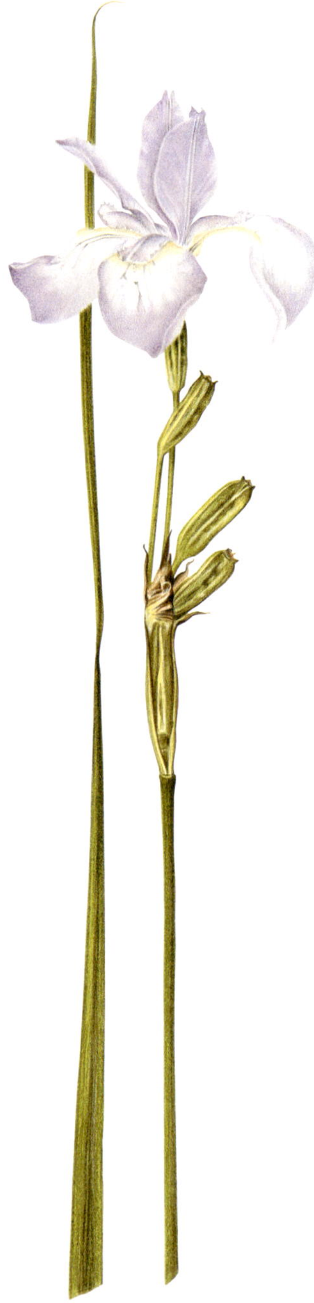

△ **Stage 4**

At this point Susan was approaching full density. She used only a very delicate layer/tint of Prismacolor Verithin Purple over the previous blue layers. Then, to return the colour to its required blue hue, she reapplied a further delicate layer of Royal Blue and continued until she felt she had achieved the desired shade. She made sure to maintain the fine paler edge to the back-view standard petal to give a sense of depth. Using a clean finger, she gently rubbed over the blue areas to smudge the colour blend, making sure not to go over the edges, though they could be cleaned up with a putty rubber if needed. It is a subtle process – note here the right fall petal had not yet been smudged. This process had to be completed before any pattern markings were added.

A Light Violet tint was blended into the blues on the style crests and a tint on the lighter areas, keeping colour almost transparent, then a touch of Teal Blue blended over to return to a blue hue. Yellow on the falls was strengthened with just a touch of Venetian Red where there was a cast shadow.

Light layers of Sap Green and Moss Green were blended into the mid-green areas of the stem, leaf and seed pods and Chartreuse into the areas where most light falls, but still keeping the colour semi-transparent. More density was added to the drying part of the calyx using Venetian Red with the addition of Chocolate Brown to the darkest shadows.

▷ **Final Stage**

The vein positions and 'splashy' markings were marked in with gentle pressure and a fine line, using a tint of well-sharpened Blue Grey; a 'fidgety' line avoided too stiff a pattern. Caran d'Ache Supracolor Purple was used to darken the heaviest markings in the centre of the falls and on some of the veins on the curled edges of the fall petals (over the yellow). On less significant veins towards the edges of the fall petals Royal Blue was used gently over the Blue Grey. A tint of Felt Grey softened the white areas between the darker pattern markings.

Susan continued to intensify all the shades of green on the stem, leaf and seed pods to create a solid depth of colour that would contrast with the delicacy of the petals. She used Caran d'Ache Supracolor Lime Green to help the density on the highlights, including those on the calyx. More Blue Grey intensified the darkest tones in the shadows.

She ensured the background was totally clean, using a clean plastic eraser and small pieces of putty rubber kneaded into the appropriate shape to clean awkward corners.

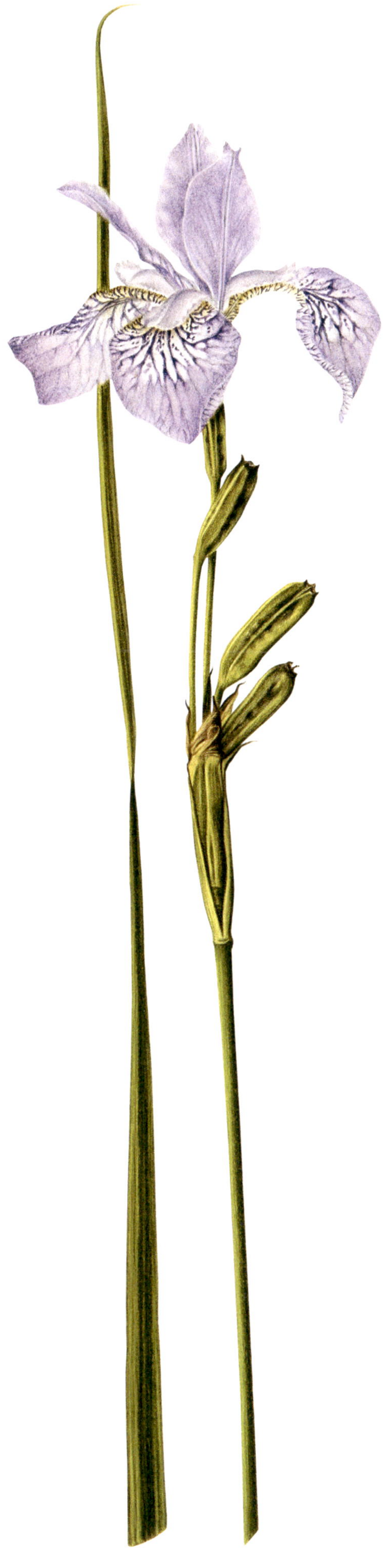

IRIS SIBERICA

37 × 9.5 cm (14½ × 3¾ in)

Susan Christopher-Coulson SBA

CHAPTER 5

PURPLE

Described by many students as 'frightening', the secondary colour of purple is of great importance to the botanical palette. So many flowers come into this colour range, from palest lilac to rich violet.

Like the blue derived from lapis lazuli, purple was an expensive dye, manufactured from the mucus of a particular type of snail and known as Tyrian Purple. Not surprisingly it was only affordable by the wealthiest, hence its association with royalty. The people of Tyre paid a different price as they lived with the stench that emanated from the piles of mollusc shells stewing in the sun!

We tend to forget what a drab place the world would have seemed to the ordinary person prior to the nineteenth century, at least to our eyes. Vegetable dyes were used to colour garments and natural mineral dyes provided pigments, with an exception or two such as the cochineal beetle, which gave its life by the trillion to produce carmine. There again, that was for cardinals' robes and it is doubtful if most people ever actually saw a cardinal. Flowers provided the colour and, of course, there were far fewer varieties than we see today.

All this was to change in 1856 when an eighteen-year-old chemist, William Henry Perkin, discovered mauveine, the first synthetic pigment. The effect on industry on both sides of the Atlantic was immense and led to the distillation of coal tar, from which aniline dyes were developed. These aniline dyes revolutionized the textile and fashion industry, making colour more affordable for the lower classes. Above all, a range of synthetic pigments gradually became available, thus widening the palette in a way that had seemed unthinkable before a teenager showed the way.

▷ BEARDED IRIS
48 × 26 cm
(19 × 10¼ in)
Vicky Mappin SBA

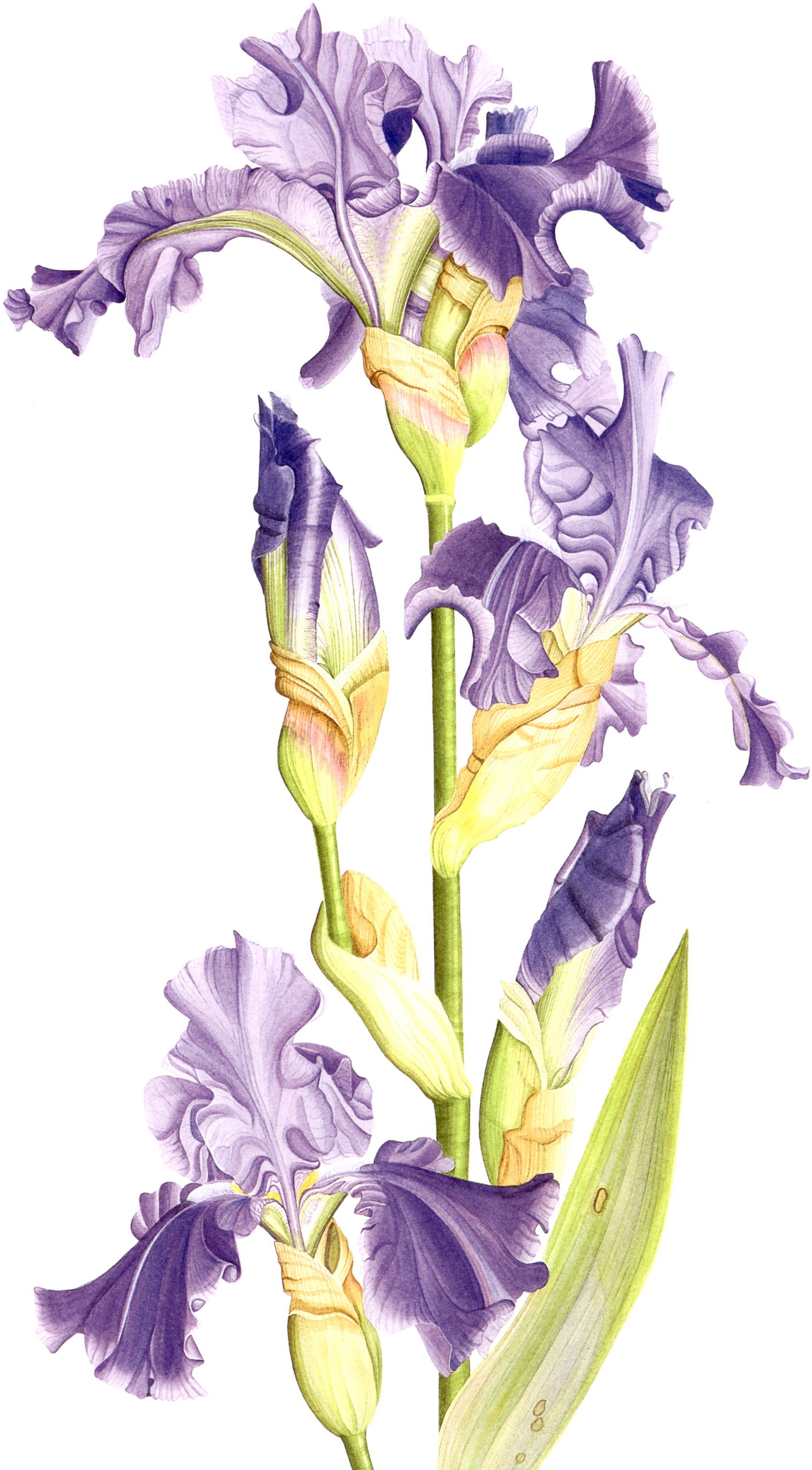

COLUMBINE

Aquilegia

Valerie Baines FSBA

Although its common name Columbine traditionally links this flower with the dove, it is actually derived from the Latin *aquila*, meaning eagle, in reference to the often long, elegant spurs. These dainty flowers have a cottage garden appeal and it does not take much imagination to see each flower as a small flock of doves.

PAINTS

WINSOR & NEWTON
Winsor Violet
Permanent Rose
Scarlet Lake
Alizarin Crimson
Winsor Lemon
Cobalt Blue
Payne's Grey

BRUSHES

WINSOR & NEWTON
Designers' sable sizes 2, 1 and 00

SURFACE

FABRIANO
Artistico HP 300 gsm (140 lb)

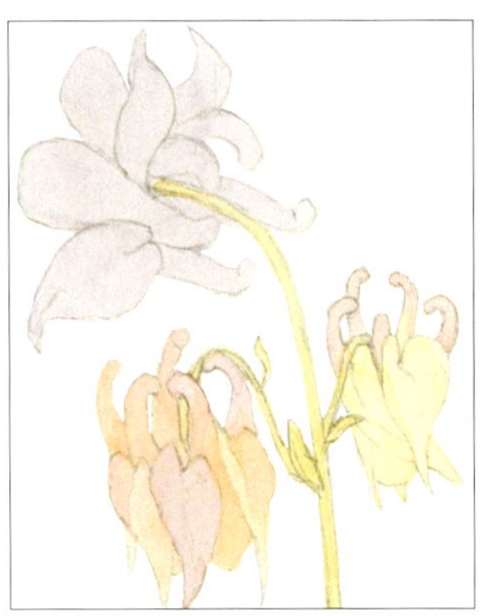

Detail from Stage 1: Starting with a very pale wash ensured that the delicate areas of colour were established and could be maintained as the flower was built up.

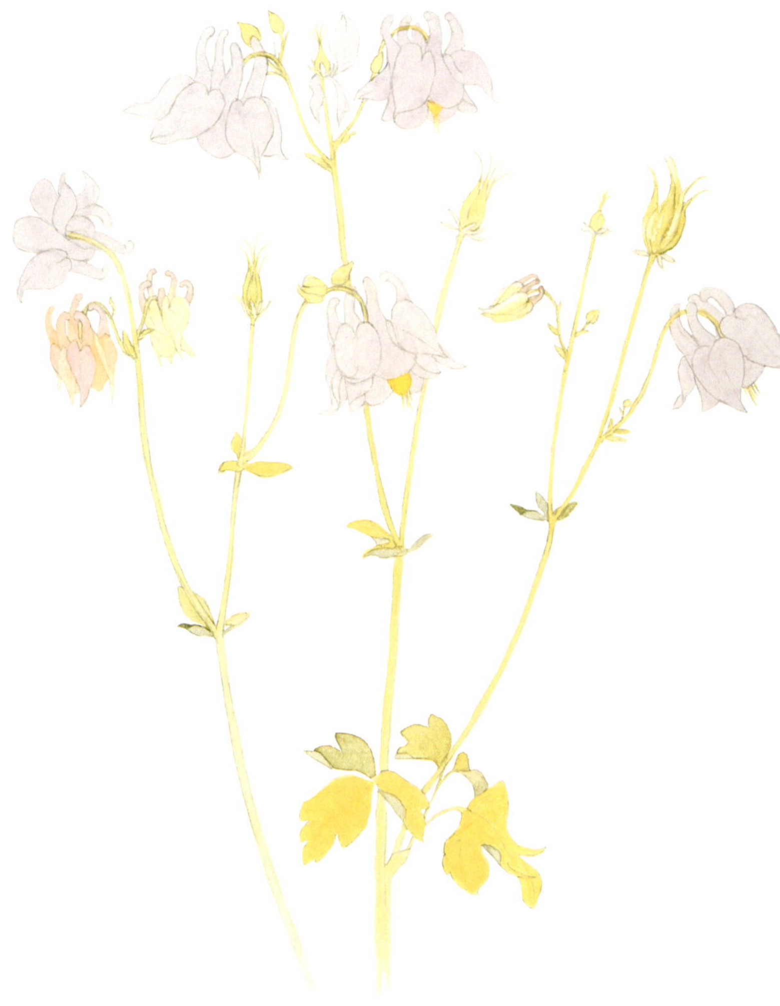

△ **Stage 1**
Valerie worked out her drawing first on tracing paper, studying the plant from all angles to find the best arrangement. When she was happy with the composition she transferred her drawing onto watercolour paper. Then, using a size 2 brush she began to apply the palest washes of mainly mixed colours. For the majority of the flowers this was a mixture of Winsor Violet with a small amount of Permanent Rose.

The pollen showing in just two flowers was Winsor Lemon slightly warmed with a touch of Scarlet Lake.

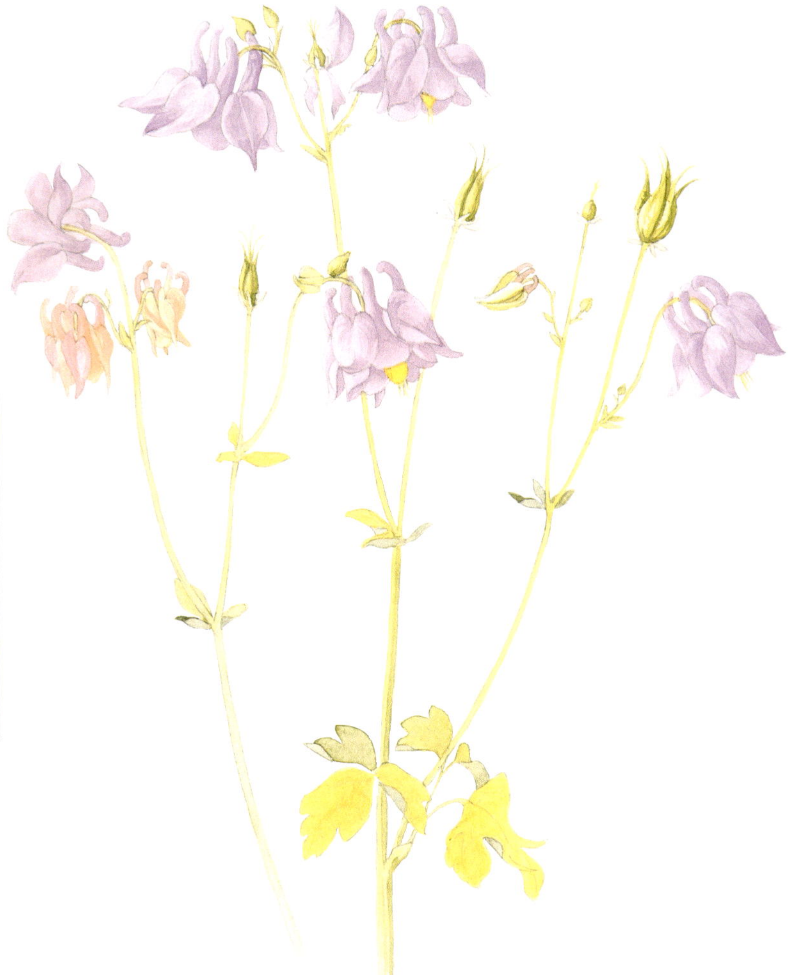

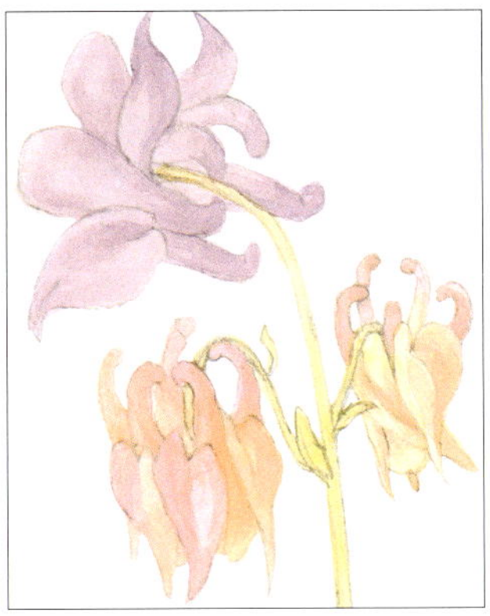

Detail from Stage 2: Sometimes only the merest hint of a pigment, in this case Payne's Grey, is needed to alter the age of a flower.

The colour of the buds was more varied and required the application of a very pale yellow-green made with Winsor Lemon with a touch of Payne's Grey.

The bud on the extreme left used a pale mix of Winsor Lemon and Scarlet Lake with a touch of Winsor Violet to cool it. Some of the spurs were Winsor Violet warmed with a little Alizarin Crimson, again very pale at this stage.

The stems, seed heads and leaves were washed with a mix of Winsor Lemon with a very little Payne's Grey added.

Where light shone through the leaves quite strongly, and where light shone on them, more Payne's Grey was used.

The undersides of the leaves required Payne's Grey with a touch of Cobalt Blue and Winsor Lemon.

Valerie turned the paper sideways to achieve more flowing lines and make painting easier.

△ Stage 2

Form was given to the flowers by shading with several layers of Winsor Violet and Permanent Rose. The flower on the left was moving towards the vertical as it faded and was starting to assume the position of the seed head which it would become. This required a wash of very pale Winsor Lemon, Scarlet Lake and just a hint of Payne's Grey to give the faded effect. The same mix, but deeper, was used to shape the two buds below it, with a pale mix of Alizarin Crimson and Winsor Violet on the spurs and the darkest one and a half petals.

A second wash of the green mix (Winsor Lemon and Payne's Grey) was applied to the thickest central stem. A paler green mix was used to give shape to the buds and seed heads; then Valerie picked out the crevices in the seed heads using a darker mix that contained more Payne's Grey.

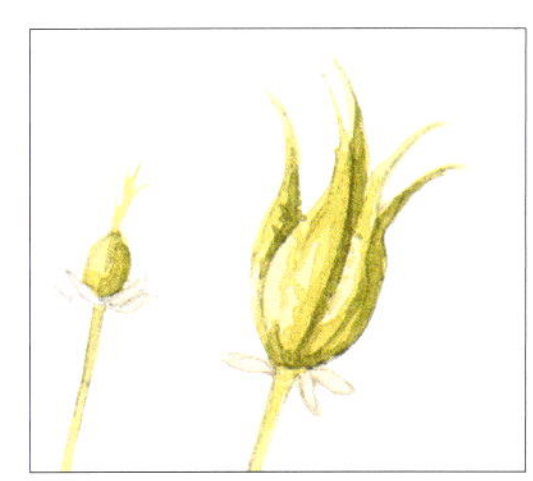

Detail from Stage 2: Picking out the crevices in the seed heads gives them form.

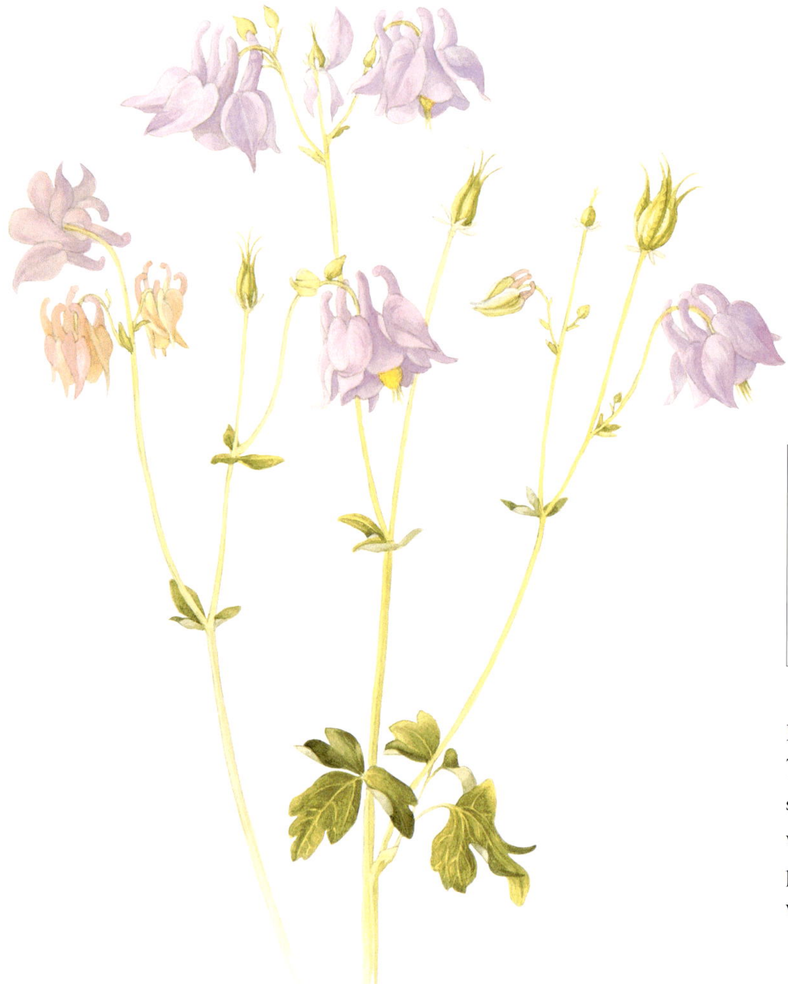

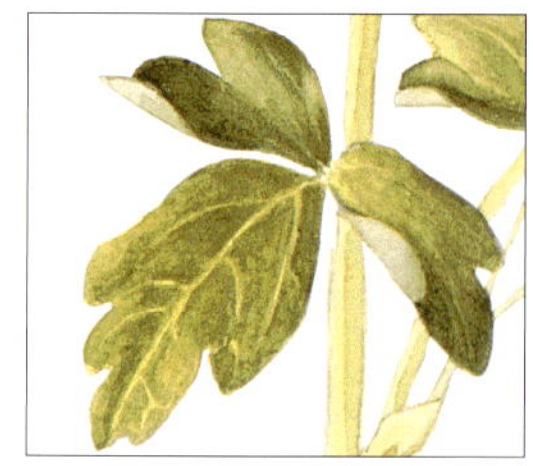

Detail from Stage 3: The light wash beneath shows up to depict the veins as Valerie carefully painted to them with varying darker tones.

△ **Stage 3**

Valerie put in the shadows on the right-hand side of the flowers and buds with a glaze of pale Cobalt Blue, still using a size 2 brush.

She also completed the leaves using Payne's Grey on top of the previous yellow-green wash, sometimes with a hint of Winsor Lemon, grading the strength of the colour where necessary and painting around the veins in the leaves.

▷ **Final Stage**

The fine details of shaping the stems and buds were added with a mixture of Scarlet Lake and Payne's Grey, using a size 1 brush. The colour was darker on the higher stems and paler on the lower ones. For touches on the top of the seed pods Valerie used a size 00 brush.

The same Scarlet Lake and Payne's Grey mix was used on the tops of the spurs and a mixture of Alizarin Crimson, Winsor Violet and Payne's Grey, varying from light to quite dark, was used to give more texture and marking on the lower part of the petals below the spurs. On the central flower Winsor Violet was omitted from the mix, resulting in a warmer tone.

The yellow pollen in two of the flowers was given shape and shadow with a pale mixture of Winsor Violet with a touch of Payne's Grey using a size 00 brush.

Finally Valerie made the usual checks to ensure that all outlines were crisp and clean and that there were no stray pencil marks.

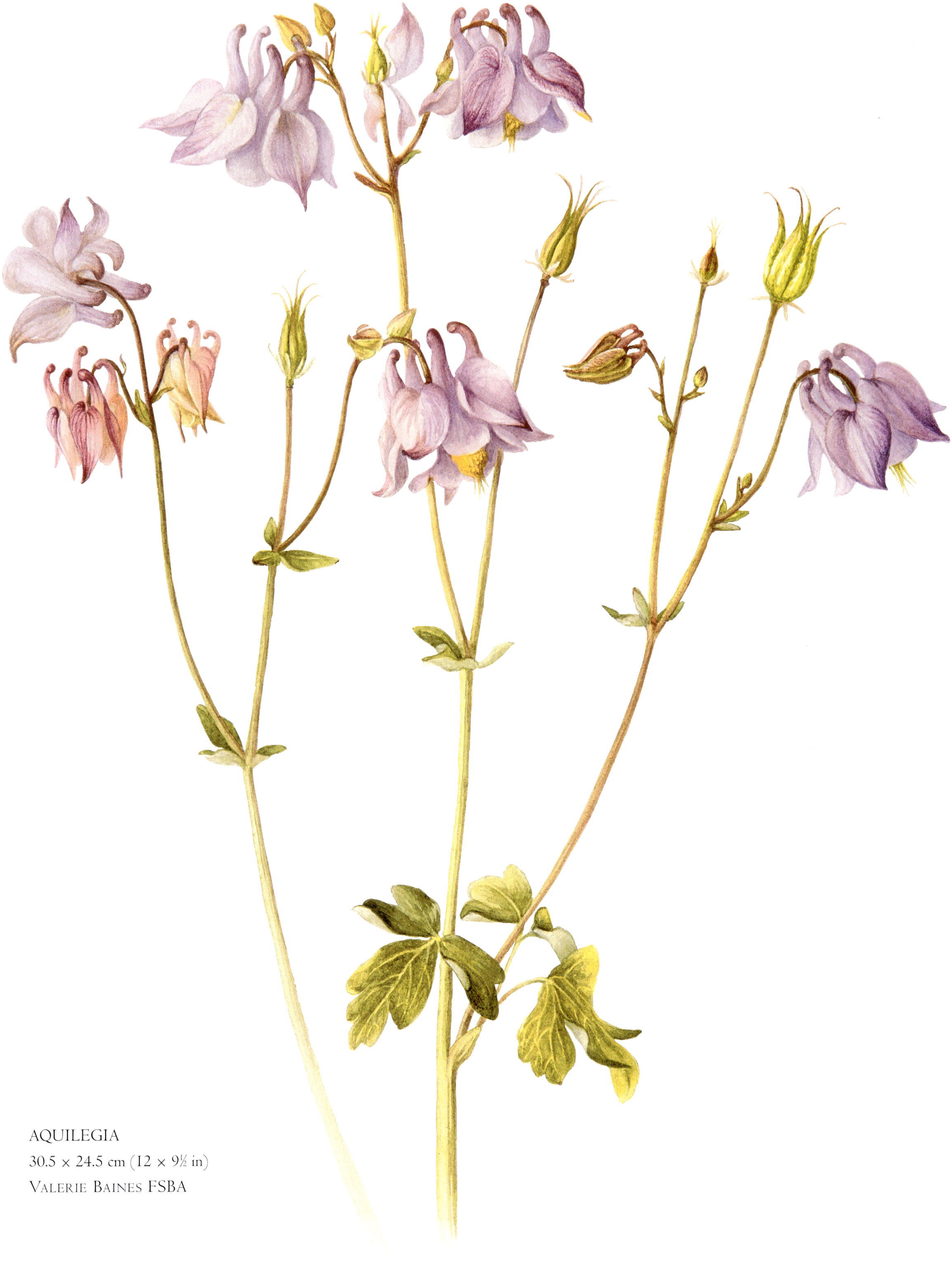

AQUILEGIA
30.5 × 24.5 cm (12 × 9½ in)
Valerie Baines FSBA

CLEMATIS

Clematis 'Star of India'

Brenda Watts SBA

There are so many wonderful Clematis cultivars that a visit to the garden centre leaves one spoilt for choice. When Brenda was invited to paint a purple specimen she chose three, including the old familiar 'Jackmanii' with its dark tones, but eventually settled on 'Star of India' for its dramatic colouring and beauty.

PAINTS

WINSOR & NEWTON
Permanent Rose
Cadmium Red Deep
Ultramarine Violet
Winsor Violet
French Ultramarine
Cerulean Blue
Winsor Blue (Red Shade)
Winsor Green (Yellow Shade)
Permanent Sap Green
Cadmium Yellow Pale
Burnt Sienna
Raw Sienna
Burnt Umber
Raw Umber

DALER-ROWNEY
White gouache

BRUSHES

WINSOR & NEWTON
Series 7 sizes 000, 00, 2, 4 and 6

SURFACE

FABRIANO
Artistico 300 gsm (140 lb)

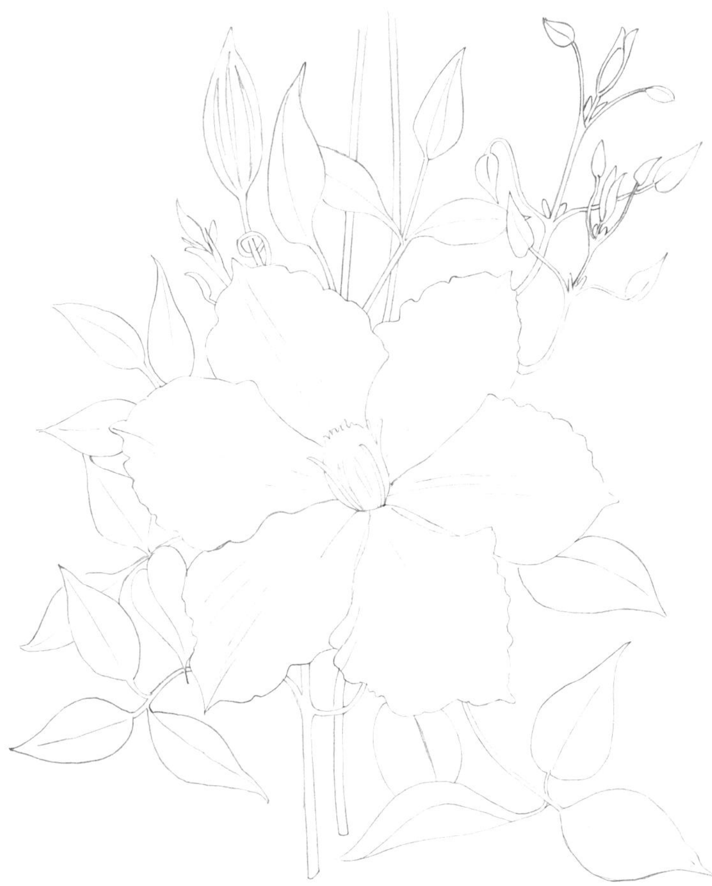

△ **Stage 1**
Brenda started with a pencil drawing, taking great care to create a pleasing composition, in which the buds, leaves and delicate tendrils would provide a foil for this 'in your face' flower. The pencil drawing would also allow her to 'feel' her way around the various shapes.

▷ **Stage 2**
She then started painting, using a size 6 brush flooded with Permanent Rose to apply the first wash to the flower.

The tips of the petals were painted with a hint of Cadmium Red Deep. Further washes were added and the ribs and shaded areas indicated with Permanent Rose.

The bud was washed with Cadmium Yellow and the leaves with Winsor Green (Yellow

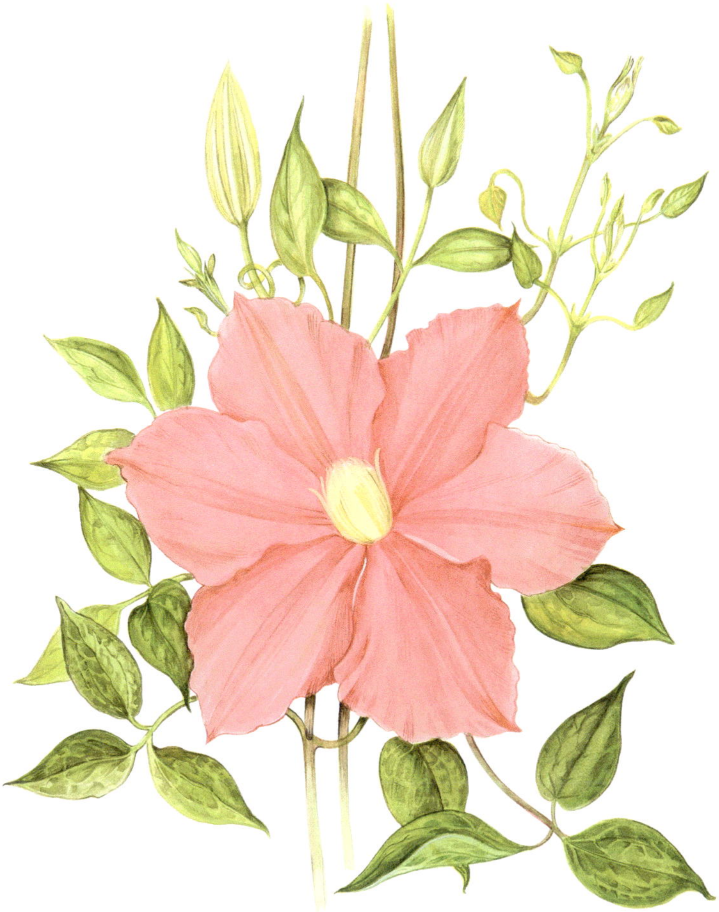

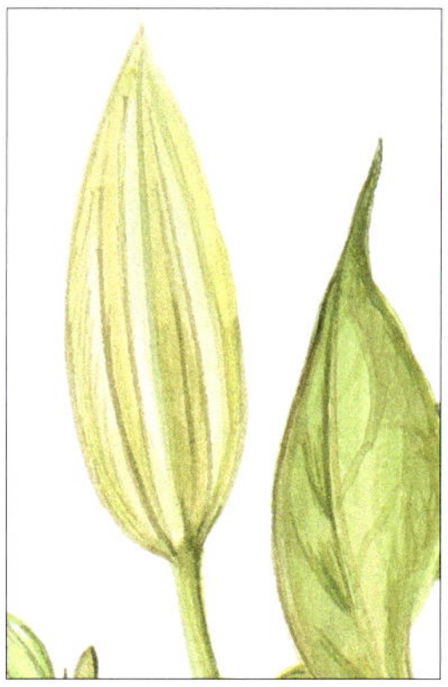

Detail from Stage 2: Cadmium Yellow Pale was used for the first wash on the bud.

Shade), to which Cadmium Yellow Pale was added as they dried and in places French Ultramarine and Raw Sienna.

The attractive long woody stems were painted with Permanent Rose, Winsor Green (Yellow Shade) and Burnt Sienna.

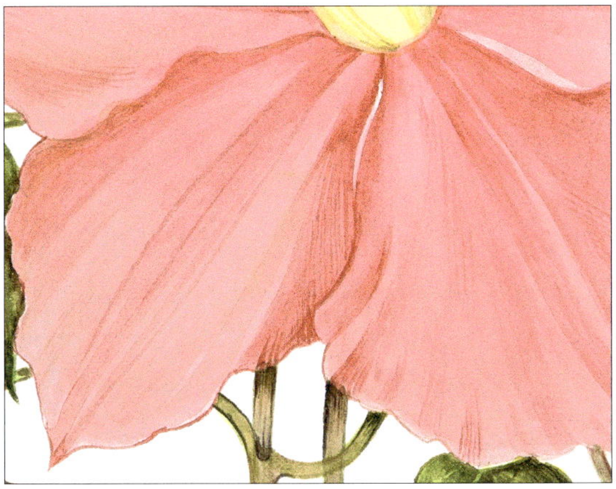

Detail from Stage 2:
Permanent Rose provided the foundation on which a glowing purple could later be built.

Stage 3 (see overleaf)
Using a size 4 brush, three thin washes of Ultramarine Violet were used to build up the flower colours, carefully avoiding the ribs and filaments. The ribs were heightened by adding touches of Cadmium Red and Permanent Rose, using a size 2 brush. To emphasize the petals, they were stroked with Winsor Blue (Red Shade) and Ultramarine Violet on the curved shapes, using the size 2 brush and going deeper into the shadows.

Brenda added a mixture of thin Cadmium Yellow with a tinge of Permanent Sap Green onto the filaments, allowing a hint of Permanent Rose to shine through. Using a 00 brush she started to indicate the veins on the petals, making sure she kept a steady hand throughout this delicate work.

Further touches of Permanent Sap Green and Raw Umber, with a little Permanent Rose for warmth, were added to the leaves and buds, thus building up depth of colour.

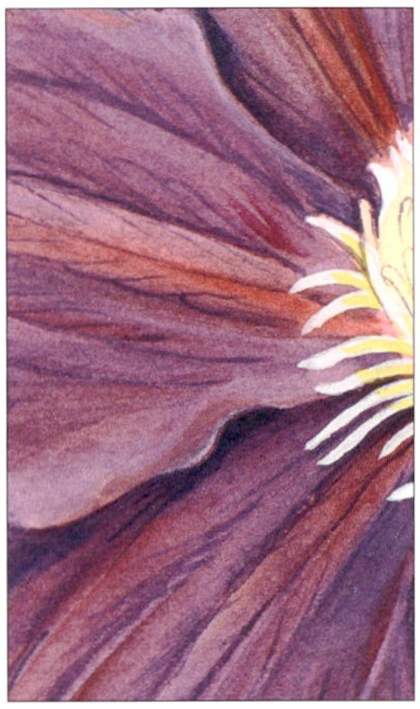

Detail from Stage 3: Thin washes of Ultramarine Violet were carefully applied to build up a rich colour around the filaments.

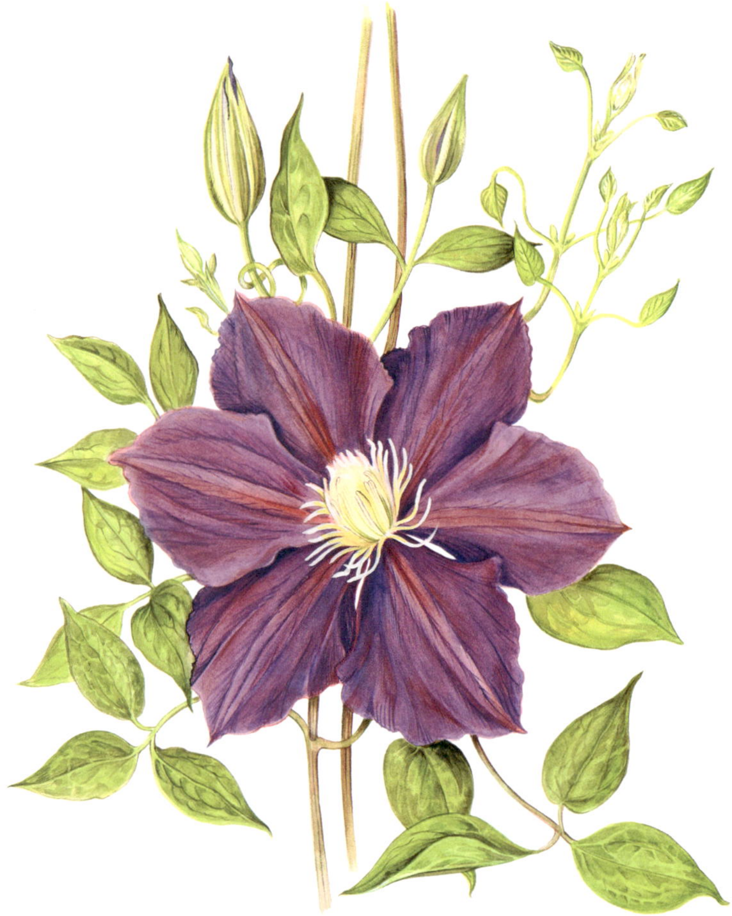

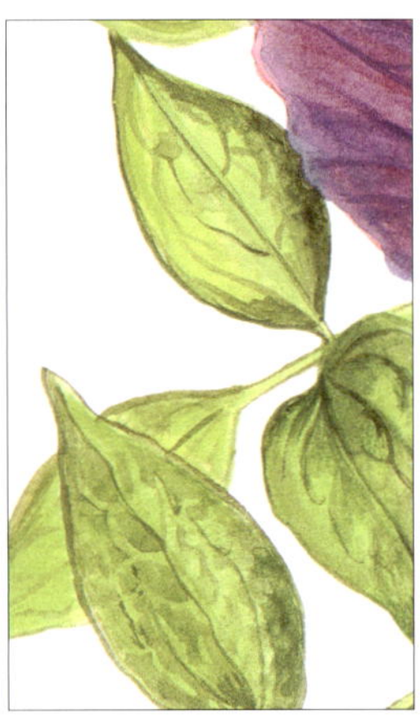

Detail from Stage 3: The leaves were darkened with a mix of Permanent Sap Green and Burnt Umber.

△ **Stage 3** (continued)
Using a size 2 brush, Brenda put another thin glaze of Winsor Blue (Red Shade) and Winsor Violet, a warmer colour than the Ultramarine Violet, on the petals, mostly at the tips, avoiding some of the ribs. With a size 00 brush she used small strokes of Cadmium Red Deep and Permanent Rose near the tips of the petal ribs.

She also indicated more sepals using a mix of Ultramarine Violet and Burnt Umber, leaving most of the work for the final stage.

Turning her attention to the leaves Brenda painted them a darker hue using a mix of Permanent Sap Green and Burnt Umber. The stems were also darkened using Burnt Umber and Permanent Rose.

▷ **Final Stage**
Starting with the buds, Brenda used dry brush technique and white gouache to crosshatch the buds and stalks, then with the tiny 000 brush she painted in the hairs. (Artists' gouache in Chinese white was a more suitable paint to use for this than Designers' body colour.) The technique required a very steady hand and the use of a magnifying glass.

Next she painted the filaments as these would be the focal point of the painting. Again she used white gouache and the tiny brush. The green base of the filaments was painted with Cadmium Yellow Pale and a tiny amount of Cerulean Blue.

Finally Brenda looked at the clematis as a whole, deciding where to put the shadows on the petals, using a mix of Permanent Rose and Winsor Violet. The leaves required further highlighting and this was done with a mix of Permanent Sap Green, Raw Sienna and a touch of Winsor Violet.

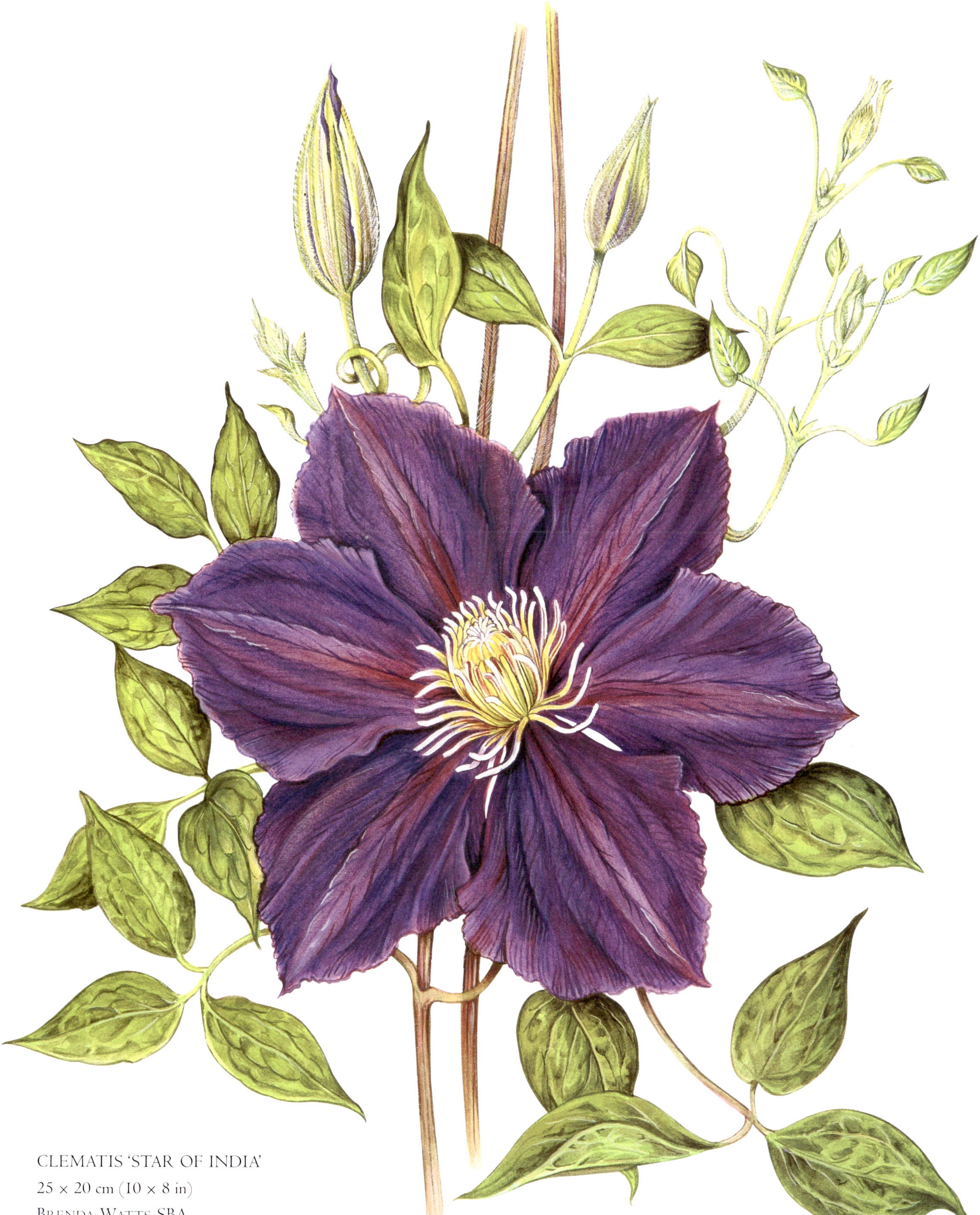

CLEMATIS 'STAR OF INDIA'
25 × 20 cm (10 × 8 in)
BRENDA WATTS SBA

Project *Clematis* 'Star of India'

The drawing for this has been simplified slightly, with fewer leaves and tendrils. This clematis provides an excellent subject on which to practise building up colour and for using the underlying hue to achieve the final shade, which is first apparent to the eye. So many times in botanical painting you need to analyse the colour before you – 'X-ray' it with your eyes and work out your starting point. Failure to do this will generally lead to disappointing results. Of course this is not always the case, but it often is with those flowers that seem to glow as if lit from within.

This project also gives excellent practice in painting leaves as they are a straightforward shape with clearly marked veins, while the small lengths of stem will be helpful in developing brush control.

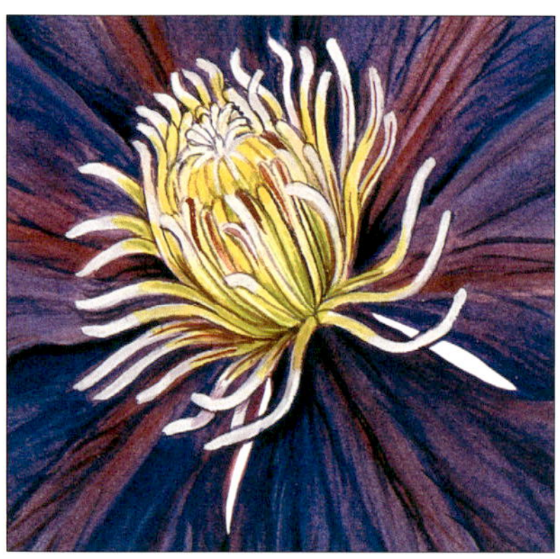

Detail from Final Stage: The filaments were given substance with careful brushwork, using Artists' white gouache, Cadmium Yellow Pale and Cerulean Blue.

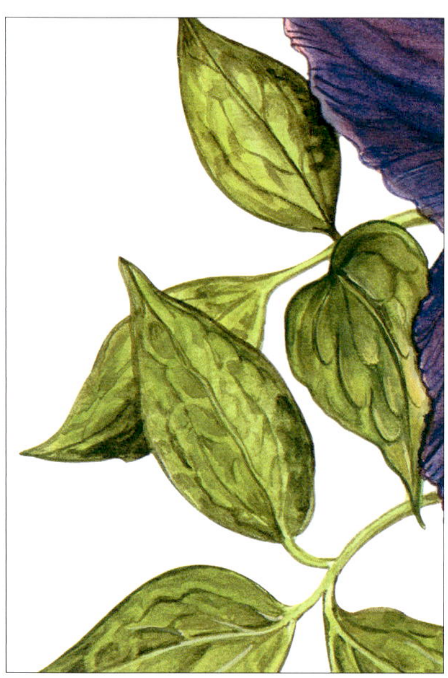

Detail from Final Stage: The leaves were given more detail and form by darkening shadows and veins.

Colour Chart

FLOWERS AND SEPALS

- **1** Permanent Rose
- **2** Cadmium Red Deep over Permanent Rose
- **3** Ultramarine Violet + Permanent Rose
- **4** Winsor Blue (Red Shade) over **3**
- **5** Cadmium Red Deep
- **6** Ultramarine Violet
- **7** Winsor Blue (Red Shade)
- **8** Winsor Violet
- **9** Permanent Rose + Winsor Violet

STAMENS

- **1** Cadmium Yellow
- **2** Permanent Sap Green
- **3** Cadmium Yellow + Permanent Sap Green over pale Permanent Rose
- **4** Cerulean Blue

LEAVES AND STEMS

- **1** Winsor Green (Yellow Shade)
- **2** Cadmium Yellow Pale + Winsor Green (Yellow Shade)
- **3** French Ultramarine + **2**
- **4** Raw Sienna + **2**
- **5** Permanent Sap Green + Burnt Umber
- **6** Burnt Umber
- **7** Raw Sienna
- **8** French Ultramarine

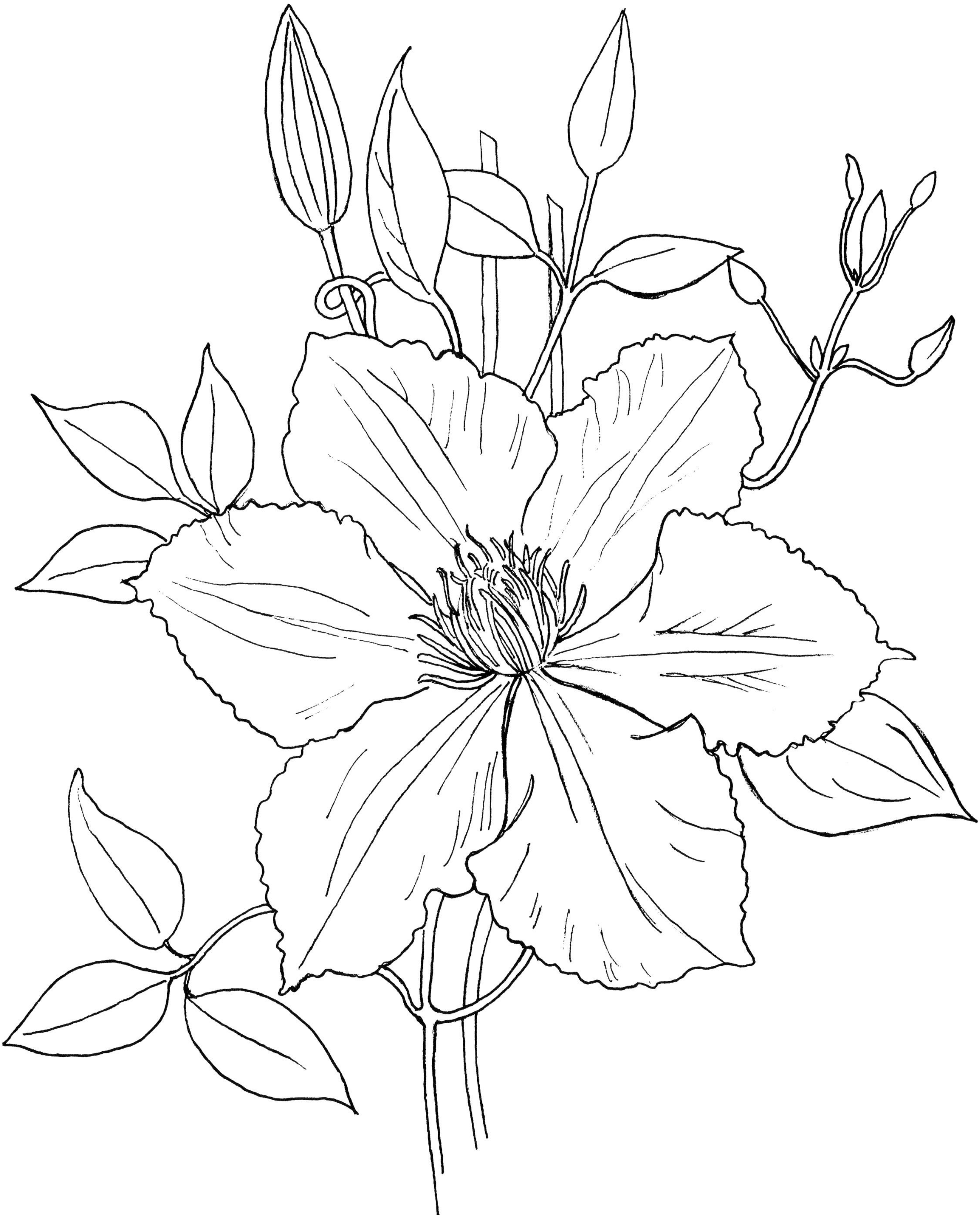

CHAPTER 6

RED

RED IS NO LONGER a luxury pigment reserved for illuminated manuscripts or as an expensive dye for ceremonial robes or military tunics.

Vermilion, originally a mineral pigment made from cinnabar, which dates from pre-history, is still available from Sennelier as both Chinese Vermilion and the brilliant French Vermilion. Carmine, dependent in Europe on the kermes insect until after 1492 when the discovery of the Americas introduced the cochineal insect to our shores, is still farmed in South America to the present day. The insect's diet of nopal cactus produces the colour. Although beautifully transparent the colour will fade in strong light; some artists continue to use it sparingly and trust in the common sense of their clients to care for their paintings properly. Finally, Madder, a vegetable dye from the madder plant, along with its synthetic substitute alizarin, has been an important part of the palette since Egyptian times.

Many other hues, mainly of chemical source, are available to the artist today, but few carry with them the romance of their origins in quite the same way as those mentioned above.

On a practical point, sometimes brilliant colours disappoint when they dry to a duller finish. A few drops of gum arabic in the water will help to avoid this and also enable the paint to flow freely from the brush – useful for larger washes of colour. Remember that the whiter the paper the more the pigment will reflect light and the harder the paper surface the less chance there is of it absorbing the paint like blotting paper. Finally, sometimes a glaze of another colour can work wonders. Schmincke Translucent Orange works well over reds and can lift the colour to another dimension.

▷ RED HEMEROCALLIS DAY LILIES
38 × 28 cm (15 × 11 in)
VALERIE WRIGHT VPSBA

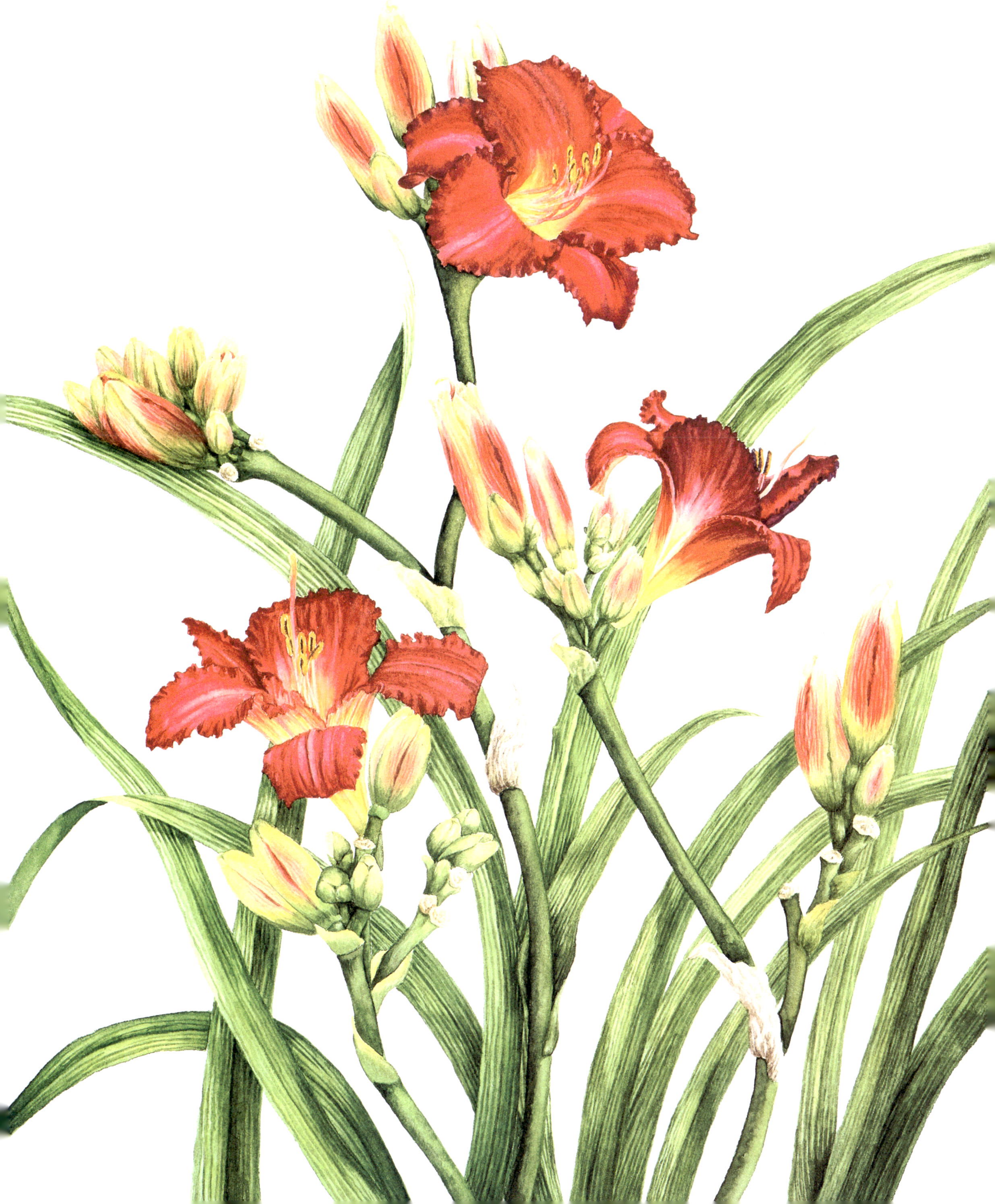

CYCLAMEN

Cyclamen persicum

Jennifer Jenkins SBA

Cyclamen are popular with experienced painters and students alike; artists are drawn to their wide range of clear bright colours coupled with a variety of leaf shapes, colours and patterns. These plants also provide interesting subjects to paint in the dark days of winter before the spring flowers give more choice than we can cope with in a season.

PAINTS

WINSOR & NEWTON
Permanent Sap Green
Raw Umber
Permanent Rose
Winsor Violet
Quinacridone Magenta
Cadmium Lemon

SCHMINCKE
Prussian Blue
Cadmium Red Light
Burnt Sienna
Magenta
Permanent Carmine

BRUSHES

WINSOR & NEWTON
Series 7 sable sizes 5, 2 and 0

SURFACE

ARCHES
Aquarelle HP 300 gsm (140 lb)

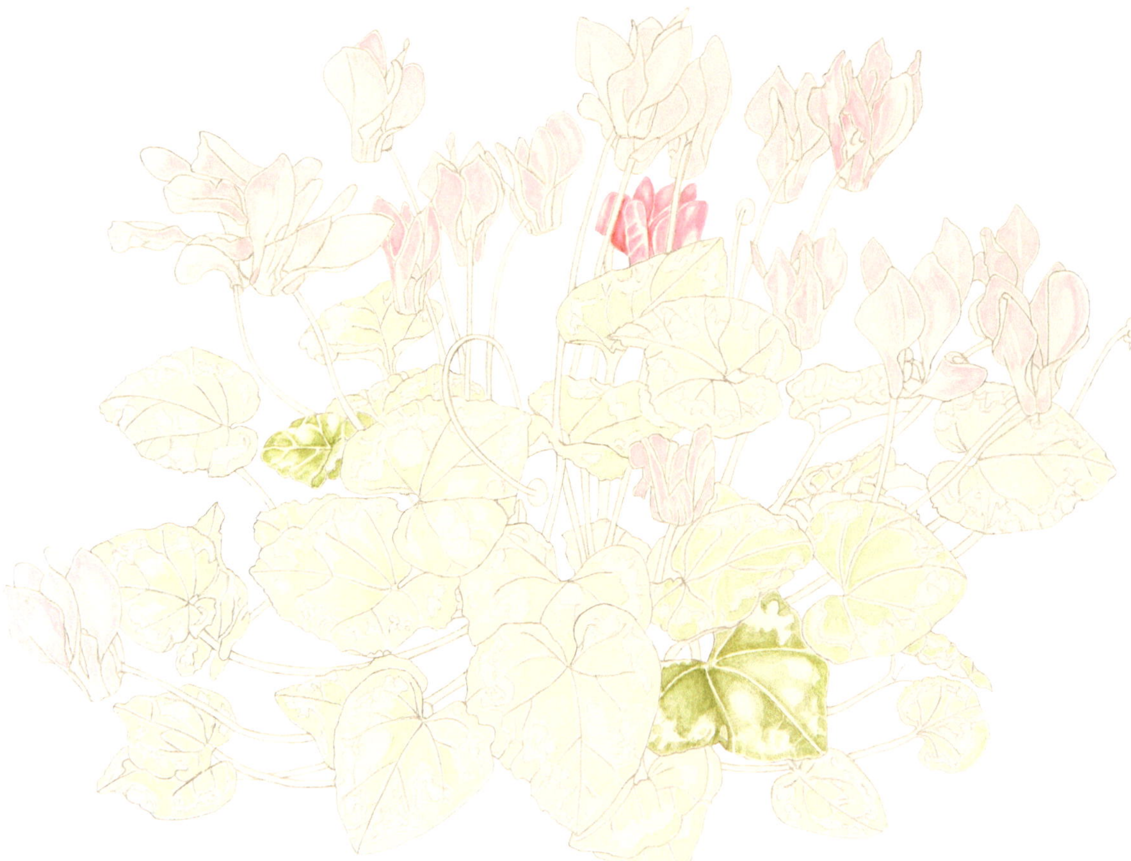

△ **Stage 1**
A delicate pencil outline was drawn using a 0.3mm Pentel; this included all the major veins and gave an indication of the skeleton veins and patterns. Jennifer then applied a watery wash of Permanent Sap Green mixed with Raw Umber, using a size 5 brush with a fine point, which holds a fair amount of paint. She was careful to avoid all pencil lines and left the patterns white, including highlighted, lighter areas.

While laying down the wash Jennifer had a clean, damp size 2 brush ready to take up any surplus paint if necessary. She then worked on one or two leaves to build up the painting a little by adding a touch of Prussian Blue to the previous green mix, again being careful not to let the paint touch the pencil lines.

The flowers were washed over with a very pale mix of Permanent Rose with a little Magenta, except for two, which were washed

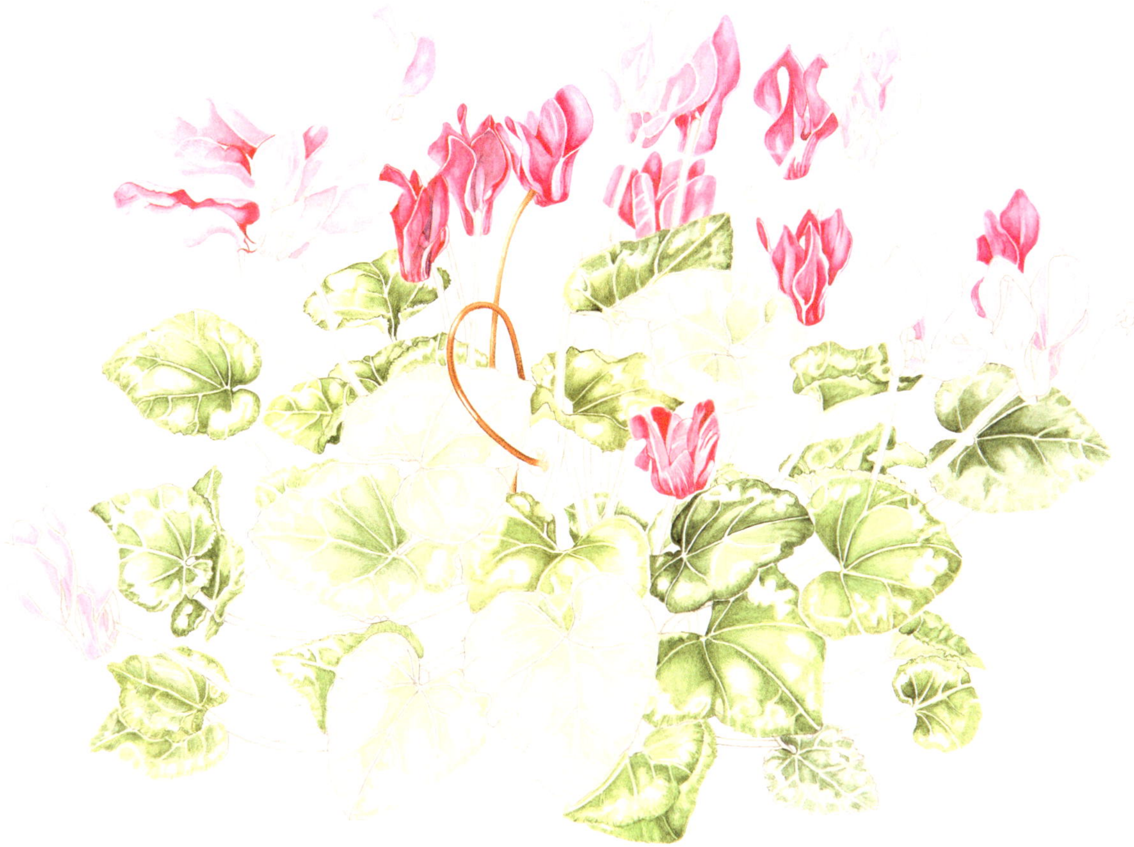

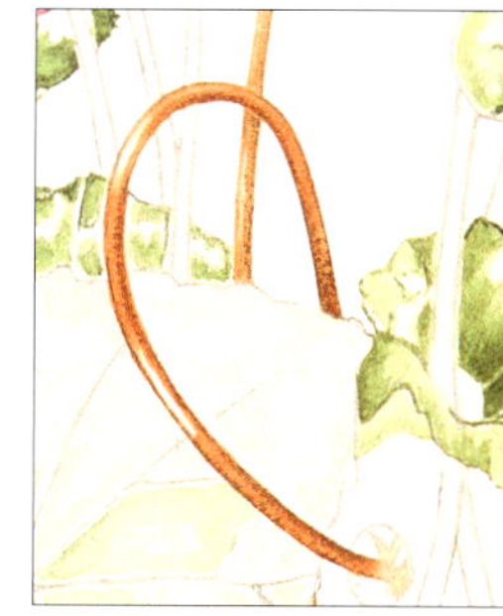

Detail from Stage 2: Time spent on carefully painting and shading stems is vitally important. This curved beauty needed a steady flowing hand to control the brush. Every stem required the same attention to detail.

with a mix of Permanent Rose and Permanent Carmine as they were a different colour. Two leaves and two flowers were developed a little to indicate the next stage of the painting.

△ Stage 2

Leaves were intensified with a wash of Permanent Sap Green, Raw Umber and Prussian Blue with, in some cases, a touch of Cadmium Red Light, blending in around the lighter areas and softening with a clean, damp brush. Pencil lines were gradually removed.

Two stems were painted using Raw Umber and Burnt Sienna. A very pale glaze was first applied with the size 2 brush. On the thicker stem a very fine line was painted on either side using a size 0 brush, pulling the colour carefully from one side of the stem to give a rounded appearance and to show its rich colour. The size 2 brush was used to define the veins on some of the leaves and the colour pulled out on either side with another, slightly damp, size 2 brush, which blended the edges.

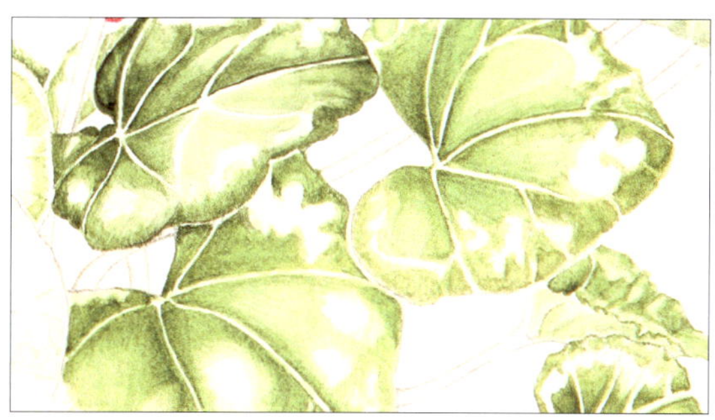

Detail from Stage 2: More leaves were worked and veins delineated as colour was blended around them.

The older blooms were painted first with a mix of Permanent Rose and Magenta, then a little Winsor Violet was added as the petals were deepening with age. Jennifer knew it was important to capture older blooms quickly in this study, in case she lost them prematurely, which might have spoiled the composition.

Younger blooms were washed with a paler colour that was a thin mix of Permanent Rose and Quinacridone Magenta.

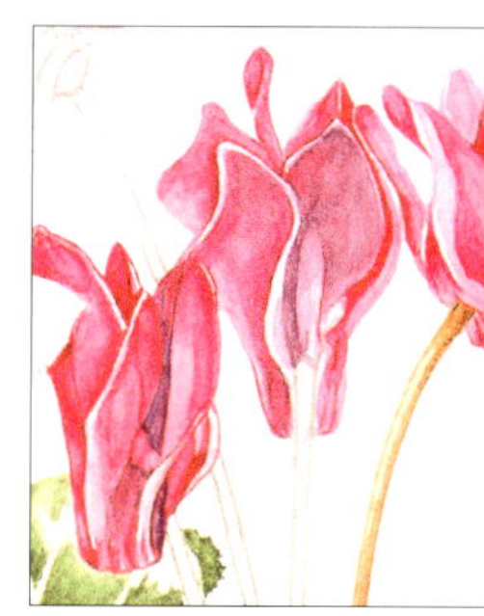

Detail from Stage 2: Older blooms needed to be painted early on in order to capture their changing colour before they faded.

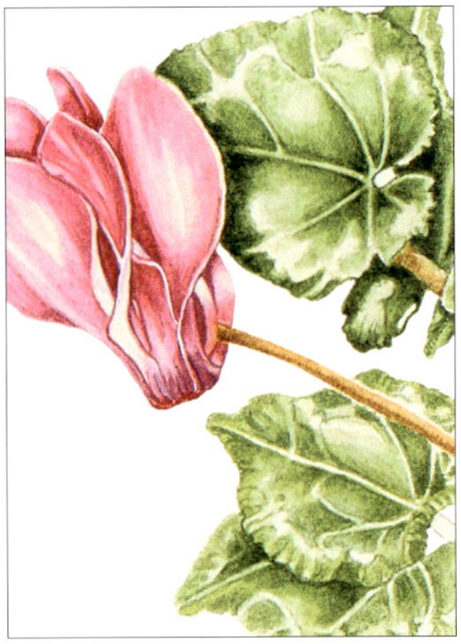

Detail from Stage 3: More detail of veining and colour was added to this group of leaves. Note the strong shadow cast by the flower, giving the sought-after three-dimensional effect.

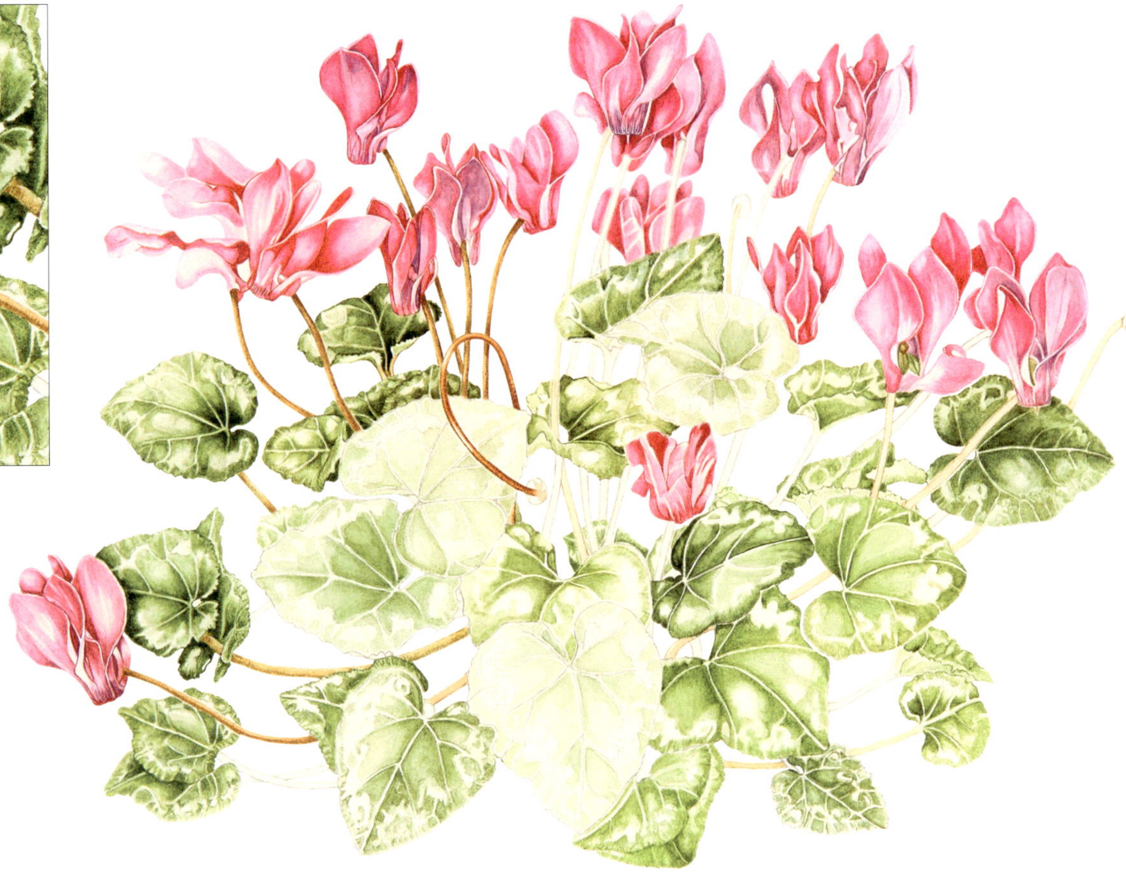

△ **Stage 3**

All the flowers were intensified in colour and detail before they faded. Permanent Carmine and Winsor Violet were used to strengthen deep shadow areas.

Some stems were glazed thinly with Raw Umber and Burnt Sienna, outlined on one or two sides in Burnt Sienna.

More leaves were intensified with a stronger wash than before, keeping the pencil lines in place. The leaves on the left-hand side were intensified, the pattern closely observed and defined, and all pencil lines were removed.

▷ **Final Stage**

Jennifer used a mix of Burnt Sienna and Raw Umber to outline the flower stems strongly on one side, then glazed overall with a light wash of Burnt Sienna. She used sizes 0 and 2 brushes. The stems were shaded below and between the leaves.

Leaf stems were washed lightly with Raw Umber, then rounded with the leaf green mix and pale Permanent Rose. The bud stems and bud heads were given a stronger mix of Raw Umber and Burnt Sienna in different areas. Green was again used in the central bud and the stem at its base section.

Jennifer continued to work in the leaves, keeping carefully to the pattern and removing pencil lines as she worked. Observing the direction of the light, she used a mix of Raw Umber, Permanent Sap Green and Prussian Blue, with a small amount of water. Next she modelled the areas around the veins, strengthening one side of the main veins with stronger green to give texture. The deep shadows were intensified with an additional touch of Cadmium Red Light. Some leaves had slightly raised sections, while others had a flatter appearance. Two leaves were pink on the underside, which required a thin wash of Magenta and Permanent Rose.

The serrated edges of the leaves were crisped up and clear water washed over any patterned leaf areas left white.

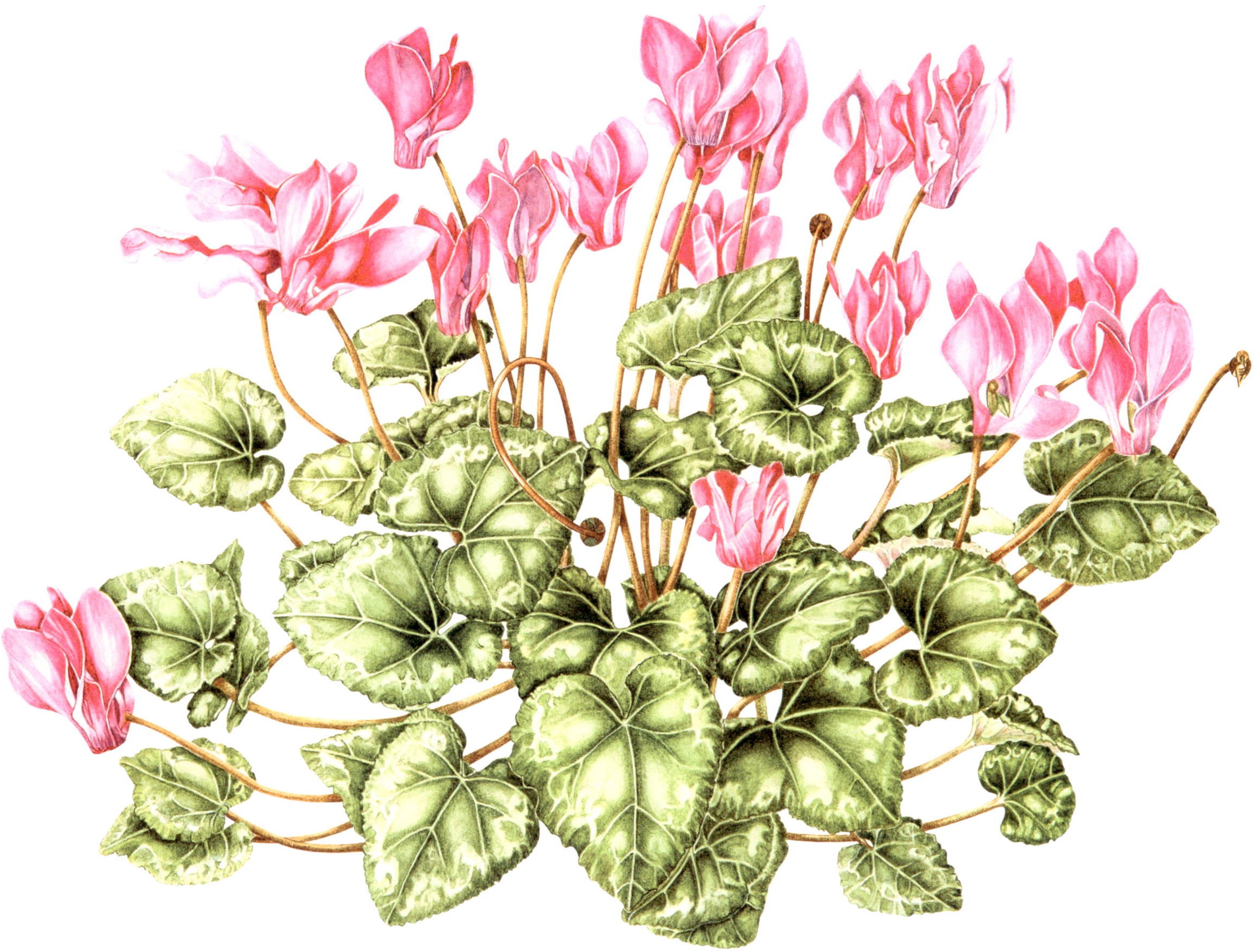

CYCLAMEN PERSICUM
18.8 × 25.5 cm (7½ × 10 in)
JENNIFER JENKINS SBA

POPPY

Papaver orientalis

Sandra Wall Armitage SBA

This flower is the ultimate red challenge for the artist. Not only are the petals an intense colour, but the hirsute and intricate leaves all require great attention to detail. Above all, you will need the ability to work quickly as the flower will drop and you may well hear the petals softly hit the table before you have finished.

PAINTS

SCHMINCKE
Translucent Orange

TALENS REMBRANDT
Alizarin Crimson

HOLBEIN
Compose Green 3
Green Grey

WINSOR & NEWTON
Scarlet Lake
Winsor Red
Winsor Violet
Perylene Violet
Payne's Grey
Permanent Sap Green
Olive Green
Oxide of Chromium
Perylene Green
Yellow Ochre
Permanent White gouache

DALER-ROWNEY
Perylene Red

BRUSHES

DALER-ROWNEY
Diana Kolinsky sable sizes 6, 4 and 2 (for the main painting)
Series 43 sizes 2 and 1 (for finer details, hairs and veins)

SURFACE

FABRIANO
Classico 5 HP 300 gsm (140 lb)

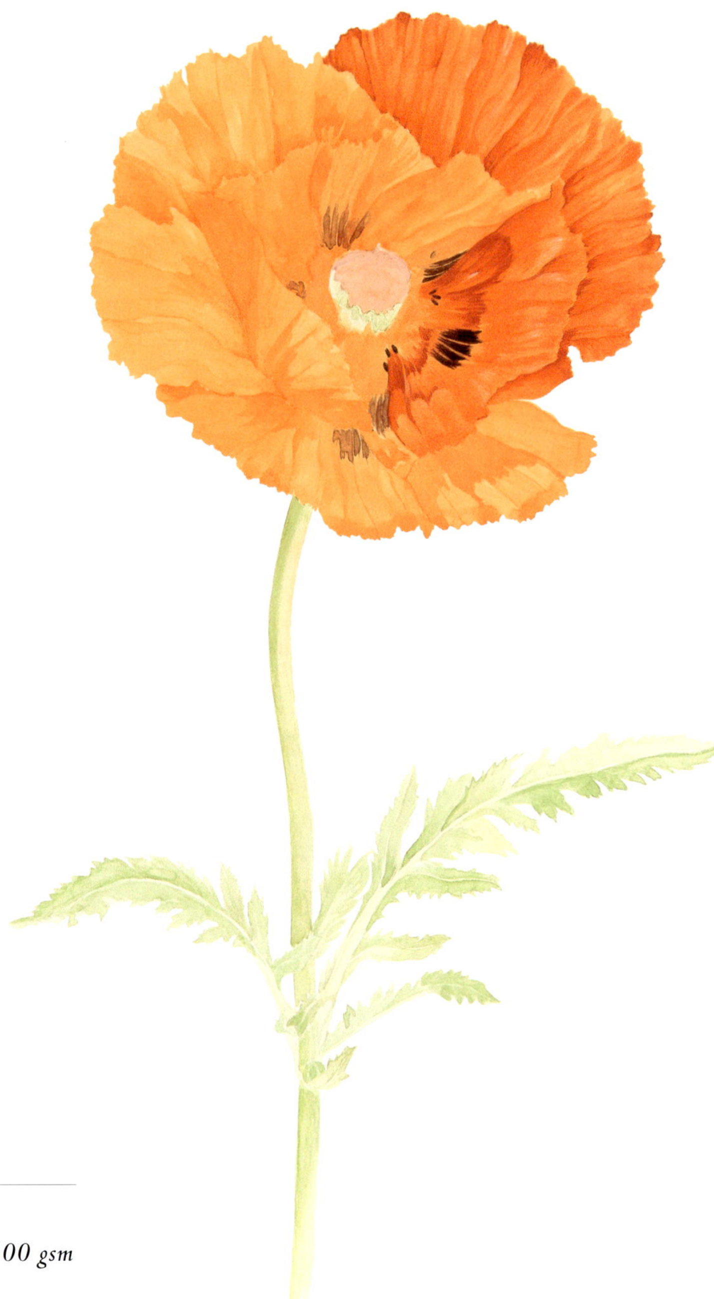

◁ **Stage 1**

Because of the transient nature of the petals, and to preserve the poppy head for as long as possible, Sandra first dipped the stem into hot water, then plunged it quickly into ice cold water. She drew the image first onto tracing paper, which allowed her to correct and adjust the proportions before transferring it onto a stretched sheet of Classico 5 HP paper.

She then applied a wash of the palest Translucent Orange, adding an additional layer in selected areas to define the form of the flower while retaining some of the lightest colour to emphasize the light falling on it. Further layers of colour were added to record some of the detail, using a mix of Translucent Orange and Scarlet Lake.

As Sandra added further colour she used pure Scarlet Lake and Winsor Red, and sometimes a combination mix of the two. Additional depth of shade was created by introducing either Alizarin Crimson and/or Perylene Red with a touch of Perylene Violet. Throughout she applied translucent glazes of Translucent Orange, which married the colours together while emphasizing the radiant glow of the petals.

The leaves and stem were given a weak wash of Permanent Sap Green, using a deeper wash to show tones and shadows, which also gave them some initial form.

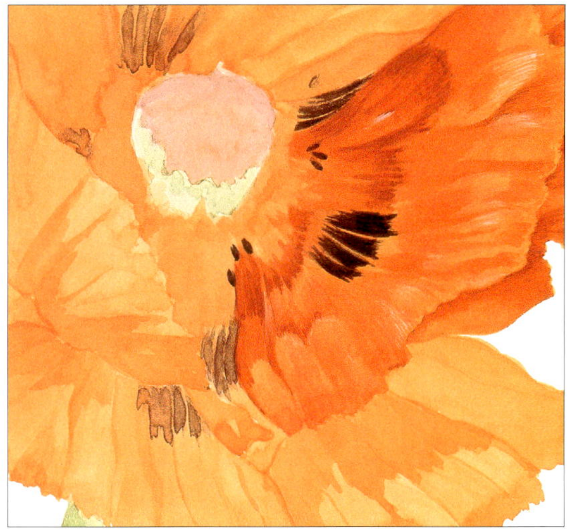

Detail from Stage 1:
The first detailed petals were worked up in order to check the colour and set the tone for the whole flower.

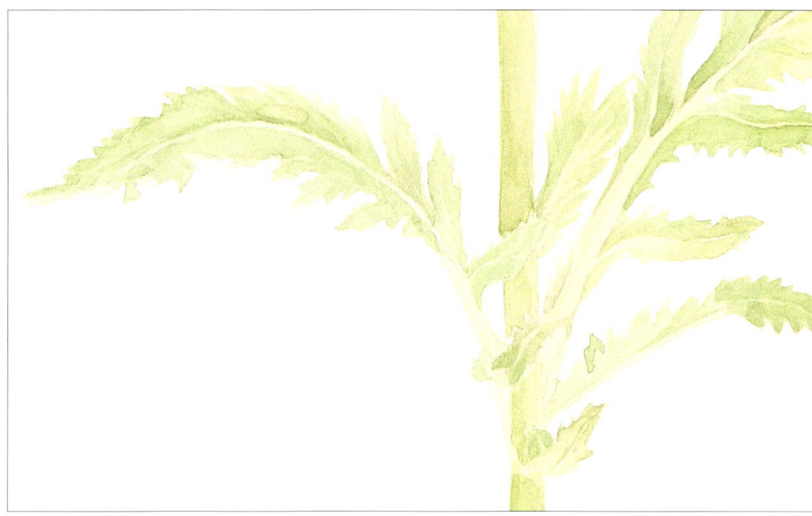

Detail from Stage 1:
Preliminary washes were applied to the leaves. Sandra used long sweeping strokes while retaining brush control, in order to preserve the serrated leaf edges.

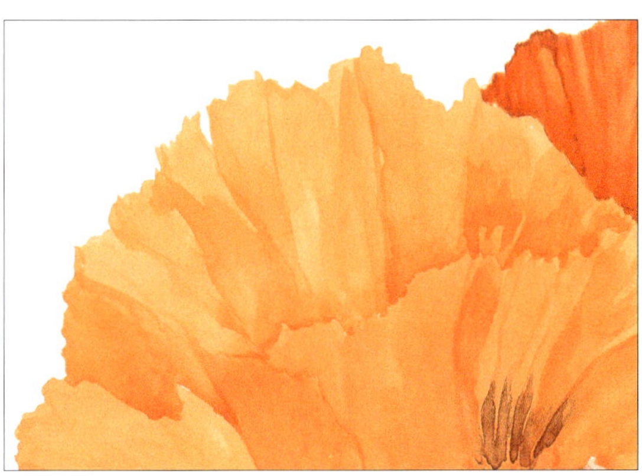

Detail from Stage 1:
First washes of colour were applied using Translucent Orange in varying intensity.

▷ Stage 2

Sandra turned her attention back to the main flower and continued to build up all the petals in the manner described. She paid particular attention to all the frilly edges and folds, and also to the cast shadows for one petal overlapping another. She continued to use the Translucent Orange glazes to keep the colour vibrant, making sure the underlying washes were dry before applying further layers.

The centre was painted with pale Oxide of Chromium for the cup and Perylene Red mixed with Winsor Violet on the top. The radial marks required a mix of Perylene Red and Payne's Grey, which also served for the blotches on the petals.

For the stamens Sandra used Perylene Violet with the addition of either Alizarin Crimson and/or Perylene Red to a greater or lesser degree as required.

Permanent White gouache was used to show highlights on the petals, very carefully blended into the red. It also highlighted some of the stamens laying in the cup of the petals.

With the flower safely completed, Sandra turned her attention to the foliage, adding an extra leaf at the back and applying washes as in Stage 1. It was important, however, to capture the opening bud, so that was quickly drawn in and washed with Permanent Sap Green before using Oxide of Chromium, Olive Green or Green Grey to make a variant green wash with which to mould the form of the sepals.

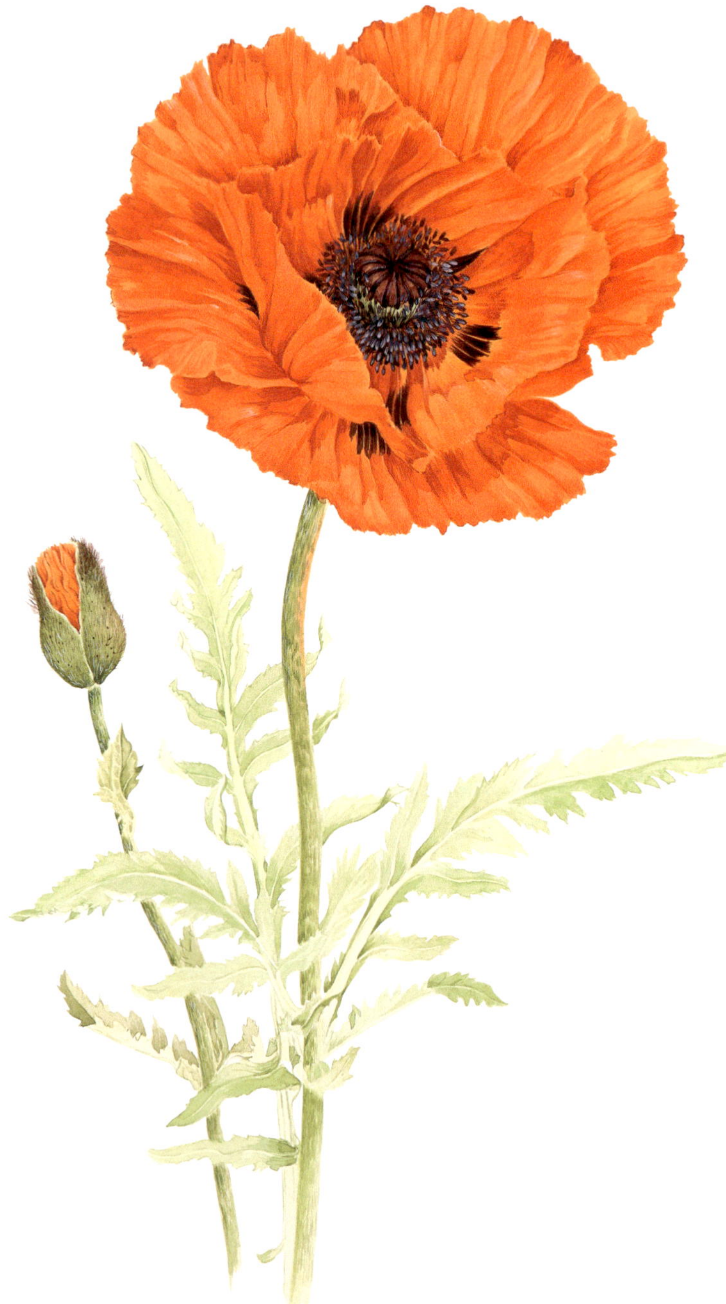

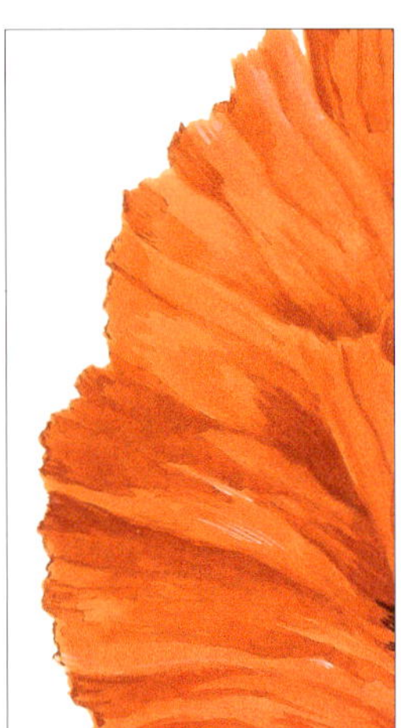

Detail from Stage 2: Pleats and creases on the petals were carefully shaded with Translucent Orange used as a glaze so that the colours would merge together.

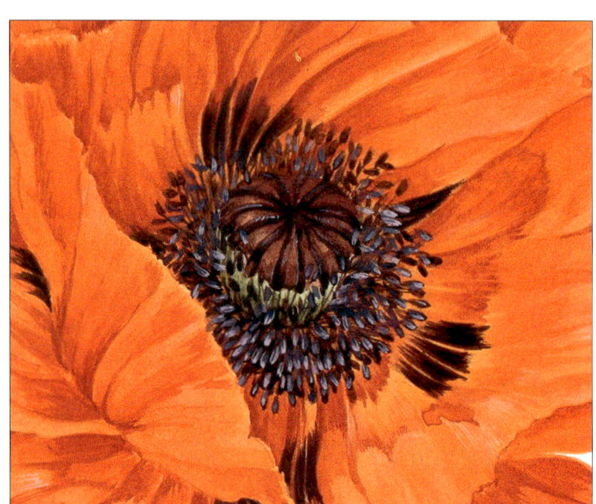

Detail from Stage 2: The centre of the flower was taking shape, with Permanent White gouache highlighting the foreground stamens. This created the slightly violet tinge of the pollen as it caught the light.

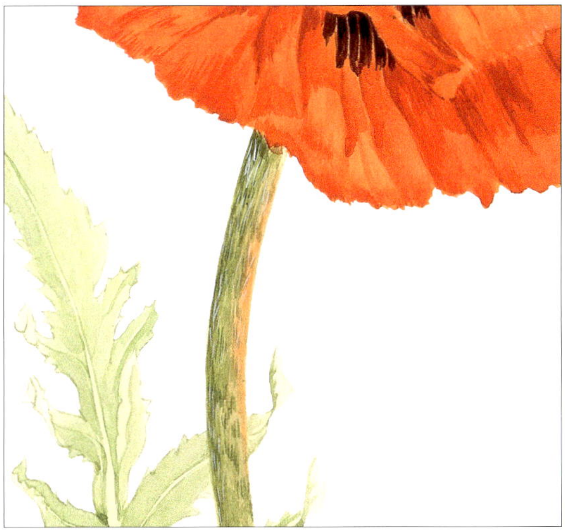

Detail from Stage 2:
Sandra painted in the reflection of the petals on the stem.

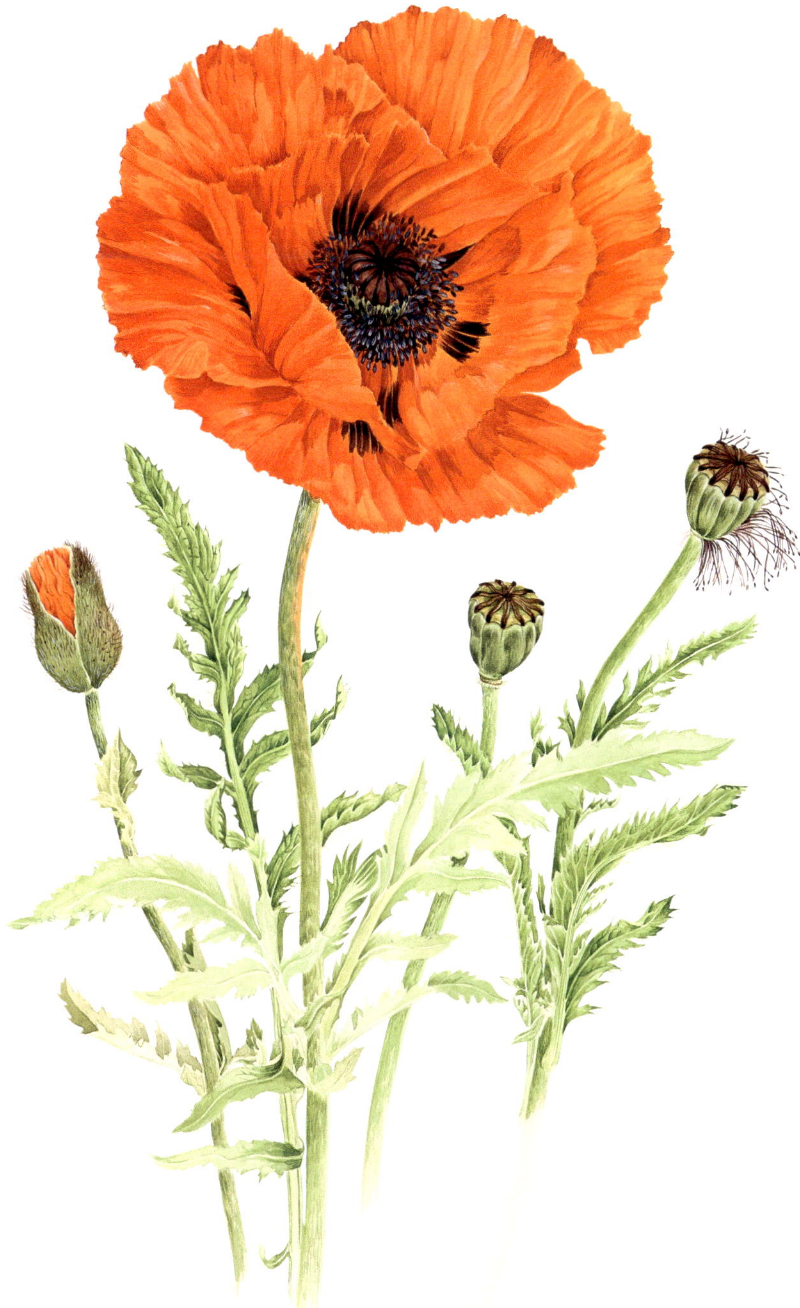

A weak mix of Perylene Red and Perylene Violet was used to lightly draw in the fine hairs of the bud, using a size 1 brush.

The emerging petals were painted in the same manner as the main flower.

Sandra used the darker green wash to shade both stems, applying the paint in an irregular, stippling fashion in order to create texture. She dropped in a little Translucent Orange on the right-hand side of the flower stem where the petals were reflected.

▷ **Stage 3**

Sandra started to build up the composition by adding two seed heads, with extra foliage. The cups of these seed heads were painted mainly with Oxide of Chromium with a little Permanent White gouache added to give the blue-green waxy bloom and highlights. The crowns of the seed heads were painted with a little Yellow Ochre over the pale green wash. This was tinted with Alizarin Crimson and the inner area was washed with the same colour. The stamens were painted with Perylene Violet and a mix of Alizarin Crimson and Perylene Red. The filaments were delicately drawn using the same mix and a size 1 brush.

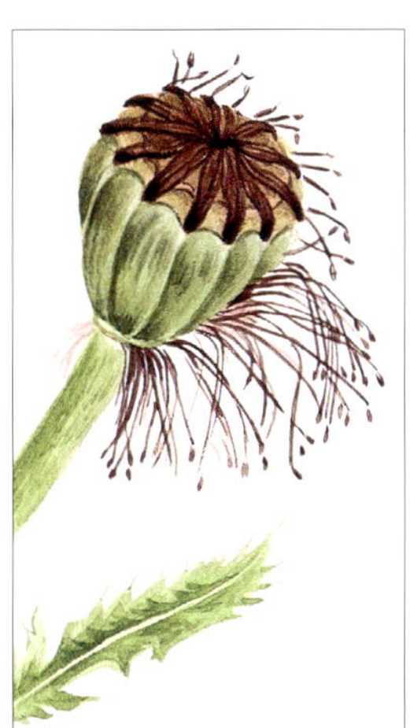

Detail from Stage 3:
The addition of seed heads began to fill out the composition, particularly when one had lots of shaggy stamens still attached to it.

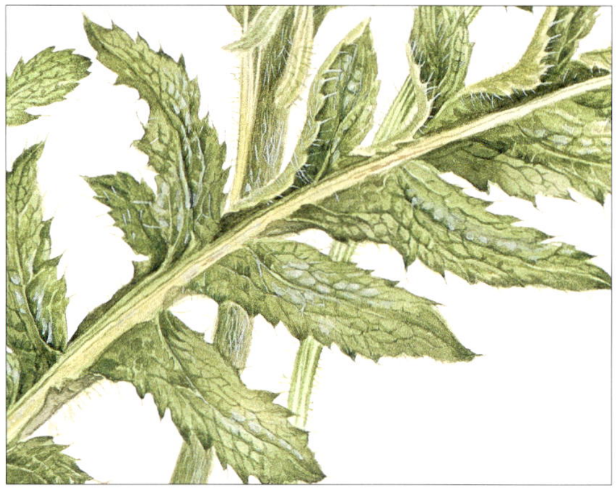

Detail from Final Stage:
Attention was focused on the leaves with their sculptural quality of line.

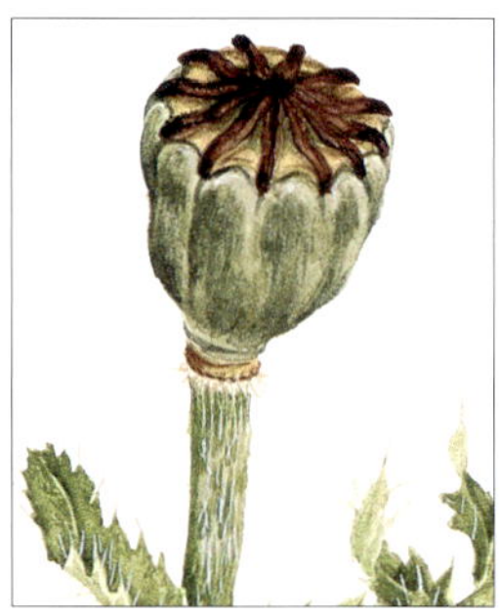

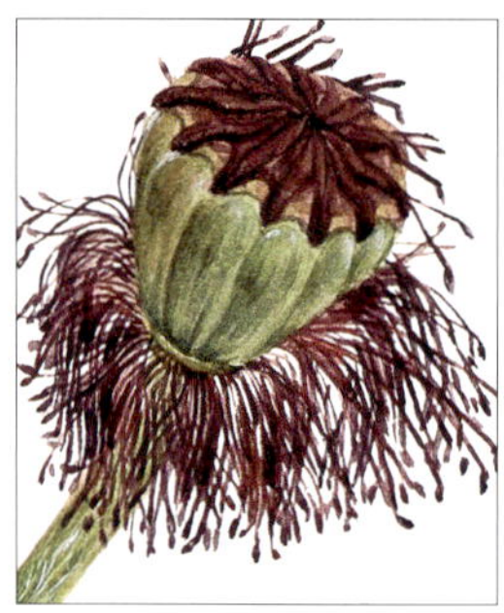

Details from Final Stage:
Both seed heads were tightened up prior to adding more stamens.

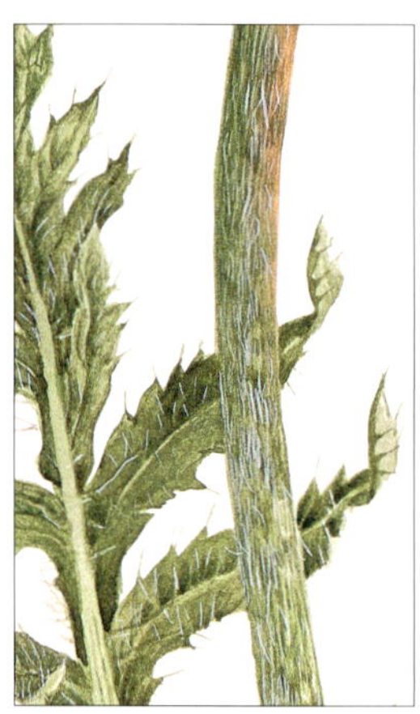

Detail from Final Stage:
Finally Sandra added hairs, with a steady hand and a very well-tipped size 1 brush.

▷ Final Stage

Now Sandra could turn all her attention to the leaves. She added two more at the lower right of the picture to balance the flower, which otherwise looked top heavy. From the pale green base wash she gradually built up the colour, giving tone and form. She mostly found that a mix of Permanent Sap Green and Compose Green 3 gave the required colour. The latter is a good strong colour, but needed to be softened and Permanent Sap Green did this well. In some areas one pigment needed to predominate and in others the reverse was the case. Where a flatter, more opaque, green was needed Oxide of Chromium worked well. For additional deep shadows and definition of some veins Green Grey combined well with the Oxide of Chromium or Permanent Sap Green.

All stems were worked with the same combination of greens and carefully shaded to show their rounded appearance. Both seed heads were crisped up and additional stamens were added to the one on the right.

With a size 1 brush and Permanent White gouache Sandra carefully added the hairs to stems and leaves. These rest against the stems rather than stick out in the manner of field poppies. The gouache was also useful for where the hairs showed up against a darker area on the leaves. Any that stood proud, from the tips of the serrated leaves, for example, she painted with a little very pale green mixed in places with a minute touch of red to tone it down to a more neutral shade.

Painting this in a heat wave required a cool head and added to the challenge that Sandra faced, but pulled off admirably.

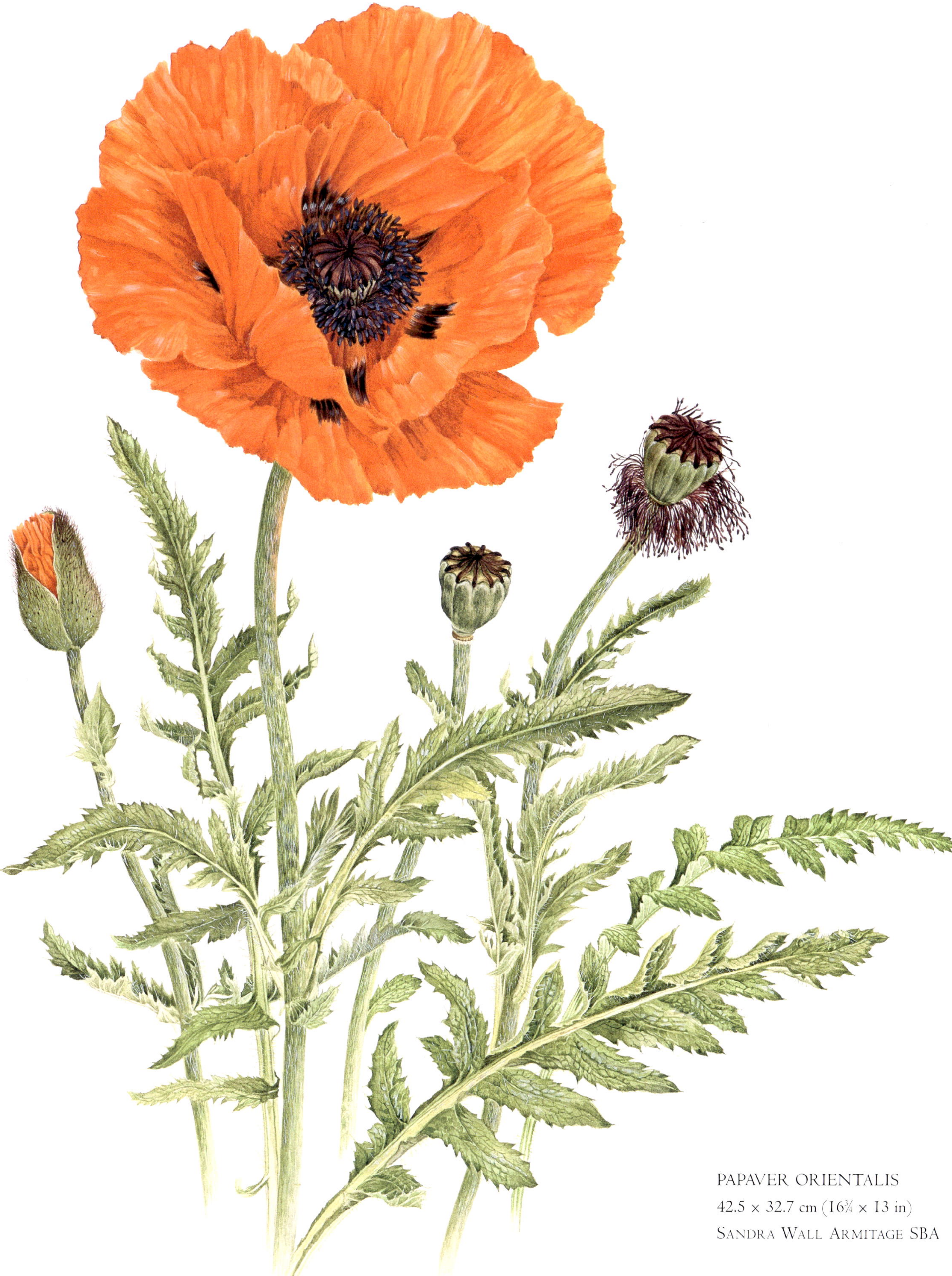

PAPAVER ORIENTALIS
42.5 × 32.7 cm (16¾ × 13 in)
Sandra Wall Armitage SBA

Project *Papaver orientalis*

The drawing has been simplified in order to tempt you into trying it. It is in that frightening colour, red, if I am to believe the response to my questionnaire (see page 11), so I did not want to make it more off-putting by making the design too complicated. Here you have the key elements of flower, foliage, bud and seed heads, which gives you a chance to try out Sandra's colours and method. Work on the flower one petal at a time and when you have them all at a similar stage of development make sure the paint is dry before applying the Translucent Orange glaze. You can do that as often as necessary to bring the work up to a finished standard. Remember you do not have either a transient flower or a heat wave to contend with, so the gods are already smiling on you.

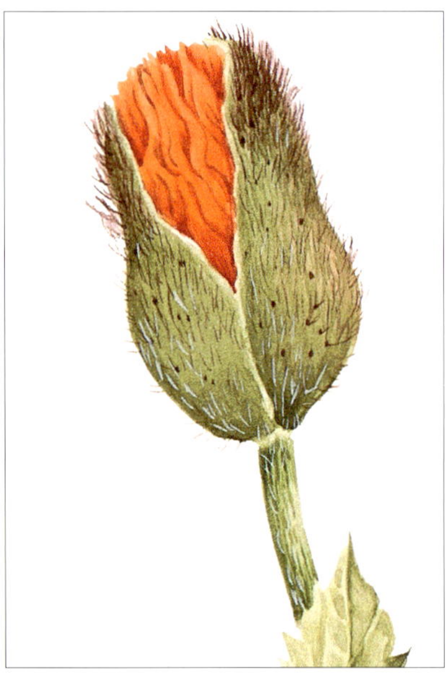

Detail from Stage 2: The bud is painted in one go, so speed is essential. Make sure that you leave the lighter greenish-white edge to the sepals and use a mix of Perylene Red and Perylene Violet to paint the fine hairs.

Colour Chart

FLOWERS

1 Schmincke: Translucent Orange
2 Schmincke: Translucent Orange
3 Translucent Orange + Scarlet Lake
4 Scarlet Lake
5 Winsor Red + Scarlet Lake
6 Winsor Red
7 Rembrandt: Alizarin Crimson
8 Daler-Rowney: Perylene Red
9 Perylene Red + Winsor Violet
10 Perylene Violet
11 Perylene Violet + Payne's Grey
12 Perylene Red + Perylene Violet

LEAVES & BUDS

1 Permanent Sap Green
2 Olive Green
3 Sap Green + Olive Green
4 Holbein: Compose Green 3
5 Compose Green 3 + Sap Green
6 Oxide of Chromium
7 Sap Green + Oxide of Chromium
8 Oxide of Chromium + Payne's Grey
9 Sap Green + Holbein: Green Grey
10 Sap Green + Perylene Green
11 Olive Green + Yellow Ochre
12 Permanent White gouache

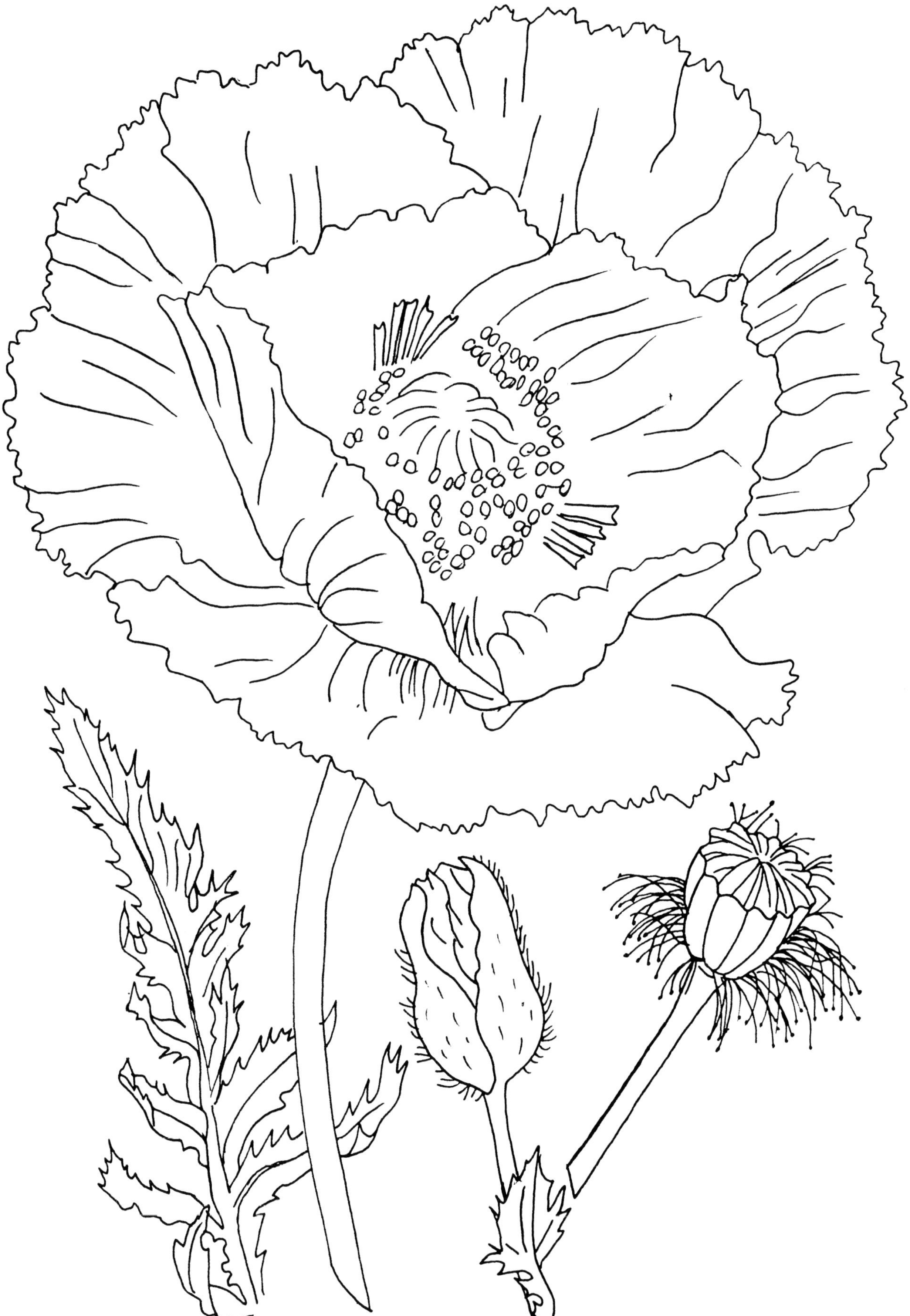

PEONY

Paeonia

Susan Hillier FSBA

This study of an old-fashioned double peony, familiar from many a cottage garden, gives an excellent opportunity to explore the deeper burgundy shades of red. The rich colour and silky sheen on the many petals contributes to a flower of great beauty to which Susan has more than done justice.

PAINTS

DALER-ROWNEY
Perylene Maroon
Permanent Magenta
Permanent Mauve
Carmine

WINSOR & NEWTON
Transparent Yellow
Permanent Sap Green

BRUSHES

DALER-ROWNEY
Series 4 Kolinsky sable sizes 1 and 2
Series 40 Kolinsky sable size 6

WINSOR & NEWTON
Series 7 Kolinsky sable size 3

SURFACE

ARCHES
Aquarelle HP 300 gsm (140 lb)

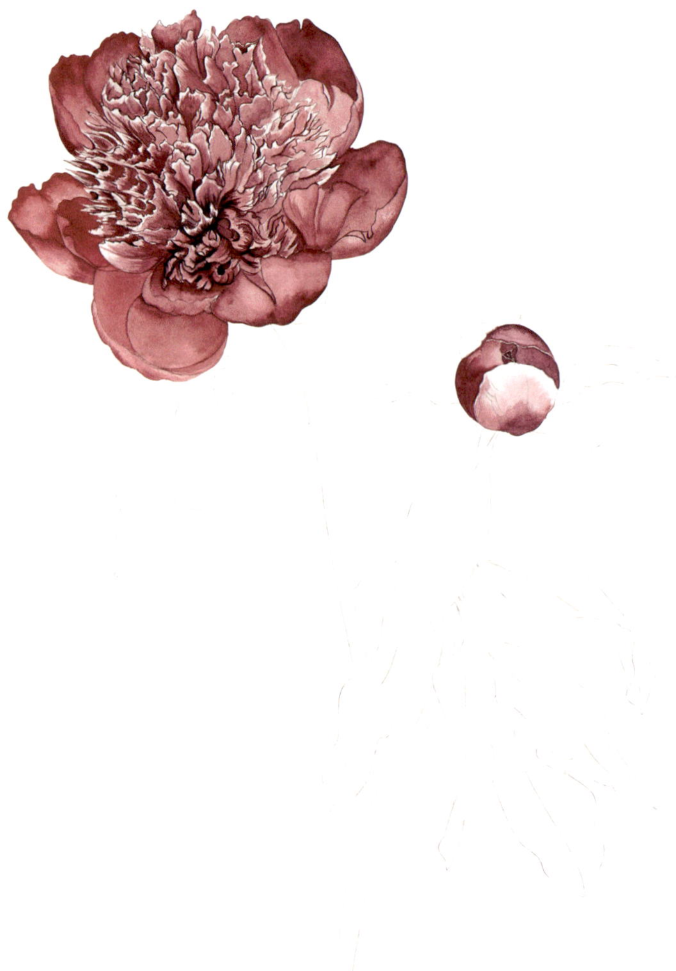

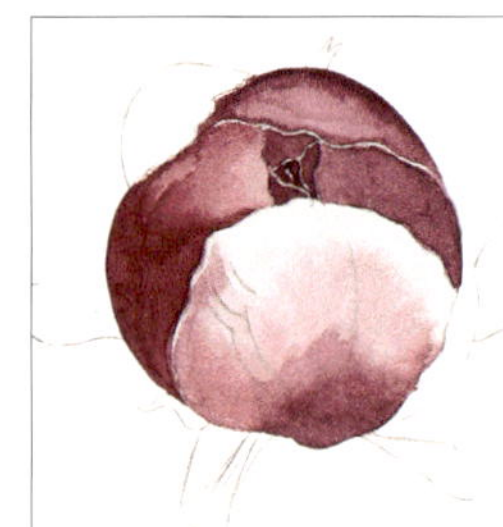

Detail from Stage I: Catching the bud before it opened, Susan put on the first washes and basic shading on the petals.

△ **Stage I**
Susan made a basic outline drawing using an HB pencil. She then mixed Perylene Maroon, Permanent Magenta and Permanent Mauve to use as a pale first wash all over the flower, but took care to leave white paper where light was catching the tips of some petals.

Now, with a mix of Perylene Maroon, Permanent Magenta and Carmine, Susan worked over the flower again with a mid-tone wash, this time leaving the white areas and some pale first wash sections, but defining the inner petals more. Some variation of colour and tone would be fine at this stage and there

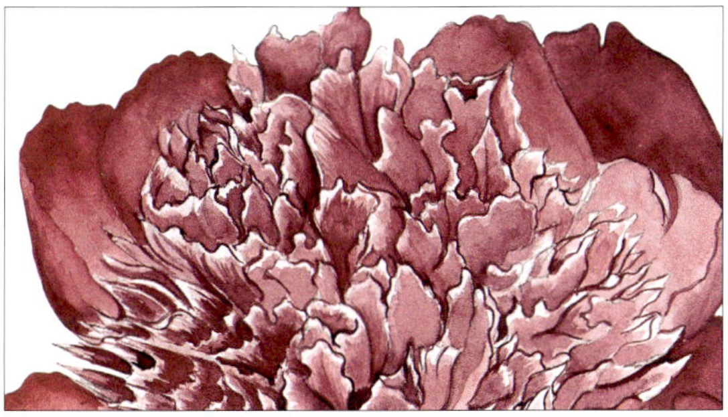

Detail from Stage 1:
Some definition was added and wet-in-wet technique allowed initial shading of the outer petals.

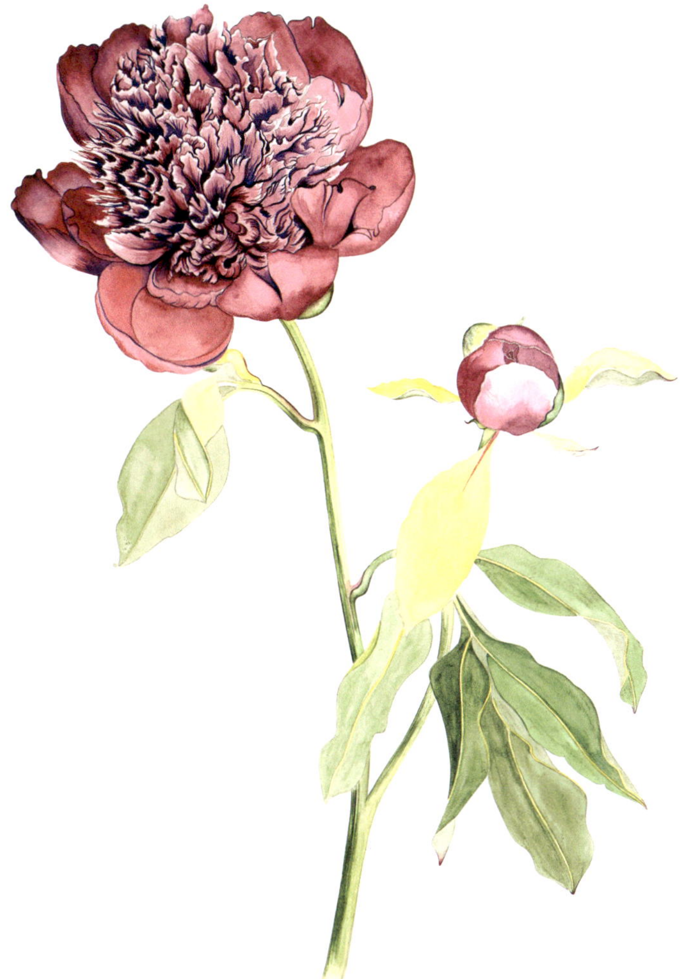

were large areas that required wet-in-wet technique, particularly the outer petals.

Susan also applied the first washes to the bud, which would very soon open.

▷ Stage 2

Susan quickly added some of the deepest shadows to the petals, using Permanent Mauve to further define the flower, which was now very close to falling apart. Having defined the tones and colours in this way she would be able to work it up to a finish even when the inevitable happened.

She then turned her attention to the leaves, applying a first wash of Transparent Yellow, followed by a wash of Permanent Sap Green, using varying strengths of pigment to make the first definition of veins and shading. The angular stem was treated in the same manner, with the dark side clearly defined.

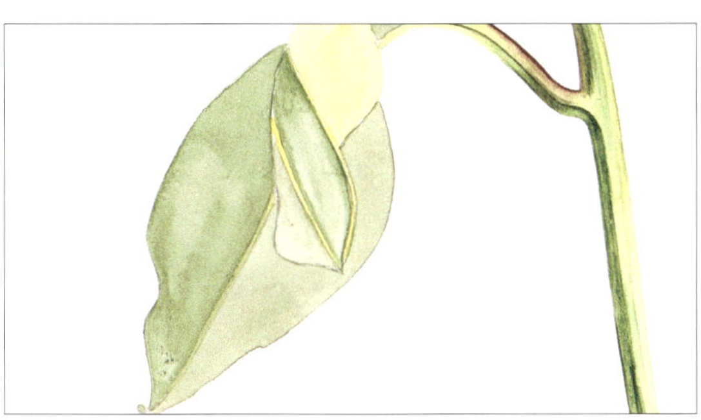

Detail from Stage 2:
The leaves and stems were given a wash of Transparent Yellow followed by one of Permanent Sap Green.

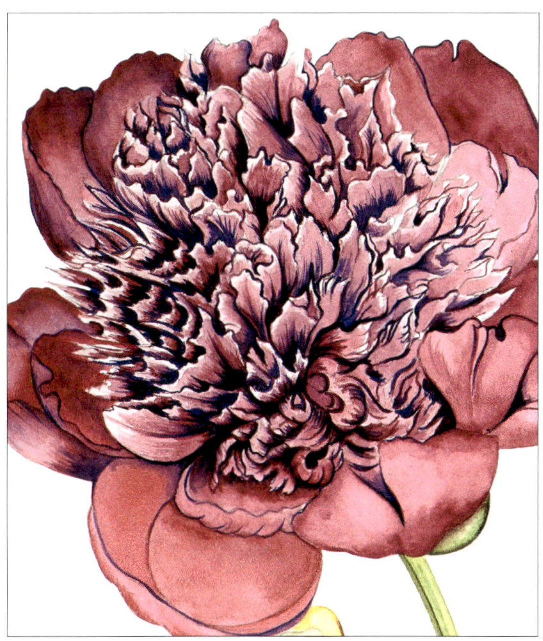

Detail from Stage 2:
Using Permanent Mauve in the mix Susan added some of the deepest shadows, aiding definition of the petals.

▽ **Stage 3**

The bud was opening fast, so Susan concentrated on that first. The flower had already fallen, but she was able to work up the colour and tone on both the flower and bud, using the same basic colours, by applying layers of washes. Note the venation on the bud, which showed up well against the high sheen.

Susan added more green shades to the leaves, using Permanent Sap Green mixed with Permanent Mauve and then glazed with Transparent Yellow.

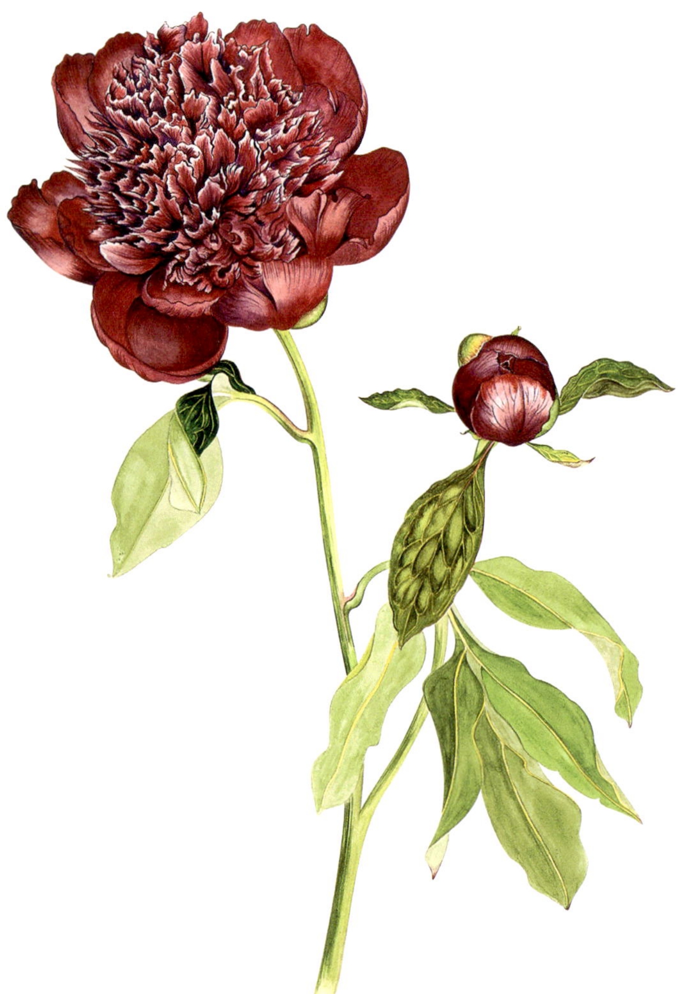

▷ **Final Stage**

The leaves and stem were worked to a finish using the same basic colours in varying degrees of density.

The veins are very prominent, so Susan made sure that these were emphasized with careful shading, using a deep tone of Permanent Sap Green and Permanent Mauve. Pigment was carefully blended into the veins thus giving texture to the leaf surface. The undersides of the leaves were lighter in colour but, as always, the veins stood proud, so they needed to be carefully drawn in with the brush to show their width. Note, too, how Susan conveyed the thickness of the leaves by the yellow edge.

Susan checked over the whole picture to tighten up and refine all detailed areas, including veins and edges. Sometimes she needed to lift off a little colour, at others a further wash over was required – these small tweaks helped to put the 'gloss' on the painting and gave it a lift out of the ordinary.

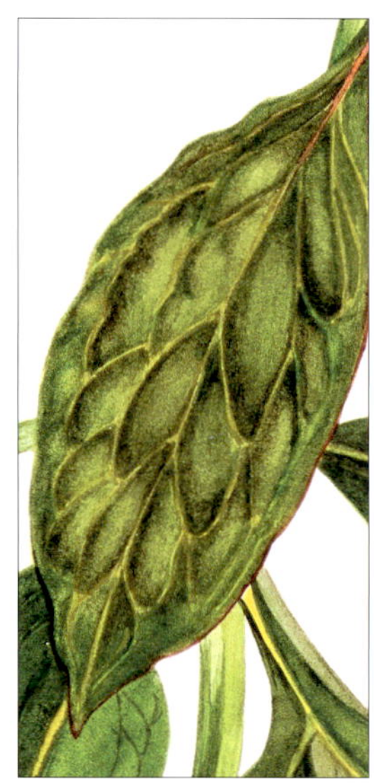

Detail from Final Stage: The reverse side of the leaves were full of interest as the veins could be seen in relief, giving an alternative texture to those on the upper side.

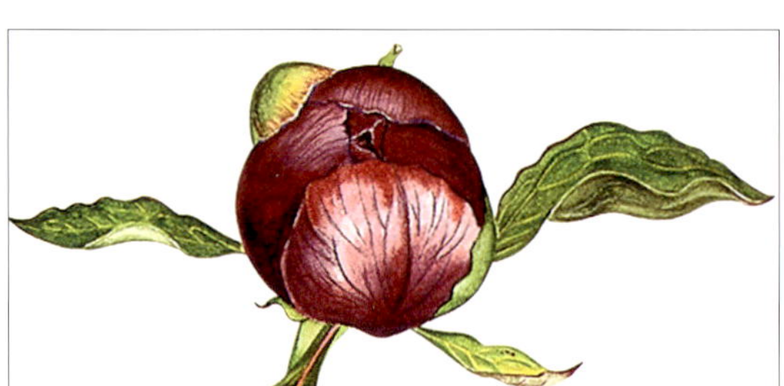

Detail from Stage 3: Susan completed work on the bud before it fully opened, carefully brush-drawing the veins against the highlighted petal.

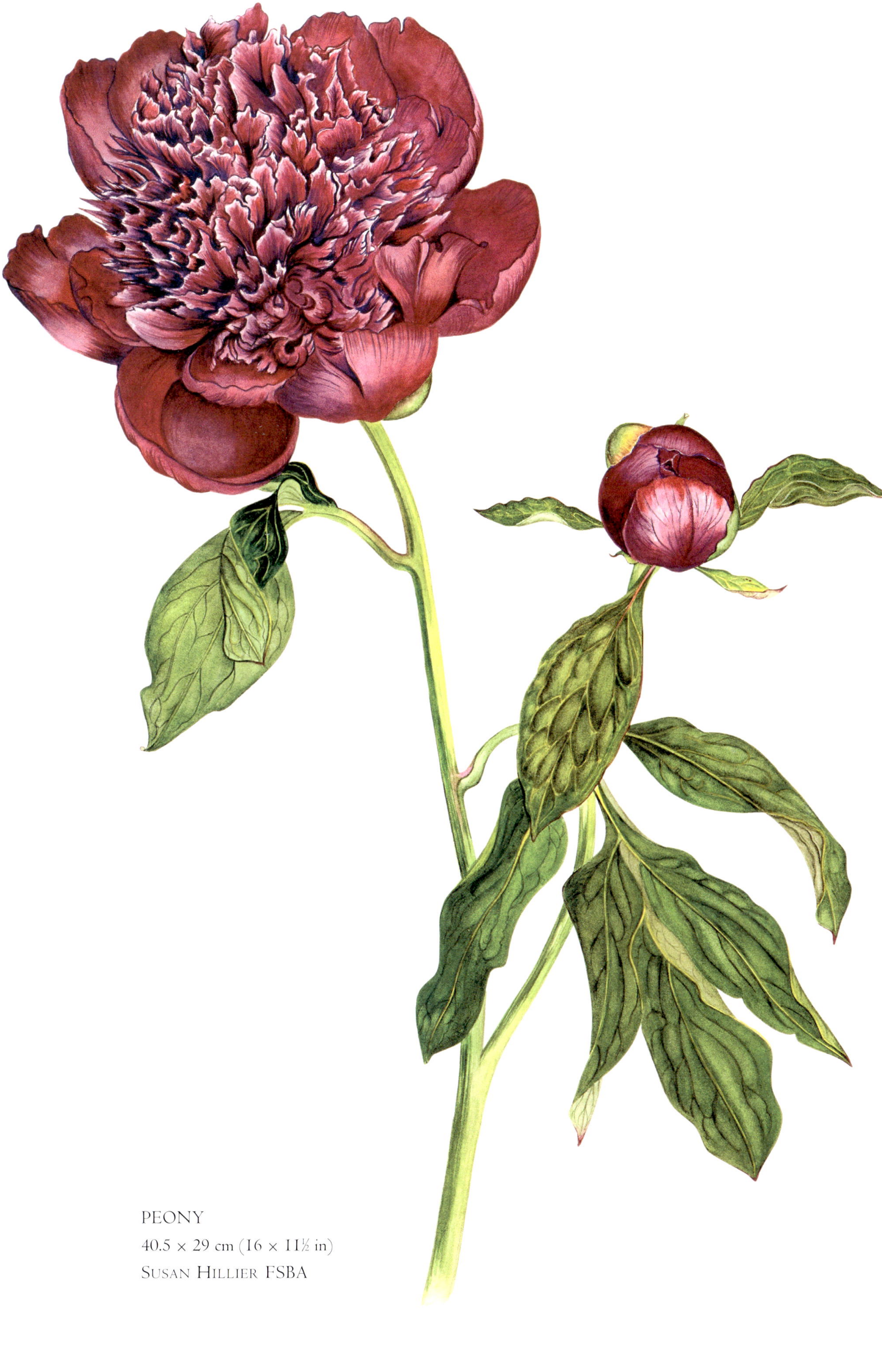

PEONY
40.5 × 29 cm (16 × 11½ in)
SUSAN HILLIER FSBA

PROJECT *Paeonia*

I have very much simplified this from the original drawing as in this case the flower needs to be the main focus for your efforts. Like the *Papaver oriental* the peony is quite a short-lived flower, particularly in a heat wave, but by using the drawing, instead of a real specimen, this will not be a problem for you. I know from experience that many students would make the initial drawing, or in this case tracing, put the first wash on and then cry 'I've spoilt it' when they see the rather patchy and uninspiring object on the paper. You have to learn to ignore that and be prepared to work up through the stages to the finish. Too often students want to put the roof on before they have dug the foundations! Be patient, and tackle each section in turn, in this case secure in the knowledge that you will not hear the gentle thud of falling petals.

COLOUR CHART

FLOWERS

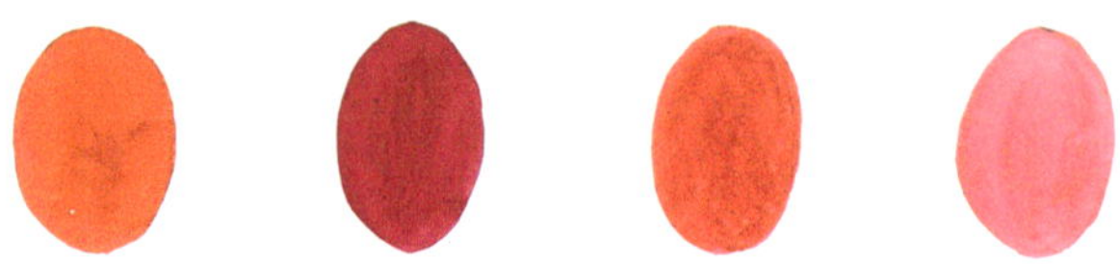

1 Daler-Rowney: Perylene Maroon

2 Daler-Rowney: Permanent Magenta

3 Daler-Rowney: Carmine

4 Perylene Maroon + Permanent Magenta + Carmine

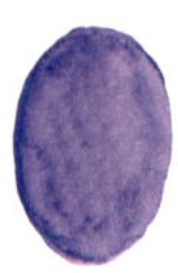

5 Daler-Rowney: Permanent Mauve

LEAVES

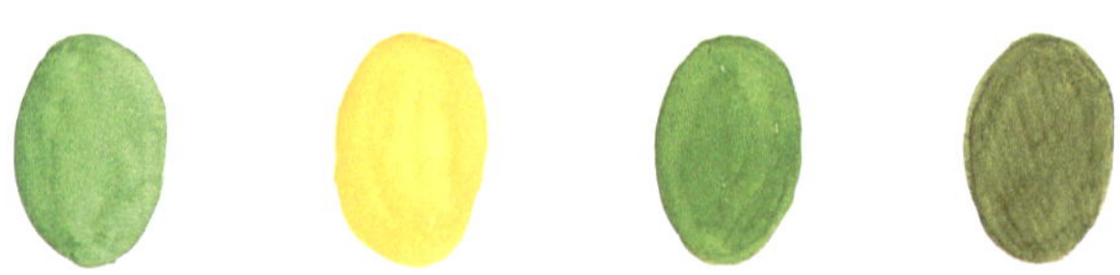

1 Permanent Sap Green

2 Transparent Yellow

3 Permanent Sap Green + Transparent Yellow

4 3 + Permanent Mauve

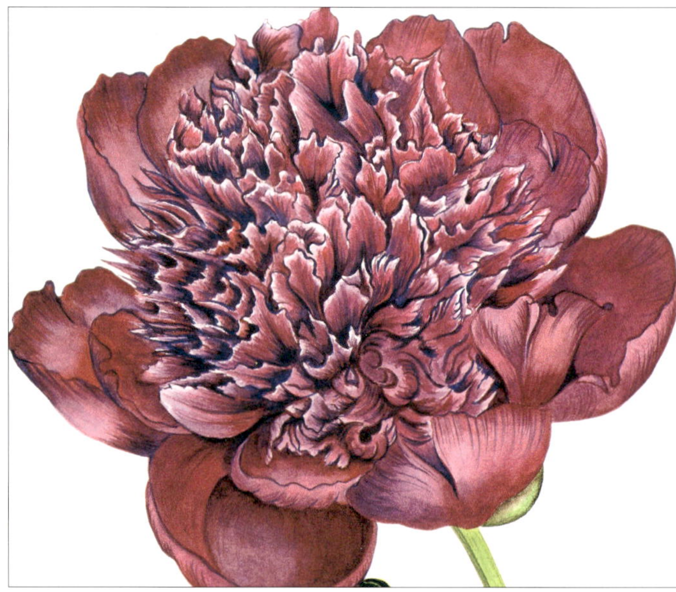

Detail from Stage 3:
The flower was worked up to completion with highlights and petal tips in perfect contrast to the deepest shadows.

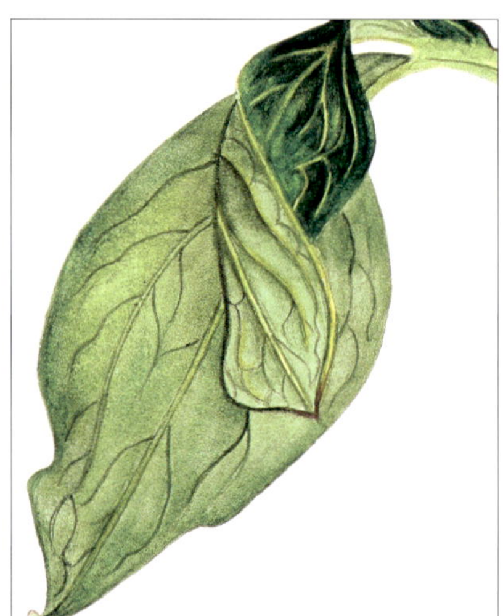

Detail from Final Stage:
The veins on the undersides of the leaves stood out in relief, so they were shaded accordingly to give a sense of texture on the surface.

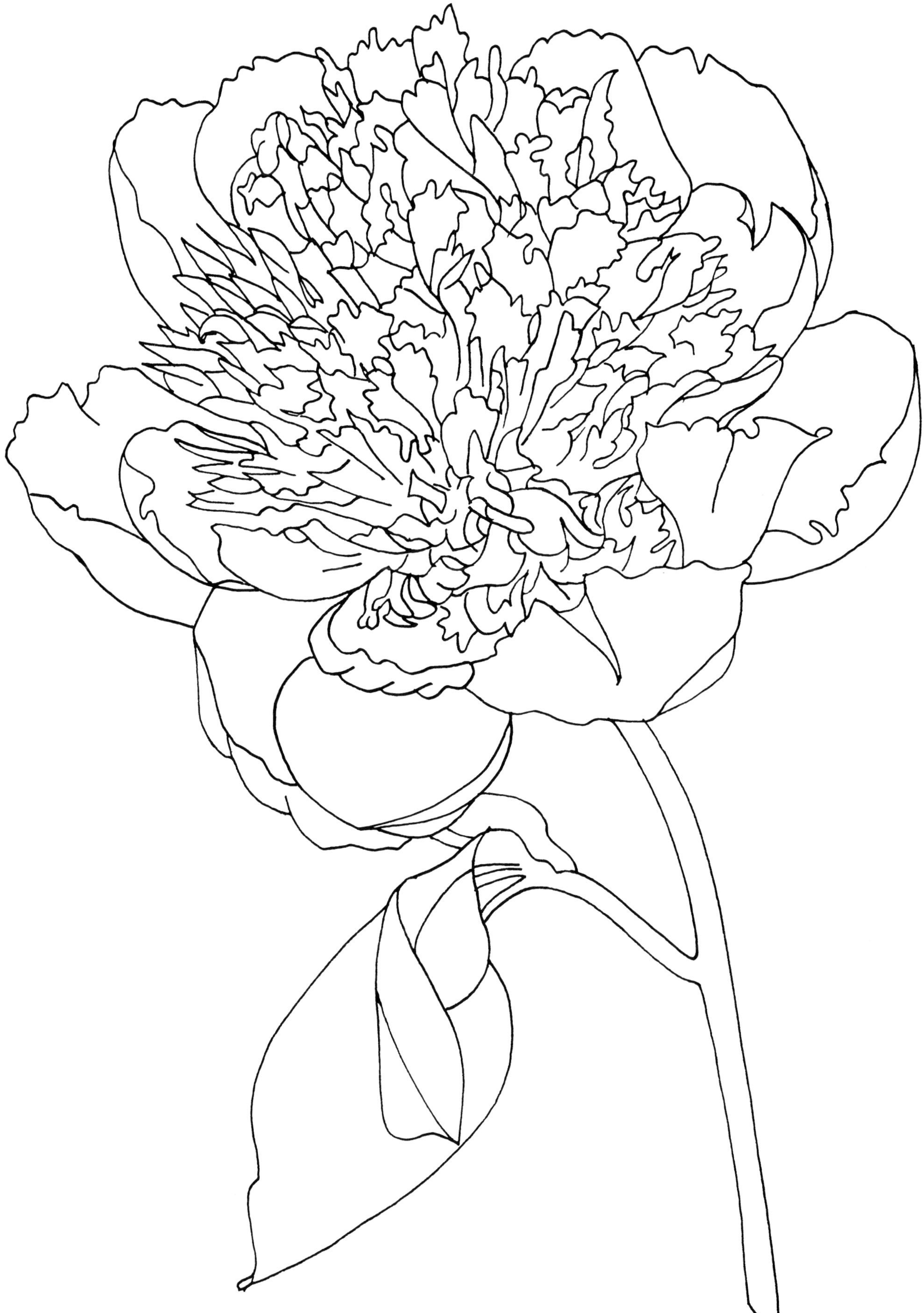

RED RHODODENDRON

Rhododendron catawbiense

Susan Martin Assoc. SBA

This hybrid Rhododendron is unusual by having young leaves that are rich brown. These become yellow-green in maturity, but still retain some of the brown pigmentation. The flowers are strikingly marked and the buds are almost black. This unusual specimen from the grounds of Inverary Castle in Argyll, Scotland, is rendered in coloured pencil.

COLOUR CHART

FABER-CASTELL POLYCHROMOS UNLESS OTHERWISE INDICATED

- Berol Karisma: Scarlet Red 922
- Berol Karisma: White 938
- Scarlet Red 118
- Chrome Green Opaque 174
- Dark Red 225
- Earth Green Yellowish 168
- Caput Mortuum Violet 263
- Apple Green 170
- Light Magenta 119
- White 101
- Ochre 184
- Soft Black 099
- Light Orange 113
- Berol Verithin: Carmine Red 21
- Berol Verithin: Dark Brown 12

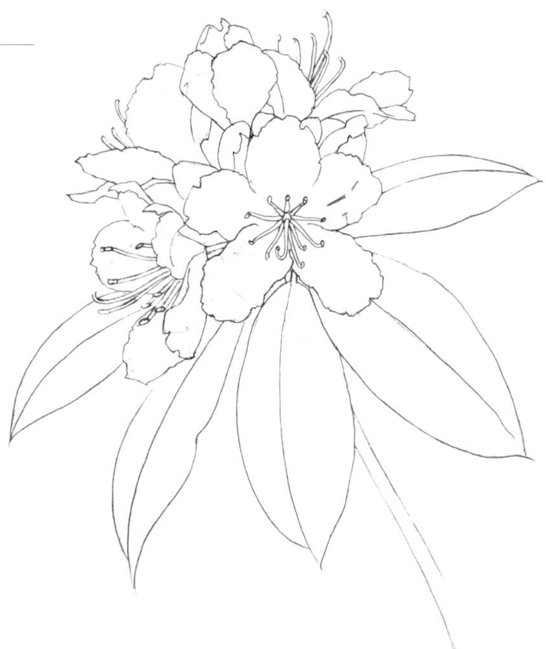

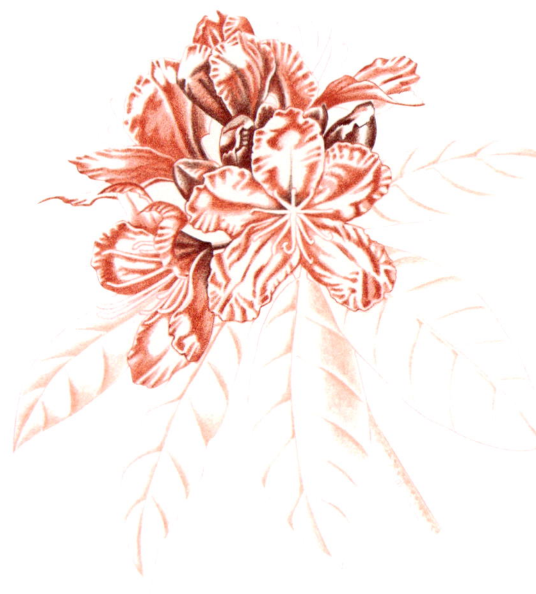

△ **Stage I**
Susan worked out the layout on tracing paper, making sure the final outline and guidelines were sharp and black. In the absence of a light box she taped both the tracing paper and her paper of choice, in this case White Rising Stonehenge, to a sunny windowpane. She was then able to trace off the image using a sharp Carmine Red 21 pencil and a very light touch. This method of transferring the image ensured that she did not have cause to erase any marks on her good drawing paper that might damage the surface.

△ **Stage 2**
Starting with the flowers, Susan neatened up the outlines wherever the stamens lay against the petals or leaves. For this she used Carmine Red 21. She then used Dark Red 225 on the shadow areas of the petals. She used a very sharp point and small circular movements to build up the shadows, increasing the pressure and working over the darkest areas. The flower buds needed to be darkened further using Caput Mortuum Violet 263.

In order to retain the brownish tint to the leaves Susan began to shade them using Scarlet Red 118. This was also used to shade the stem, varying the pressure for unevenness.

▷ Stage 3

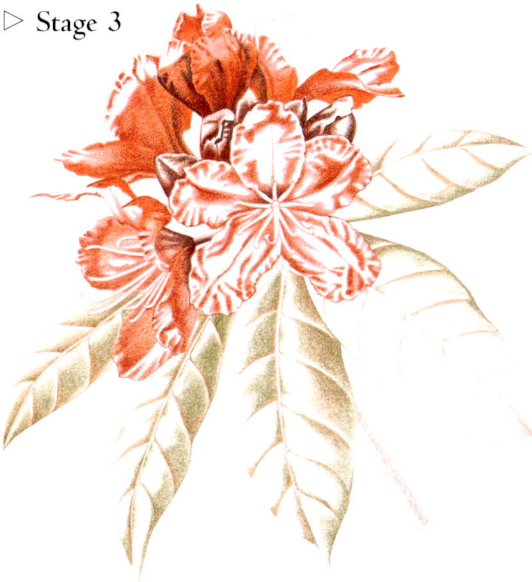

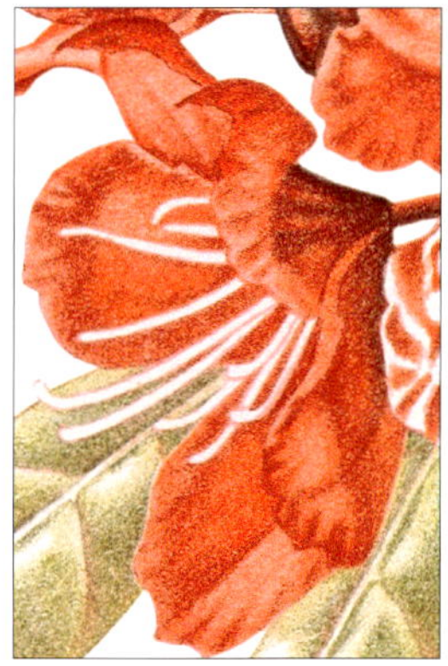

Detail from Stage 4: Areas of petals that were backlit by the sun were kept light.

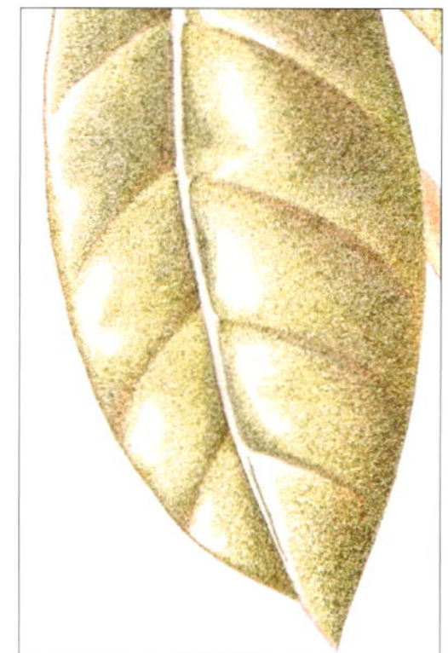

Detail from Stage 4: Care was taken to retain highlights that were on the leaves.

Detail from Stage 3: It was important to fix the direction of light at the outset and stick to it. Here it caught the tips of the petals.

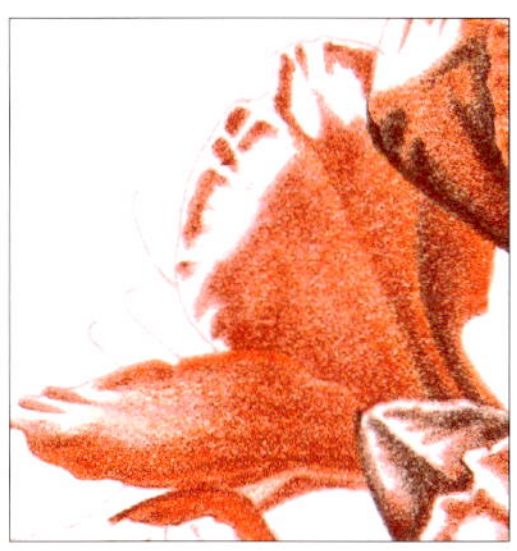

Detail from Stage 3: Scarlet Red 922 defined the veins, which again emphasized the direction of the light.

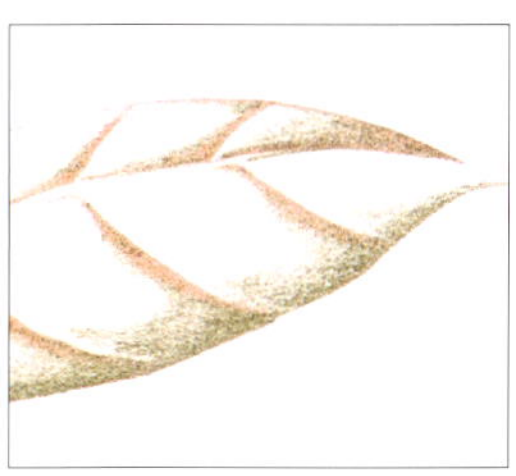

▷ Stage 4

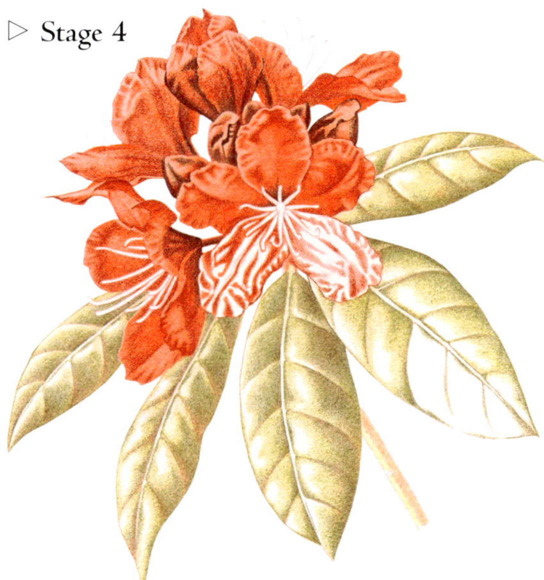

△ Stage 3

The sun was shining from the left and slightly behind the petals, which meant that it was shining through some of them. Scarlet Red 922 was used to colour these petals, and also worked over some of the shadows.

In order to add more shade to the leaves Chrome Green Opaque 174 was used, working from left to right. At this point the grain of the paper was still showing through.

△ Stage 4

The main colour on the petals was started, using Scarlet Red 118, a sharp point and the same circular movements. The work progressed from light to dark and the lightest areas would be highlights. The dark red shadows were worked over, but the areas backlit from the sun needed to be kept bright. Depth of colour was achieved by keeping a sharp point and increasing the pressure.

Using Earth Green Yellowish 168 Susan started to overlay the existing colours on the leaves, fading away to nothing while leaving the white paper as highlights. Some shadow was added to the veins using the same colour. She enhanced some of the areas of shadow against the edge of the leaves using a sharp-pointed Scarlet Red 118 pencil and a light touch. The stem was coloured with Apple Green 170.

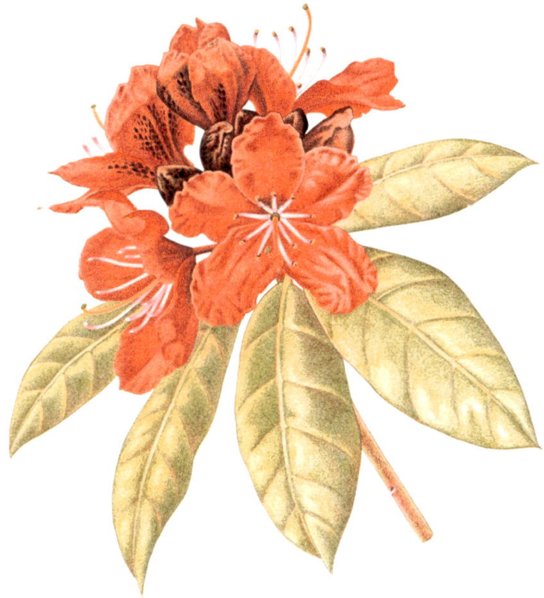

△ **Stage 5**

The petals were burnished using a colourless blender with a rounded point, cleaning it before burnishing another area, and avoiding the stamens. More Scarlet Red 118 deepened the colour. The flower buds were darkened with Soft Black 099 and creases on them were deepened to black; black dots were drawn in.

Some of the guide lines for the white stamens were lifted off using Frisket film. They were then outlined lightly with a sharp Light Magenta 119, making a slightly thicker shadow on one side. A flush of Light Magenta 119 was laid on all the filaments below the anthers, fading to nothing. They were shaded with the same colour and burnished using White 101 to blend the colour. Carmine Red 21 was used to draw in the anthers and Ochre 184 for the pollen. The style was drawn with Light Orange 113, overlaid with Scarlet Red 118, using a very sharp point. Where the style was against the red petal a minute amount of Light Orange 113 was left showing, then burnished. More Scarlet 118 was applied as shadow. The stigma was coloured with Earth Green Yellowish 168, highlighted with a dot of White 938. Shadow underneath was Dark Brown 12.

The ovary was coloured with Earth Green Yellowish 168 and shaded with Dark Brown 12, pressing heavily. Carmine Red 21 was used for detail around the filaments.

The white paper highlights were covered with Ochre 184 blended into the green areas. Most of the green areas were overlaid with Apple Green 170, blending lightly into the highlights. The veins were coloured with Ochre 184, working over the shadows. Where they caught the light Susan burnished with White 101.

For the stem she used Dark Red 225 for the shadow, fading to nothing on the right-hand side, which was catching the light and fading off to the left of the stem where there was reflected light. The shadow was built up with dots of colour and burnished. The dormant bud and leaf scar was defined with Dark Red 225 and the shadow with Dark Brown 12, which also outlined the stem.

▷ **Final Stage**

The black dots, or bee lines, were drawn onto the petals, following the lines of the veins; some are oval and some like inverted 'U's. Susan checked that the edges of the leaves were crisp; she sharpened up the shadow side with Chrome Green Opaque 174 and the highlighted side with Earth Green Yellowish 168. Finally the flower petals were sharpened with Scarlet Red 118.

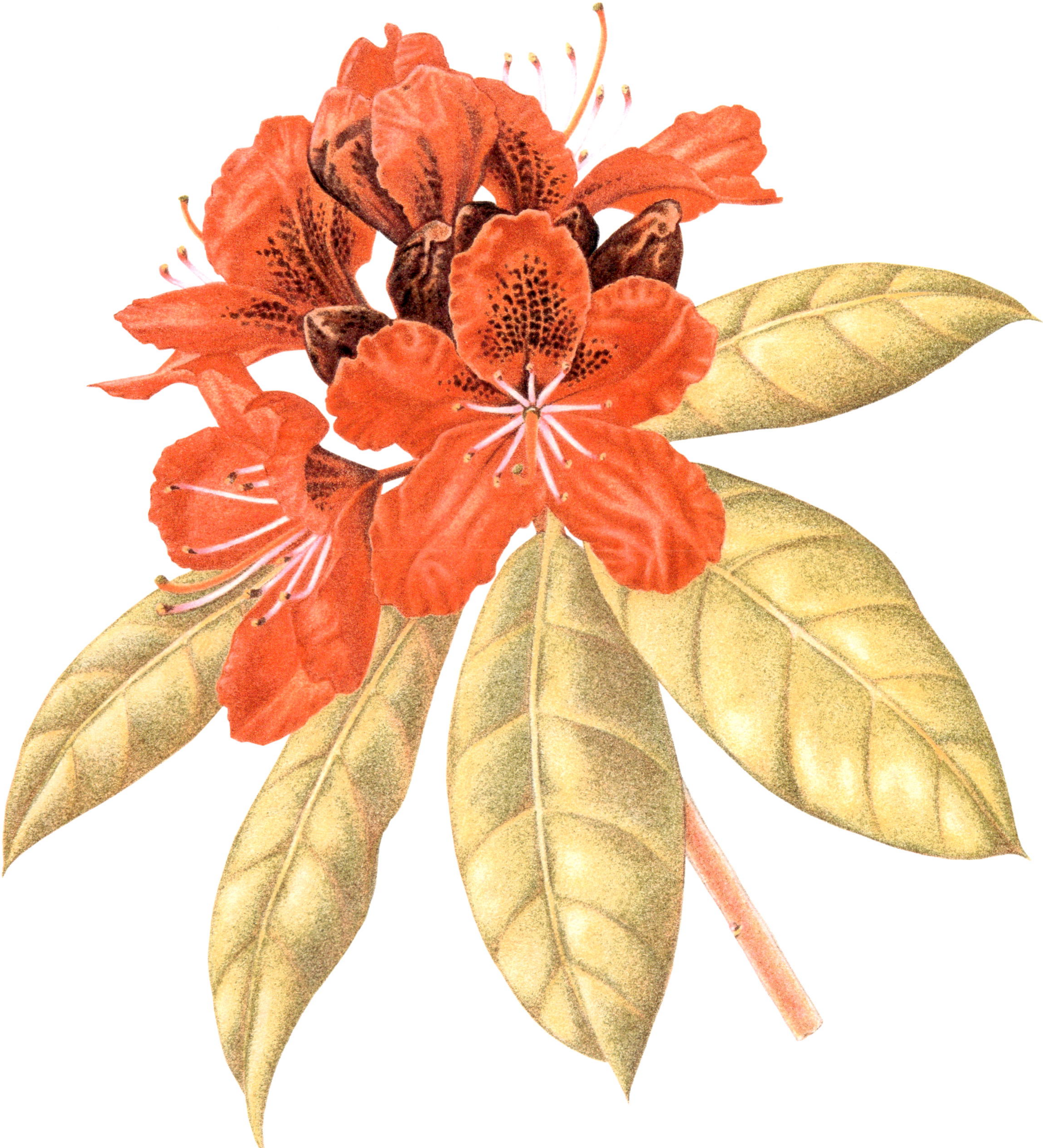

RHODODENDRON
27 × 20 cm (10¾ × 8 in)
Susan Martin Assoc. SBA

CHAPTER 7

BROWN

BROWN, OR EARTH, pigments are a stable element in the palette of every botanical artist. Used to capture the diversity of soft colours found in twigs, branches, nuts, seeds, fungi and autumn foliage, browns are also a useful aid to mixing greens.

Earth pigments are amongst the oldest known to man, dating back to the time when our cave-dwelling forbears felt the urge to create a visual image on the rock face and looked around for something with which to make their mark.

A stick from the dying embers of the fire gave a caveman charcoal, and the mud that stained his feet and legs on wet days provided various shades of brown, depending on where his hunting expeditions had led. I am guessing, of course, unless it is some kind of latent memory! Perhaps I just nagged my man for treading mud into the cave and not wiping his feet on the grass at the entrance.

The umbers and siennas, either in their natural state or heated to produce the darker burnt colours, should be in every artist's range. So, too, should be the other natural pigments of ochre in its many shades from yellow to brown and 'terre verte', green earth. These colours date to pre-antiquity, when already the raw materials were in place for the artists of today – an awe-inspiring thought.

Amongst the bearded iris we find a number of 'brown' cultivars, but, as you will see in Barbara McGirr's splendid example, the warm rich tones achieved are the result of careful mixing and glazing rather than dependent on any brown pigment. As with Clematis 'Star of India' on page 72 it is a case of searching out the underlying colour and working up the glazes from that base.

▷ ACANTHUS SEED HEADS
40 x 23.5 cm
(15¾ x 9¼ in)
KATHLEEN BAKER SBA

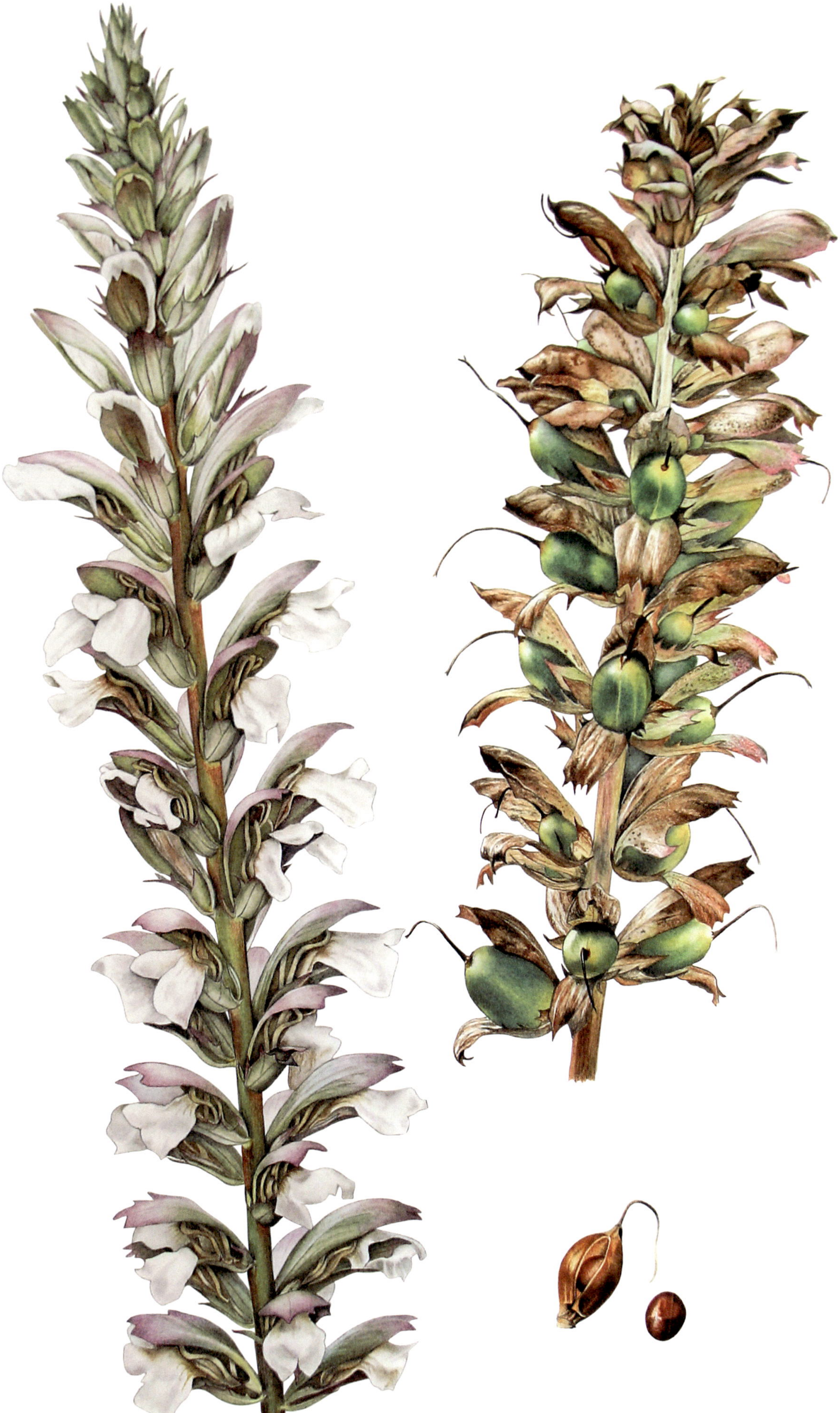

BEARDED IRIS

Iris germanica

Barbara McGirr SBA

I had greatly admired Barbara's paintings of Bearded Iris, so she was the natural choice to present this study of rich, velvety brown flowers grown to perfection in Cambridgeshire soil. To arrive at their stunning colour is to take a journey of discovery through the palette and it is one that I hope you will also take, by trying the project on page 108.

PAINTS

WINSOR & NEWTON
Cadmium Yellow Deep
Cadmium Yellow Pale
Sepia
Alizarin Crimson
Prussian Blue
Hooker's Green
Olive Green
Lemon Yellow
Raw Umber
Burnt Umber
Winsor Green (Yellow Shade)
Yellow Ochre
Cerulean Blue

SCHMINCKE
Ultramarine Finest
Purple Magenta

BRUSHES

DA VINCI
Maestro sizes 2 and 4

SURFACE

ARCHES
Aquarelle Not 300 gsm (140 lb)

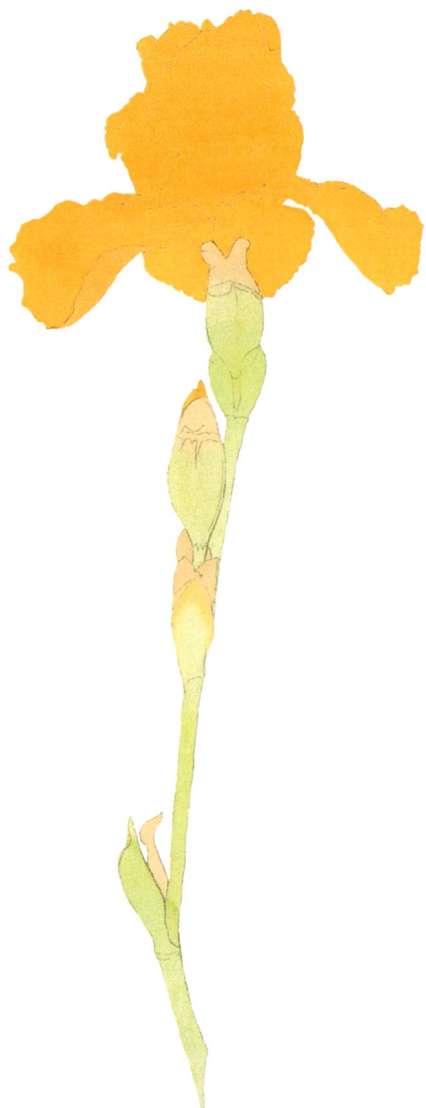

△ **Stage 1**
Barbara drew with a soft 5B pencil to discover the structure of the flowers. Drawing helped her to 'see', and 'fix' the plant in her mind.

Most of the pencil lines were then erased, leaving enough to guide the painting as it was built up with the brush. Working directly with living flowers has taught the artist to finish a flower before it moves and the buds open.

Working on a large sheet of paper enabled the composition to be built up gradually, following the upright growth habit of the iris. Barbara enjoyed using clean, bright colours; these could be toned down if incorrect, but vice versa would not be possible.

The rich glow of this brown iris comes from the underlying golden tone, probably the result of breeding from the more common yellow and purple varieties; when painting always look through the obvious to search out what lies beneath. So the first application of paint was a strong flat wash of Cadmium Yellow Deep, using a size 4 brush.

▷ **Stage 2**
Purple Magenta and Ultramarine Finest were mixed to make the lightest brown for the 'fall' and 'standards' (petals) of the flower, and also the creases in the petals. The yellow beard was carefully left. For the dark tones Alizarin Crimson was mixed with Ultramarine Finest, replacing the latter with Prussian Blue for the darkest areas. Where these dark shadows merged into lighter areas the colour was softened with a damp brush.

Barbara started painting the stem by glazing a pale base of green mixed from Lemon

▷ Stage 2

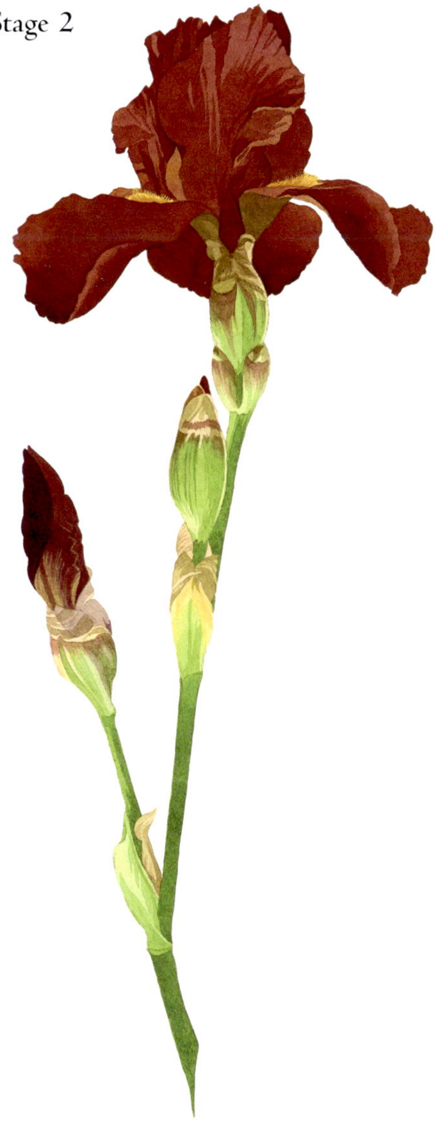

Yellow, Hooker's Green and Olive Green with brown mixed from Burnt Umber, Raw Umber and Cadmium Yellow Pale, allowing the colours to flow into each other.

The buds were built up with more glazes of green. The brown papery sheath was built up by varying Burnt Umber for warmer tones and Raw Umber for cooler tones. Where it merged with green the brown was blended with a damp brush.

A pale wash of Alizarin Crimson was added to the edge of the sheath of the opening bud and a touch of Yellow Ochre added to the shadows. Barbara moulded the stem with the original green mix, adding more Hooker's Green and Olive Green for the darkest tone. These colours were dropped in wet-in-wet, with detail added with a dry brush; that is, using minimum water.

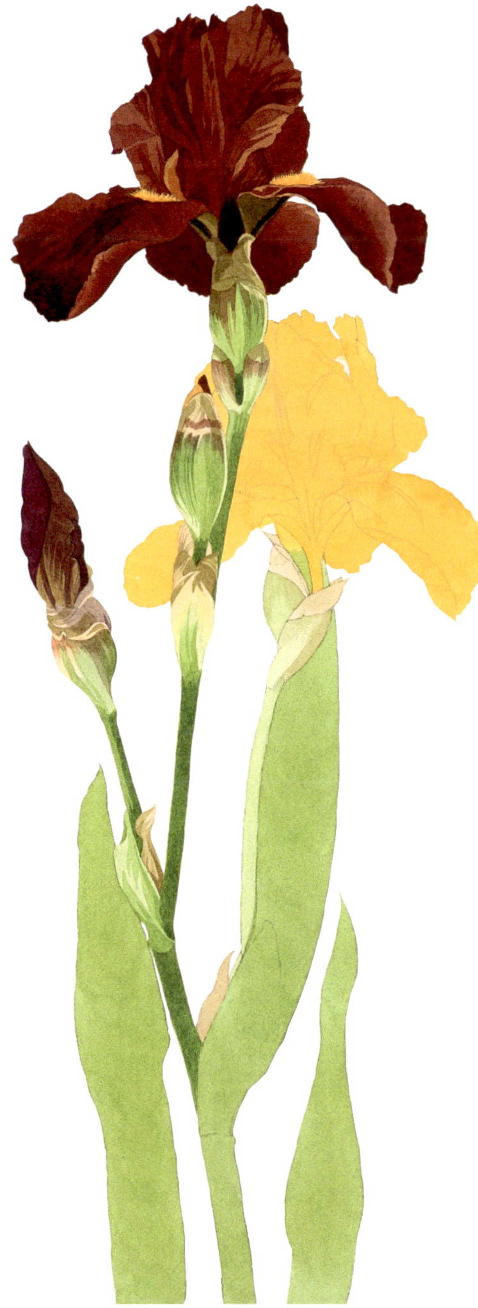

△ Stage 3

With the first stage completed the second flower, its stem and leaf could be composed, making sure that the first stem grew naturally from the main stem. This needed careful observation to ensure that the angle where they joined was correct.

The flower was then painted in the same manner as the first one. As iris leaves mostly grow lower than the flowers Barbara drew some of them in to add weight to the lower part of the picture.

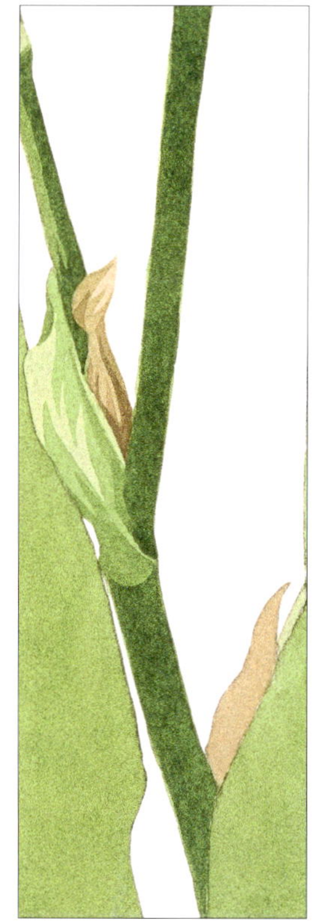

Detail from Stage 3: When adding extra stems the artist was careful to get the angles of growth correct.

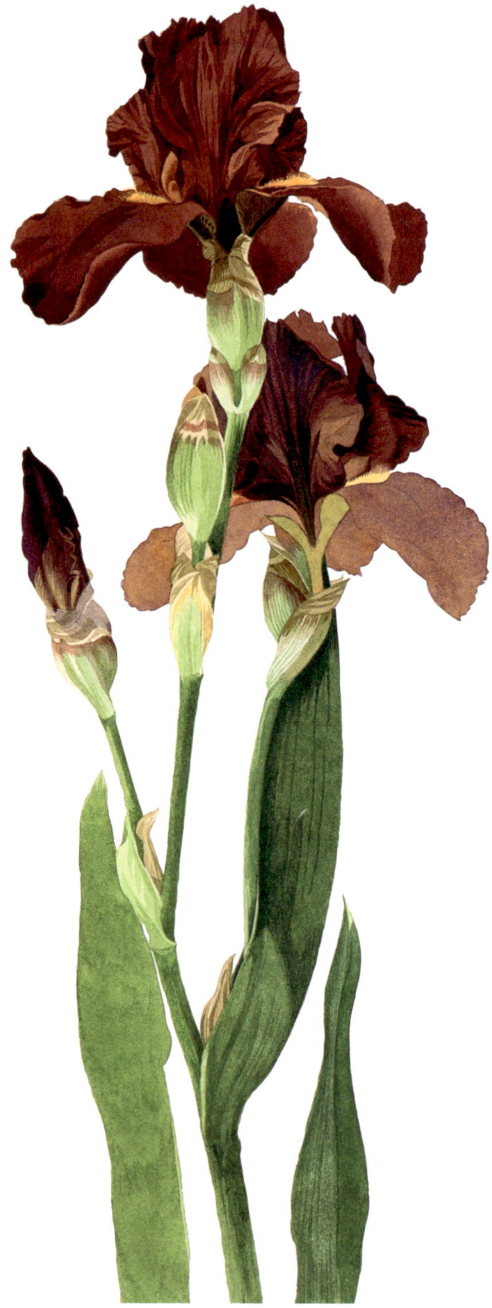

△ **Stage 4**
Barbara chose the lightest tone of the leaves and laid on a flat wash using the basic green mixture of Lemon Yellow, Hooker's Green and Olive Green. She continued to build up tone using this mix, adding a little Raw Umber when necessary.

The third leaf had more reflected blue light on it, so a mix of Ultramarine Finest and Cerulean Blue was glazed over it. For the very deepest shadows Winsor Green was added to the green mix.

▷ **Final Stage**
Barbara studied the work carefully, making slight adjustments to the occasional leaf or petal edge to ensure that they were all sharp.

Generally it is a good idea to leave your work somewhere where you can glance at it occasionally before declaring that it is completely finished, as often small points suddenly become obvious. In the same manner, holding the painting upside down or looking at the reflected image in a mirror will reveal details that you might have overlooked.

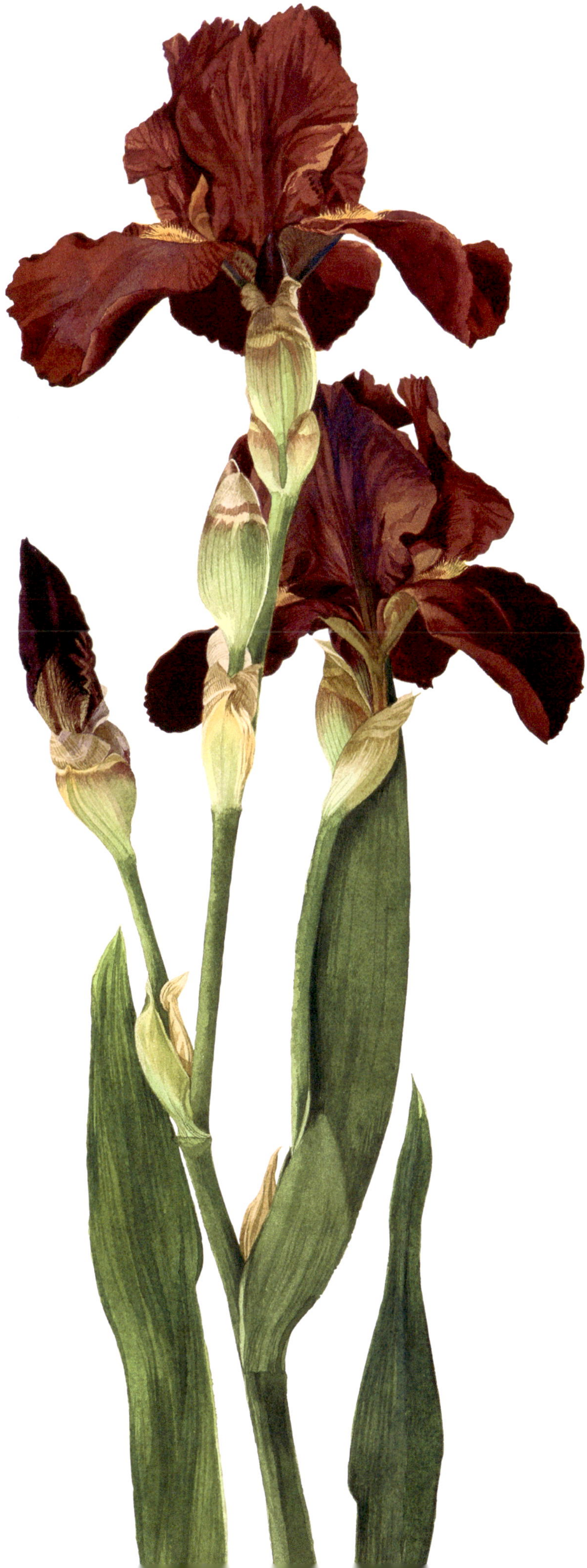

BEARDED IRIS
51 × 19 cm (20 × 7½ in)
BARBARA MCGIRR SBA

PROJECT *Iris germanica*

The colour chart together with the description of Barbara's working method should enable you to try out this project.

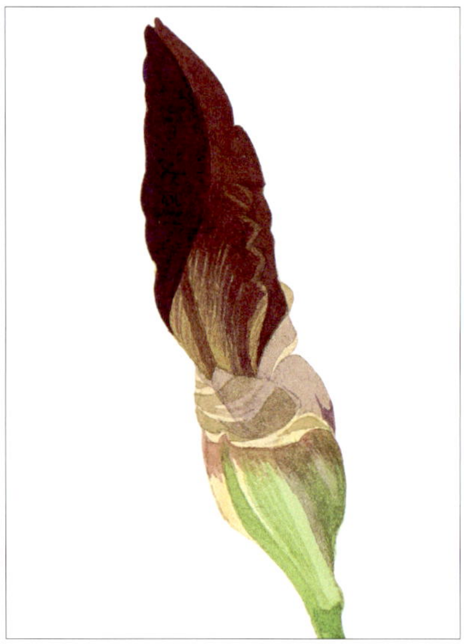

Detail from Stage 3: Early work on the bud laid down the first colour details for the petals and papery sheath.

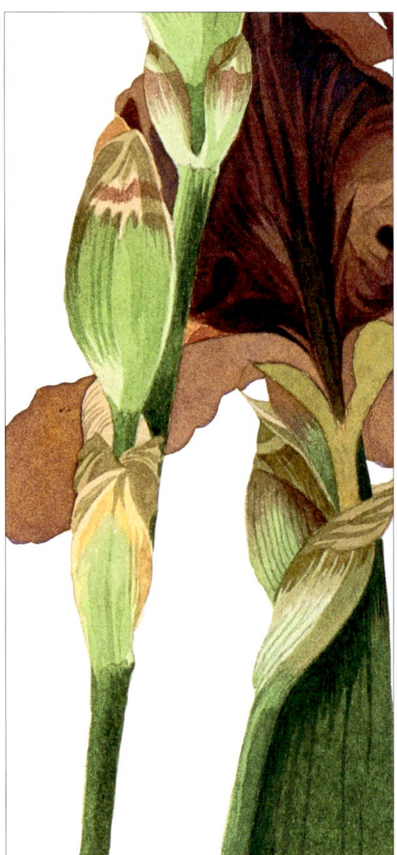

Detail from Stage 4: The main stem had the added interest of the immature buds, which were built up using the same basic colour mixes as for the one that was nearly open.

COLOUR CHART

FLOWERS

1 Cadmium Yellow Deep

2 Schmincke: Purple Magenta + Ultramarine Finest

3 As 2 + more Ultramarine Finest

4 Alizarin Crimson + Schmincke: Ultramarine Finest

5 As 4 + more Ultramarine Finest

6 Alizarin Crimson + Prussian Blue

7 As 6 + more Prussian Blue

LEAVES

1 Lemon Yellow + Hooker's Green + Olive Green

2 As 1 + more Hooker's Green

3 As 2 + more Olive Green

4 As 3 + Raw Umber

5 As 4 + more Hooker's Green

6 As 5 + Winsor Green

BUDS

1 Raw Umber + Burnt Umber

2 Raw Umber + Olive Green

3 Sepia + Burnt Umber

4 Sepia + Burnt Umber + Olive Green

5 As 4 + more Sepia and Burnt Umber

6 Sepia + Alizarin Crimson + Schmincke: Ultramarine Finest

7 As 6 + more Alizarin Crimson and Ultramarine Finest

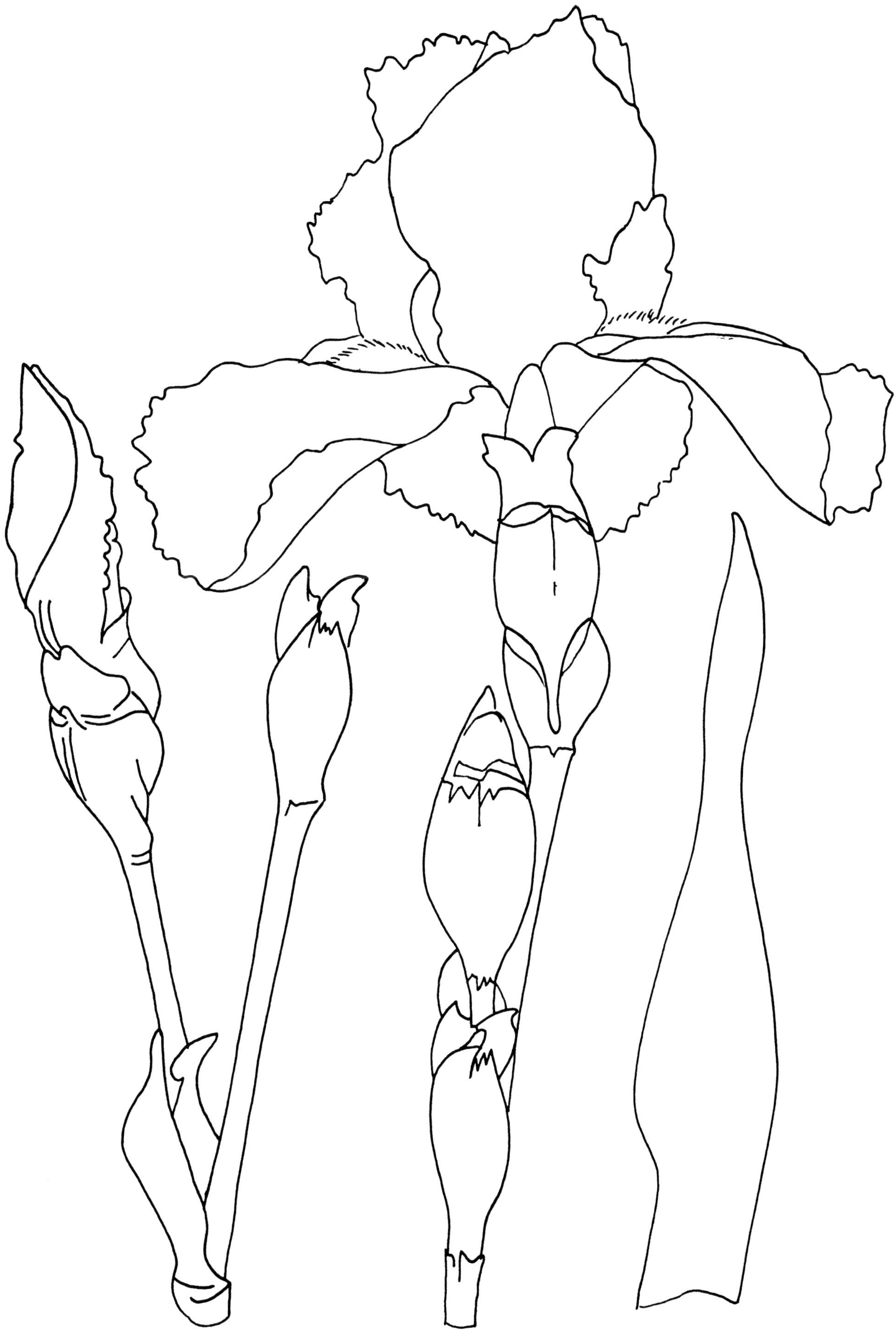

CHAPTER 8
BLACK

THIS IS A PIGMENT whose particles absorb light, so as botanical painters we do not need it in the strictest sense. However, there is a range of flowers, foliage and fruit that are thought of as black, apart from the tulips which first come to mind. Included in these is Iris tuberose, the widow iris, with its brownish, blue-black flowers, *Sambucus nigra*, the black elder, and the old favourite dahlia 'Bishop of Llandaff', with its crimson flowers shown to great advantage by its green-black foliage. There are others, of course, which make striking features in the garden, but none of them require the use of black pigment as each will show, on closer inspection, to be a mix of very dark pigments.

It would be a useful exercise to compose a black shade card in the same way as you make one for greens, only this time working with a selection of greens, purples, browns and reds. The 'shades' of black will then become apparent.

There are, of course, a number of black fruits, from elderberries and blackberries to sloes and damsons. For the first two, remember the process of ripening from green through red to black. Colours glazed in that order with a little Winsor Violet in the final mix will give the depth of colour required. For sloes and damsons there is less, if any, red involved and green, blue and purple will suffice.

Achieve bloom on any of these fruits by applying a first wash of Viridian Green, followed quickly by a stronger wash of, say, French Ultramarine and Winsor Violet, depending on the colour of your fruit. While still slightly damp lift out the area of bloom with a clean damp brush, and there it will be. Do not fuss with it; the edges must remain soft and blurred. Blot gently with a small piece of kitchen paper if needed.

▷ ARISERUM PROBOSCIDEUM
27 × 16 cm
(10½ × 6¼ in)
SUSAN HILLIER FSBA

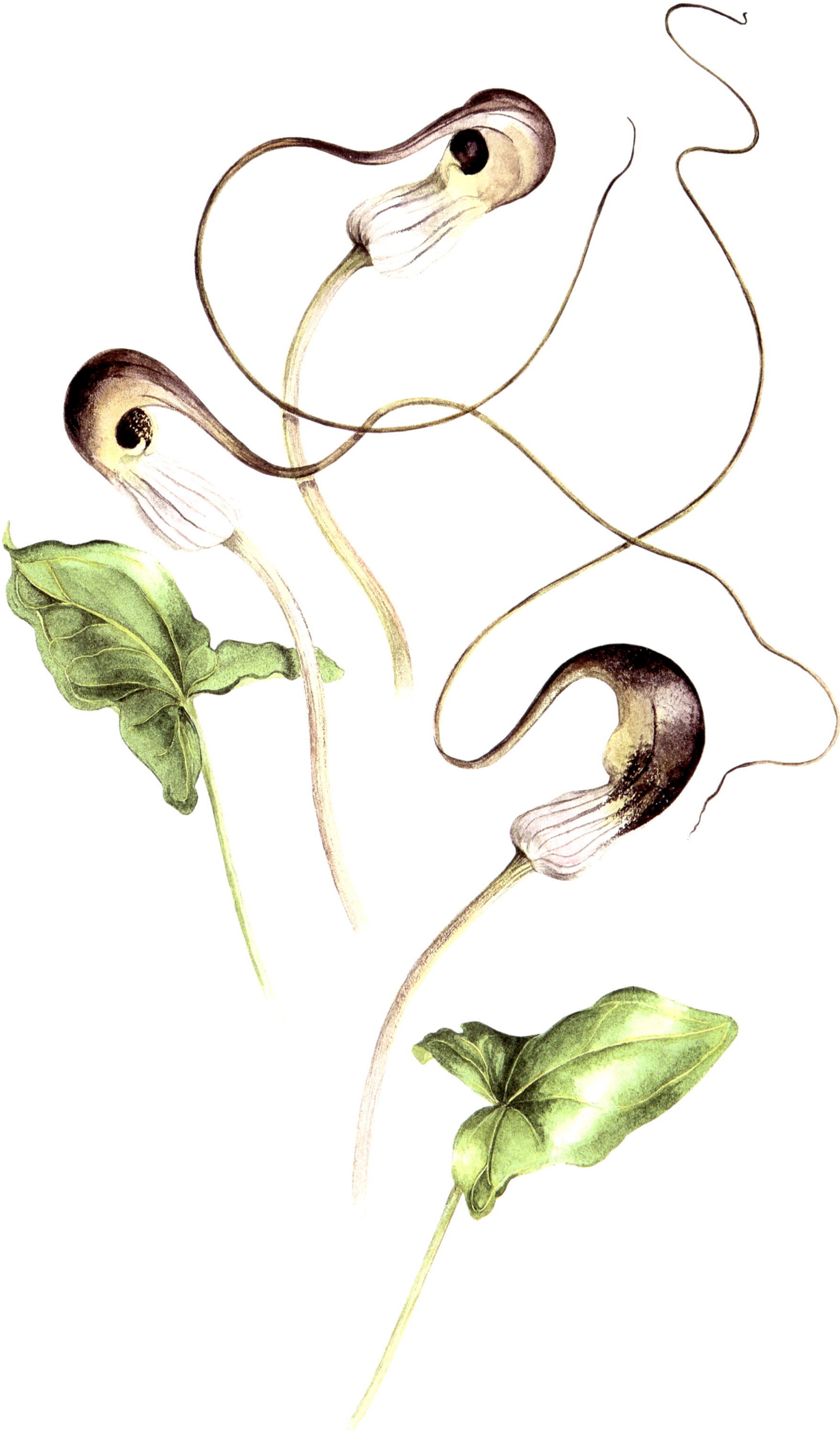

TULIP

Tulipa 'Queen of Night'

Susan Christopher-Coulson SBA

This cottage tulip is one of those which first springs to mind when a black flower is mentioned. It is an excellent subject to represent the darkest end of the spectrum and Susan's observation of the underlying colours in this coloured-pencil drawing helps to create the intense tones and the beautiful sheen so admired in this variety of tulip.

COLOUR CHART

DERWENT ARTISTS UNLESS OTHERWISE INDICATED

- Berol Verithin: Black 747
- Burnt Carmine 6500
- Cedar Green 5000
- Sap Green 4900
- Chartreuse 5130
- Indigo 3600
- Grape 2120
- Blue Grey 6800
- Spruce Green 4130
- Faber-Castell Albrecht Dürer: Dark Indigo 157
- Faber-Castell Albrecht Dürer: Wine Red 133
- Caran d'Ache: Supracolor Black 009
- Caran d'Ache Supracolor: Bluish Pale 371

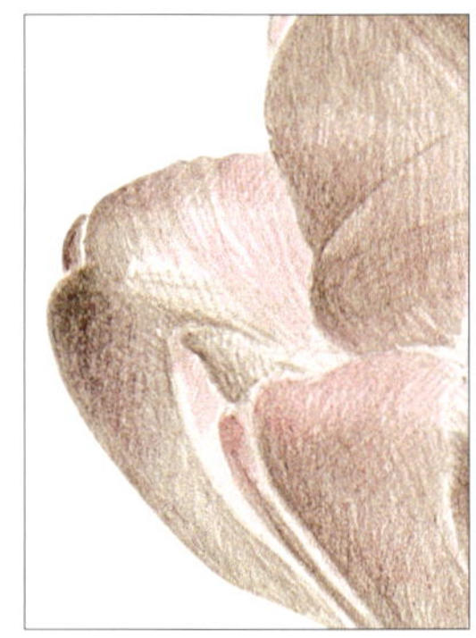

Detail from Stage I: Verithin Black was used to work in the darkest areas of tone in contrast to the white paper left for highlights.

△ **Stage I**

Before starting make sure you are comfortable with the chosen aspect and happy with any foreshortened views of your subject.

Susan selected a sheet of A3 Goldline Bristol board and using a well-sharpened soft graphite pencil (B or 2B) made a faint line drawing with minimum pressure so as not to damage the paper surface. For the purposes of reproduction the line was made heavier than would normally be used. The drawing was not made in coloured pencil as mistakes would be difficult to erase.

All the chosen coloured pencils were well sharpened before beginning. All graphite marks were erased before any colour was used, leaving just enough to guide the artist in the area on which she was working at the time.

She took care that her working hand did not press any unwanted marks into the paper or create smudges.

Using quick close-hatching strokes with very delicate pressure Susan used a Verithin Black 747 on the petals to work in the darkest areas first, leaving any highlights as white paper. This established a tonal base coat from light to shade. She added Burnt Carmine 6500 to areas with a more predominant red hue. Two or three layers were needed where the colour was most intense, with the hatched layers in contrary directions where possible. Always a delicate pressure was maintained.

For the stem and leaf Susan applied Cedar Green 5000 to darker areas and Sap Green 4900 to lighter areas, with Chartreuse 5130 for the stem highlight. In order to work on the flower a clean sheet of paper was put over the stem and leaf area so that the working hand did not besmirch it.

▷ Stage 2

Susan intensified the base coat and enlivened the deadening black with Indigo 3600 and Grape 2120. She also continued to blend in Burnt Carmine 6500 where appropriate. Working with these three colours as required she blended and adjusted colour and tone, always maintaining a delicate pressure. The base coat of black on the petals provided some initial depth for such a dark subject.

A tint of Blue Grey 6800 was used to tone down some of the lesser highlights.

A light layer of Grape 2120 was worked into the darker shadow areas of the stem and leaf, and Spruce Green 4130 worked over all. The base coat of Sap Green 4900 showed through, altering the hue.

Susan continued to add delicate layers throughout to enrich colour and add density, balancing the colours to achieve the desired hues. She did not concentrate on a single part of the subject, but aimed for equal density of coverage in all areas so that she could see the subject develop as a whole.

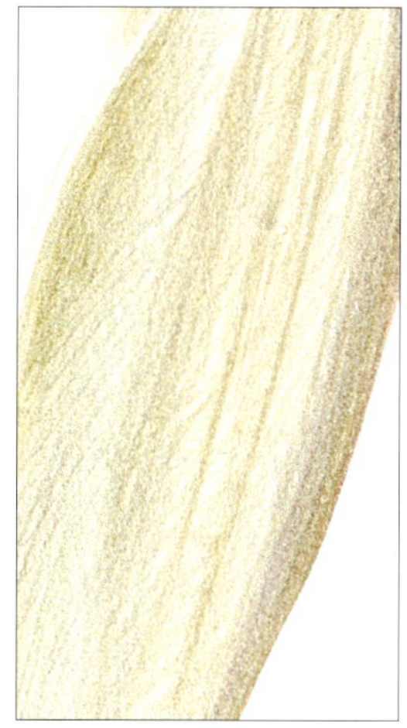

Detail from Stage 2: Spruce Green was worked over the Sap Green base, with Grape adding to the darker shadows that were away from the light.

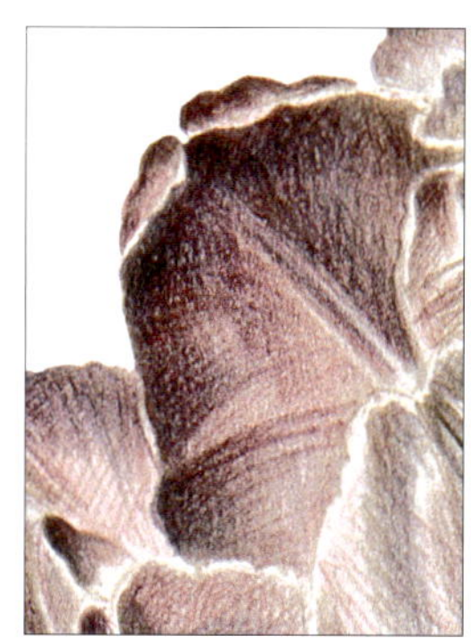

Detail from Stage 2: Indigo, Grape and Burnt Carmine over black started to create a richness in colour.

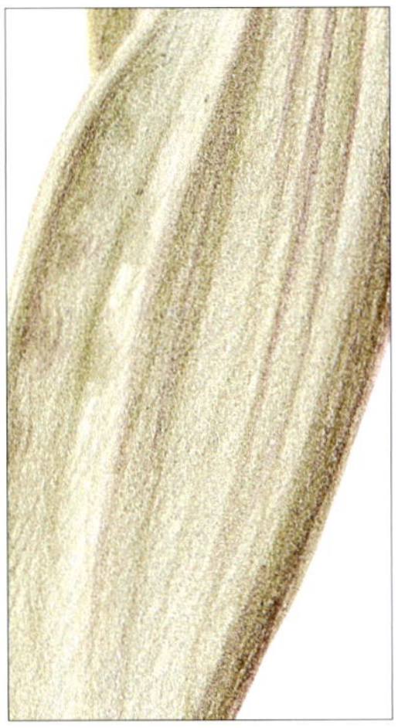

Detail from Stage 3: A layer of Sap Green helped to restore vibrancy to the leaf if the tone started to become too dark.

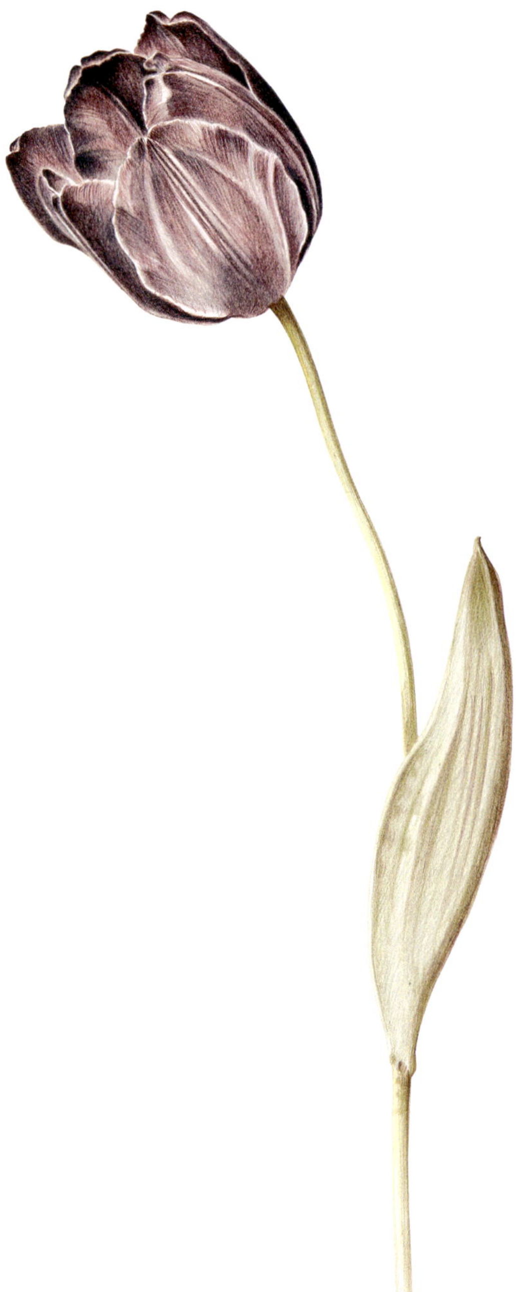

◁ **Stage 3**

Using slightly more pressure to add density to the petals, Susan continued to blend and layer between alternating colours, Indigo 3600 and Grape 2120, adding Burnt Carmine 6500 to return to redder hues as required. She checked for any highlights that needed to be toned down, adding a tint of Blue Grey, Grape or Burnt Carmine as appropriate. She made sure that all outlines were crisp, while ensuring that there were no obvious, harsh outlines.

She continued to add density and to balance the greens appropriately. For instance, if the tone was too dark or blue-green she used some Sap Green 4900 to return it to a brighter colour. Working on the drawing needed constant judgement to balance colour. Coloured-pencil artists are forced to glaze their colours in a way that watercolourists are not. This automatically gives their work an appearance of luminosity and the opportunity to exploit colour to the full.

▷ **Final Stage**

Susan used waxier pencils to ensure all colours were fully blended to the required depth for the final layer and to achieve solid colour, particularly on dark subjects. Albrecht Dürer Wine Red 133 and Dark Indigo 157 were used for this purpose and even the sparing use of Black 009 was necessary in the very darkest shadows (the interior and base of the flower). Caran d'Ache Bluish Pale 371 was blended to soften highlights and give a pinkish lavender hue. For the strongest highlights the white paper could be left; often White pencil appears more cream than true white.

A touch of Bluish Pale blended over the highlights on the veins of the leaf, and on the stem highlight, heightened contrast.

Susan ensured that the background was totally clean by using a clean plastic eraser and small pieces of putty rubber kneaded into the appropriate shape to access awkward corners.

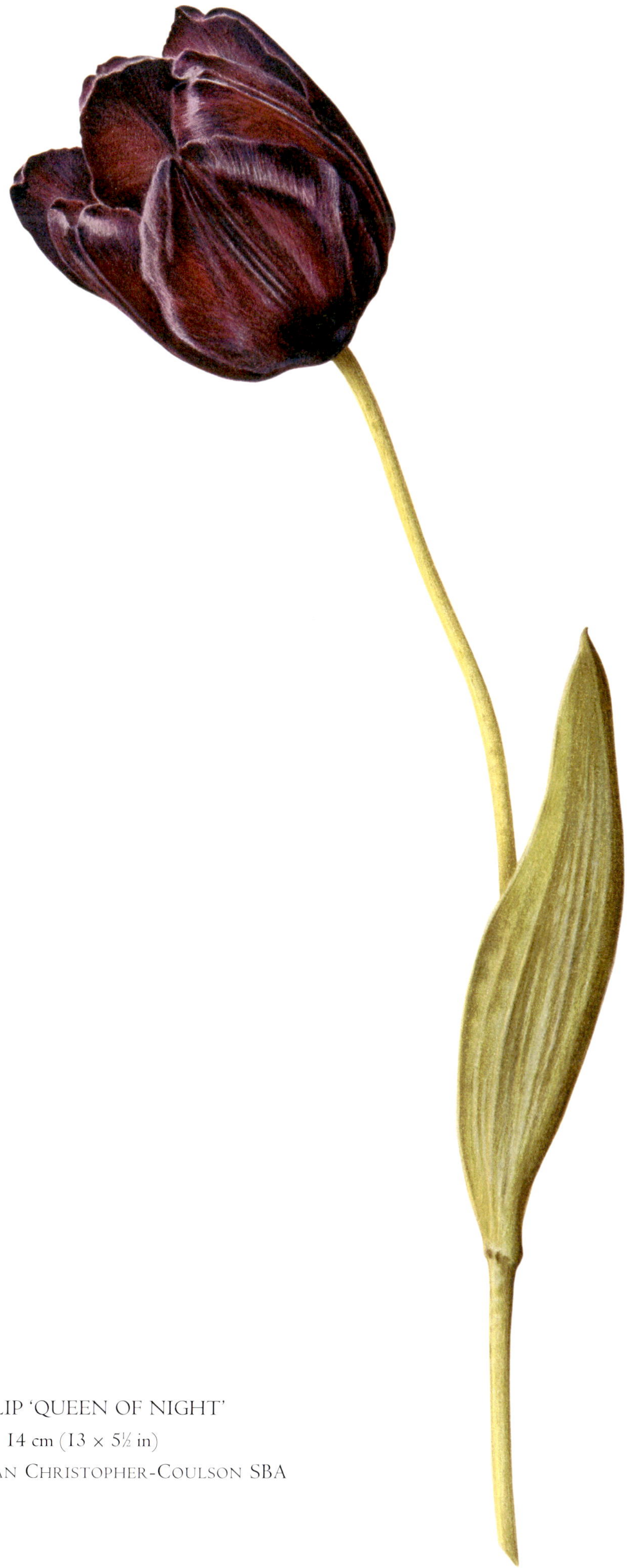

TULIP 'QUEEN OF NIGHT'
33 × 14 cm (13 × 5½ in)
SUSAN CHRISTOPHER-COULSON SBA

COLOUR COMPARISONS

THE PURPOSE of the following pages is to describe a full range of pigments by different manufacturers in words as well as with colour swatches.

To reproduce colour in print with 100 per cent accuracy is almost impossible, so the written description and comparison is there as a backup. It should also provide a useful reference source before you dash out to buy a particular colour recommended by another artist or tutor, because it may be virtually identical with one that you already have – only the name will be different. If you knew the chemical compounds of each colour that would tell you the same thing, but few of us go to those lengths and this will serve the same purpose for most of the colours you are likely to require. Also, it will tell you at a glance if the pigment is opaque or transparent, which is vital when you are glazing one colour on top of another.

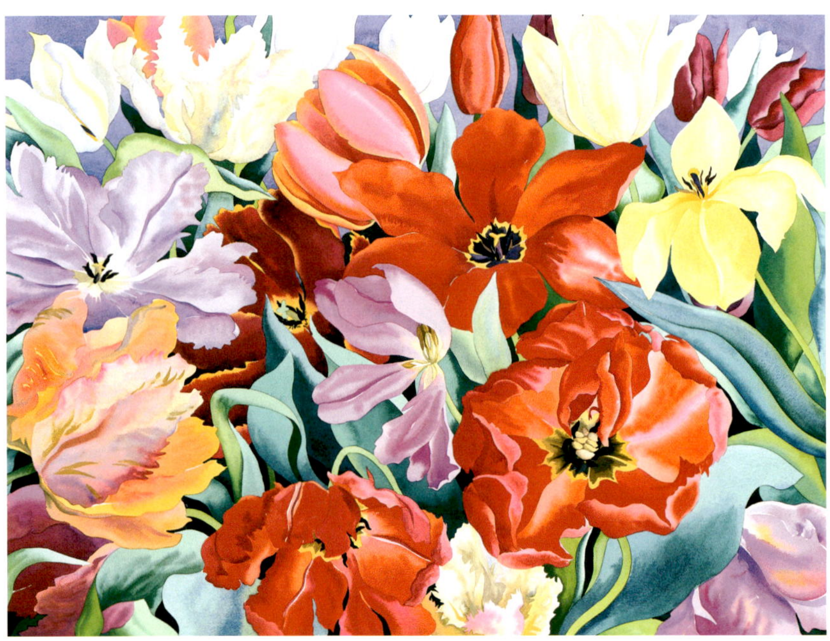

TULIPS
55 × 73 cm
(21½ × 28¾ in)
CHRISTOPHER RYLAND SBA

PURE COLOURS FOR LONGEVITY

Artists today are spoilt for choice when buying colours and it can be a daunting procedure. Perhaps as well as being beguiled by colour one should look more closely at the way paints are manufactured. For example, the French firm of Sennelier, still a family business after 120 years, chooses to use only the finest Kordofan gum Arabic as a binder, adding honey for lustre and glycerine for plasticity. These pure ingredients are mixed with the best available pigments, some sourced from the earth in time-honoured fashion, before the slow process of soaking and grinding begins. Slowly revolving granite grindstones result in fine particles, which help to create the pure and luminous colours that many artists find unbeatable. I am reminded of the colours in my father's paint box that he used at the beginning of the twentieth century.

This brings me to the subject of fugitive colours; that is, ones that cannot be guaranteed to withstand the passage of time. For botanical painters this is particularly sad as they need help to be able to match some of the wonderful flower colours found in nature. I believe that there is at least a partial solution to this problem of longevity.

First, consider using conservation glass when you have your work framed. It will filter out the most damaging ultraviolet light rays and today's specialized glass will not distort or tint your paintings in any way. It will be a little more expensive, but consider if your painting is worth it and talk to your framer accordingly.

Secondly, when you sell your work, educate the buyer. Protective glass cannot do it all and it is wrong for any painting to be hung in full sunlight where it might still be damaged, or indeed where there is high heat or humidity. Common sense has to play a part in giving your work a long life. Now use all your paints and enjoy them to their full.

COLOUR TEST CHARTS

Key to Abbreviations

Manufacturers
D-R – Daler-Rowney
Sch – Schmincke
Sen – Sennelier
WN – Winsor & Newton
Note: All pigments with the prefix Winsor are manufactured by Winsor & Newton; for example, Winsor Violet.

Opacity
O – Opaque
SO – Semi-opaque
T – Transparent
ST – Semi-transparent

Note: All colours tested were Artists' quality paints.

SHADE CARD

This small shade card shows a few of the paints from the Sennelier range that are either recorded as or considered to be fugitive. Of course they occur in every range, but in any case I believe they are there to be used, so I make a case for their enjoyment.

If you paint fuchsias you will beg for the colours **4-6**. These are moderately lightfast 'flower colours'.

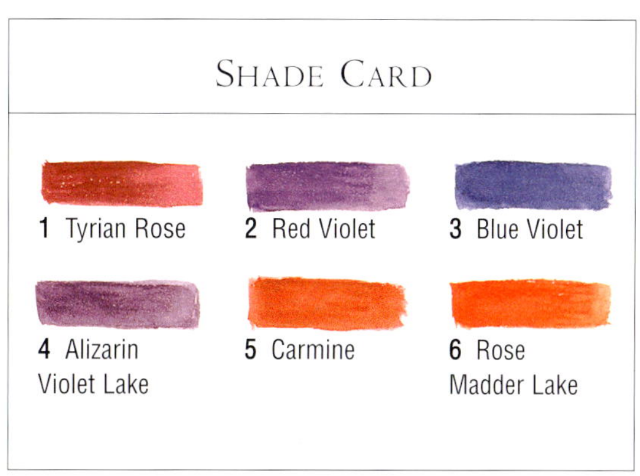

COLOUR TESTING THE YELLOWS

1 WN Naples Yellow (O) and **2** D-R Naples Yellow (O) in the tube are similar, but **3** D-R Naples Yellow (O) in the pan appears paler. **4** WN Naples Yellow Deep (O) in the same colour range is very much stronger.

5 Sen Lemon Yellow (T), **6** D-R Lemon (T), **7** Sch Lemon Yellow (ST) and **8** WN Winsor Lemon (ST) are interchangeable. The exception is **9** WN Lemon Yellow (O), which is deeper and opaque.

10 WN Winsor Yellow (ST) is almost identical to **11** Sch Pure Yellow (T). **12** WN Transparent Yellow (T) is similar to both, but less intense.

13 Sch Aureolin Modern (ST), **14** D-R Aureolin (T) and **15** WN Aureolin (T) are all different in colour, but both the latter, transparent ones make excellent glazes. **16** D-R Permanent Yellow (T) is a good substitute.

17 Sen Cadmium Yellow Light (O) and **18** Sen Yellow Light (T) are very similar, but use the latter for glazes. **19** D-R Cadmium Yellow (O) and **20** WN Turner's Yellow (O) also fit into this group, but Turner's Yellow has a slightly more reddish tinge. **21** Sch Venadium (O) is similar, but with a hint of green.

22 WN Cadmium Yellow (O) and **23** D-R Cadmium Yellow Deep (O) are almost identical. They are also very similar to **24** D-R Indian Yellow (T) and **25** WN Indian Yellow (T), but as both these are transparent these are best for glazing. Others belonging to this group are **26** WN New Gamboge (ST) and **27** WN Winsor Yellow Deep (ST), but note that they are semi-transparent.

28 WN Cadmium Orange (O) and **29** Sch Cadmium Orange (O) are very different; the first is a vibrant orange, the second has more red content. **30** WN Winsor Orange (SO) is a richer, warmer colour than **28** WN Cadmium Orange (O). **31** D-R Warm Orange (T) is a useful glaze, with a brilliant, almost vermilion red hue. **32** Sen French Ochre (T), **33** WN Yellow Ochre (SO), **34** WN Gold Ochre (ST) and **35** WN Quinacridone Gold (T) are good autumnal colours, with **32** Sen French Ochre having the strongest yellow element.

36 D-R Yellow Ochre (T) is much more yellow than **33** WN Yellow Ochre (SO).

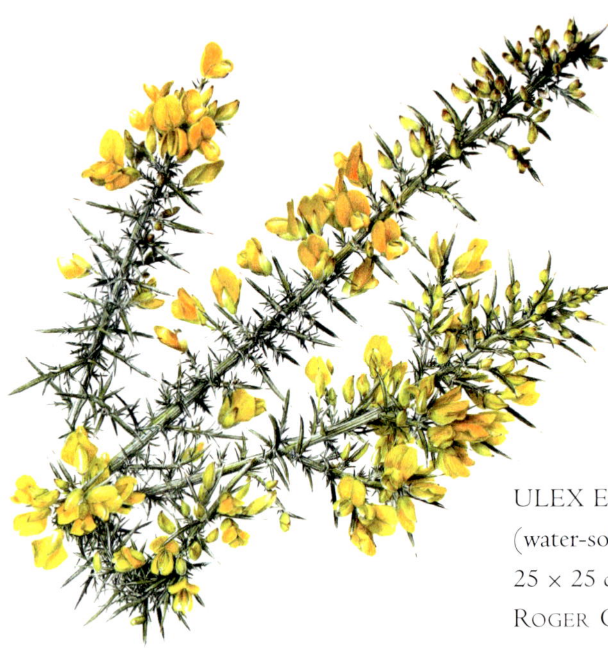

ULEX EUROPAEUS – GORSE
(water-soluble coloured pencil)
25 × 25 cm (10 × 10 in)
ROGER C REYNOLDS SBA

Colour Testing Chart – Yellows

1 WN Naples Yellow	**2** D-R Naples Yellow (tube)	**3** D-R Naples Yellow (pan)	**4** WN Naples Yellow Deep	**5** Sen Lemon Yellow
6 D-R Lemon	**7** Sch Lemon Yellow	**8** WN Winsor Lemon	**9** WN Lemon Yellow	**10** WN Winsor Yellow
11 Sch Pure Yellow	**12** WN Transparent Yellow	**13** Sch Aureolin Modern	**14** D-R Aureolin	**15** WN Aureolin
16 D-R Permanent Yellow	**17** Sen Cadmium Yellow Light	**18** Sen Yellow Light	**19** D-R Cadmium Yellow	**20** WN Turner's Yellow
21 Sch Venadium	**22** WN Cadmium Yellow	**23** D-R Cadmium Yellow	**24** D-R Indian Yellow	**25** WN Indian Yellow
26 WN New Gamboge	**27** WN Winsor Yellow Deep	**28** WN Cadmium Orange	**29** Sch Cadmium Orange	**30** WN Winsor Orange
31 D-R Warm Orange	**32** Sen French Ochre	**33** WN Yellow Ochre	**34** WN Gold Ochre	**35** WN Quinacridone Gold
36 D-R Yellow Ochre				

COLOUR TESTING THE GREENS

1 WN Olive Green (T) is paler and more yellow than either **2** D-R Olive Green (T) in the tube or **3** D-R Olive Green (T) in the pan. The pigment in the pan is a darker colour than that in the tube.

4 Sch Olive Green Yellowish (ST) and **5** Sch Permanent Green Olive (ST) are very different colours. The latter is similar to **6** Sen Hooker's Green (T) and **7** D-R Hooker's Green Dark (T). Both of these have the benefit of transparency. **8** Sch May Green (ST) is very much like **9** D-R Vivid Green (T).

10 Sch Sap (T) is a brighter colour than **11** D-R Sap (T), **12** Sen Sap (T) or **13** WN Permanent Sap (T).

14 WN Green Gold (T) is an ideal glaze. It is particularly useful for adding brilliance to an otherwise drab green and as an autumn colour. **15** D-R Midnight Green (T) is currently only available as one of a group of three ready-made greens (The Terry Harrison Collection).

16 WN Perylene Green (T) is a useful very dark green for shadows where one leaf overlaps another, and also for darkening other greens such as Sap.

17 D-R Terre Verte is an easily applied pigment, not sticky, and very useful for glaucous foliage and bulb leaves. Glazed with light violet it will give the bloom often seen on daffodil leaves and similar foliage.

COLOUR TESTING CHART – GREENS

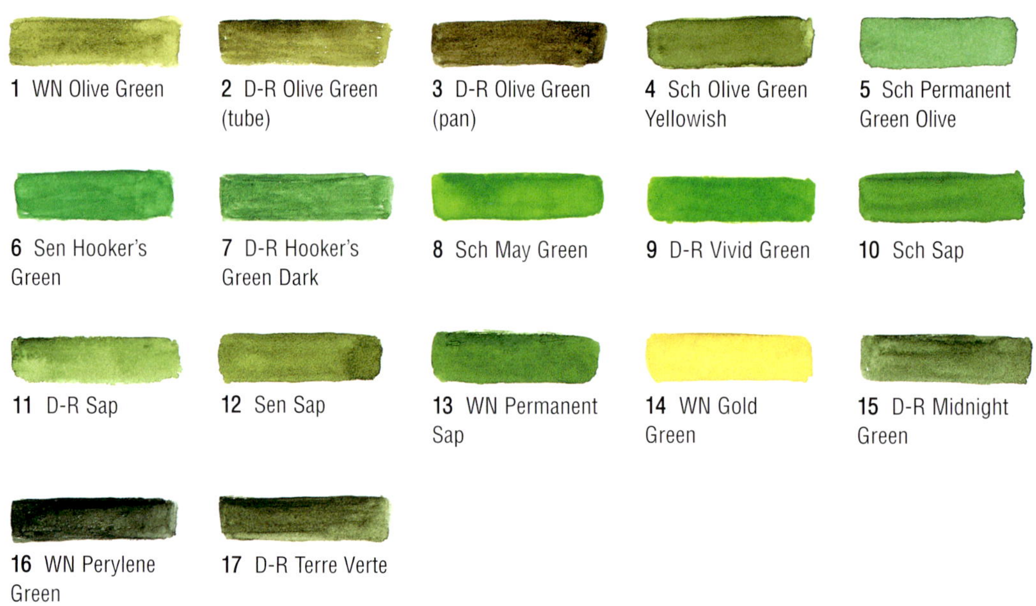

COLOUR TESTING THE BLUES

1 WN French Ultramarine (T) and **2** D-R French Ultramarine (T) are virtually interchangeable. **3** Sch Ultramarine Blue (ST) is similar, but less intense. **4** WN Cobalt Blue Deep (ST) is similar to all three. **5** Sen Ultramarine Deep (T) and **6** Sen Ultramarine Light (T) are matchless colours, giving pure transparent colour. **7** Sen Cobalt (T) is a soft transparent blue. **8** WN Cobalt (ST) and **9** D-R Cobalt (SO) are very similar.

10 Sch Cerulean Blue Tone (ST) is a clear strong colour. Less intense are **11** WN Cerulean (SO) and **12** D-R Cerulean (O), which are very similar to each other.
13 Sen Cerulean (O) is less turquoise and tends towards a softer powder blue.

14 Sch Delft Blue (SO) and **15** WN Indanthrene Blue (ST) are interchangeable.

16 WN Winsor Blue (Red Shade) (T) and **17** Sch Helio Blue Reddish (ST) are very similar, apart from the degree of transparency.

18 Sch Prussian Blue (SO) and **19** WN Prussian Blue (T) are interchangeable colours. Prussian Blue mixes to a rich green when used with various yellows, such as with Cadmium Yellow for a lively, bright colour or with Quinacridone Gold for a soft, strong green.

20 WN Antwerp Blue (T) and **21** Sch Mountain Blue (ST) are similar, but the latter is more turquoise.

22 Sch Phthalo Blue (ST) and **23** D-R Phthalo Blue (T) are interchangeable.

Colour Testing Chart – Blues

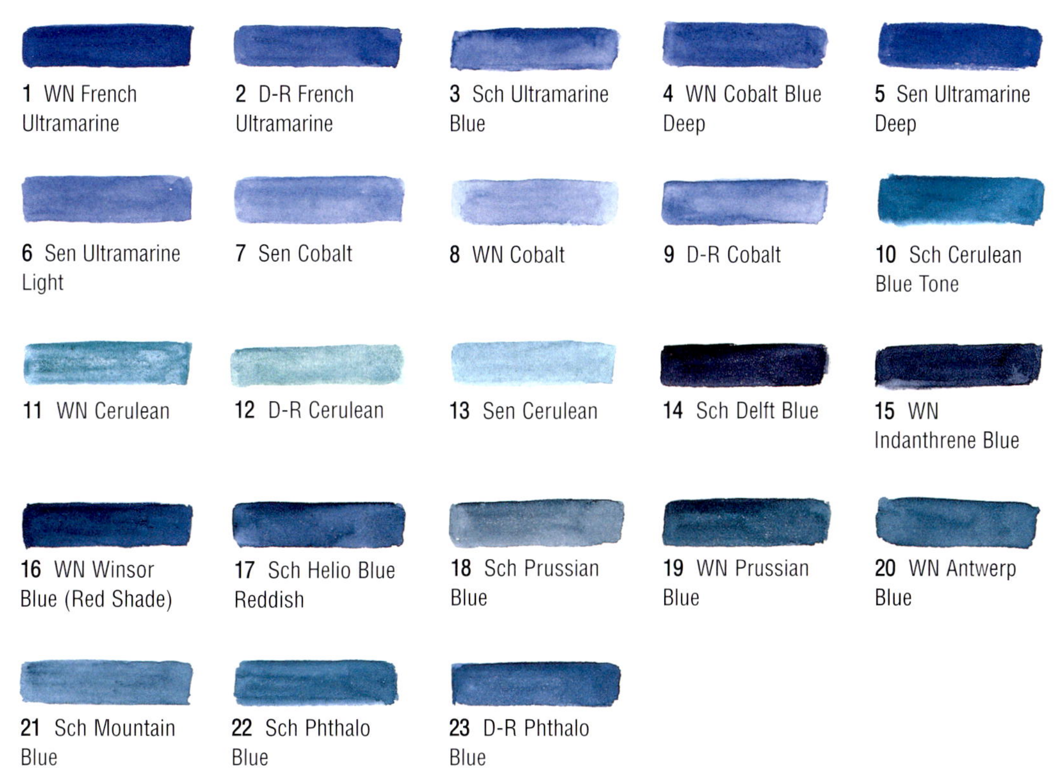

COLOUR TESTING THE REDS

1 Sch Deep Red (SO) and **2** WN Winsor Red Deep (SO) are interchangeable. **3** WN Permanent Alizarin Crimson (T) and **4** Sen Alizarin Crimson (T) are interchangeable. **5** Sch Ruby Red (ST) is very similar in colour, but less transparent.

6 WN Bright Red (SO) has been discontinued, but **7** WN Orange (Red Shade) (ST) is an excellent substitute and is not susceptible to damp. **8** Sch Scarlet Red (SO) and **9** Sen Red (T) are rich colours and interchangeable. Both are similar to **10** WN Winsor Red (ST).

11 D-R Permanent Red (ST) is slightly more orange than **12** WN Scarlet Lake (ST). **13** WN Cadmium Red (O) is a more vibrant shade than **14** WN Cadmium Red Deep (O), neither of which can be relied upon to withstand damp. The most exciting colour is **15** Sen Cadmium Red Light (O).

16 WN Quinacridone Red (T) is a warm rose with no hint of blue and is a particularly good glazing colour. Try it over very dark red – cherries or a crimson rose – and see how it makes the colour glow.

17 Sch Madder Lake Light (ST) is an equally good rose colour, but with slightly more blue. **18** WN Opera Rose (ST) is a brilliant colour, but is not totally durable. However, it is very useful as a glaze. **19** WN Permanent Rose (T) is a soft pink with blue undertones. **20** D-R Permanent Rose (T) is totally different, warmer and closer to **16** WN Quinacridone Red (T).

There is little difference between **21** D-R Carmine (T), a staining colour, and **22** WN Permanent Carmine (T).

23 Sch English Venetian Red (O) is similar to **24** WN Light Red (SO), but with purple undertones. **25** D-R Transparent Red Brown (T) is warmer and makes an excellent shadow colour with varying proportions of French Ultramarine.

26 WN Potter's Pink (SO) is a pigment from the eighteenth century, recently reintroduced. Once popular in the ceramics industry, it is a slightly grainy colour, ideal for adding a pinkish tone to stems or leaves.

27 WN Rose Dore (T) may be sticky to apply, and a similar colour can be achieved by glazing **19** WN Permanent Rose over Naples Yellow.

28 D-R Perylene Maroon (T) is a livelier colour than **29** WN Perylene Maroon (T).

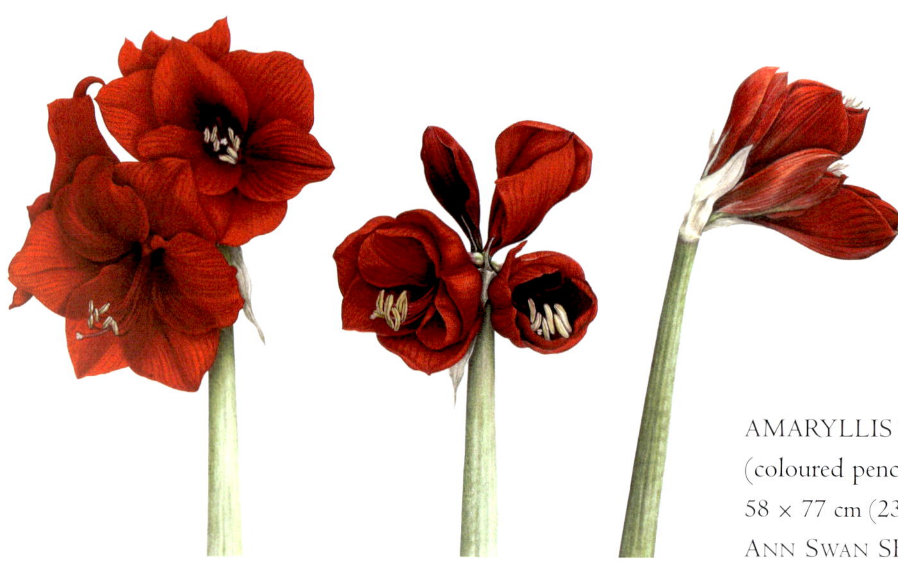

AMARYLLIS TRIO
(coloured pencil)
58 × 77 cm (23 × 30½ in)
Ann Swan SBA

Colour Testing Chart – Reds

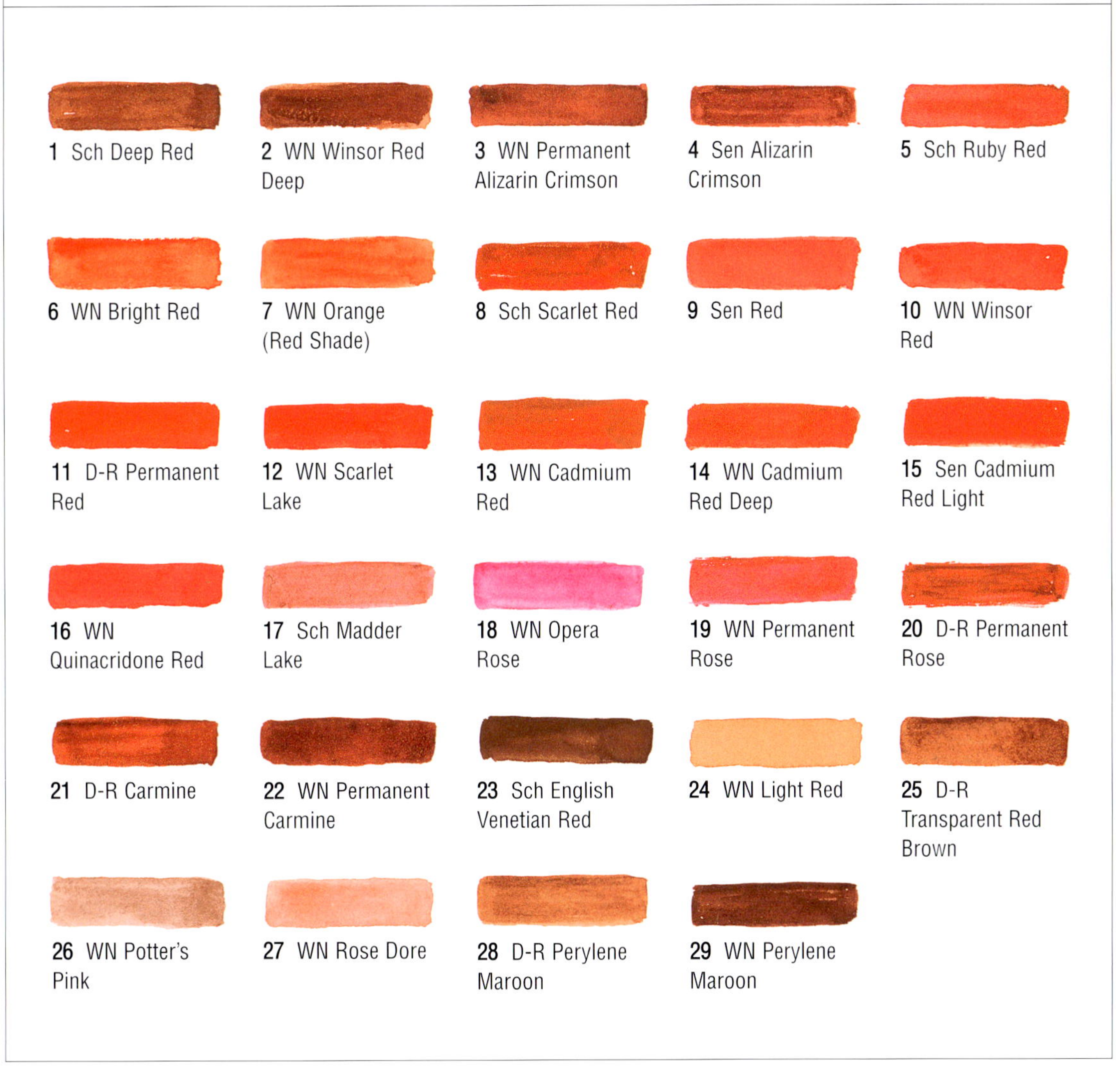

COLOUR TESTING THE PURPLES

1 WN Quinacridone Magenta (T) and **2** Sch Purple Magenta (T) are interchangeable colours. **3** Sch Magenta (ST) is very different with a dull rose appearance. **4** WN Permanent Magenta (T) is different again and appears rather flat in comparison. **5** Sch Quinacridone Violet (SO) is very similar to WN Permanent Magenta, but is a more intense colour.

6 D-R Cobalt Magenta (T) is a soft colour that is rather unique and is ideal for capturing the colour of some sweetpeas or fuchsias. **7** Sch Manganese Violet (ST) is similar to **6** D-R Cobalt Magenta, but with more purple.

8 Sen Blue Violet (ST) and **9** Winsor Violet (T) are two strong colours, but Winsor Violet has a more reddish tinge.

10 D-R Permanent Mauve (T) is close to Winsor Violet, but is also less red. **11** Sen Red Violet (ST) is an intense and beautiful colour, but must be used with care.
Note: See page 117 for information on Sen Blue Violet and Sen Red Violet regarding lightfastness.

12 WN Perylene Violet (T) is a suggested replacement for **13** WN Thioindigo Violet (T), which has been withdrawn, but there is no comparison as this colour is too drab. It would make a better substitute for **14** WN Purple Madder (T), also withdrawn. It pays to search the art shops in the hope of tracking down some of these lovely colours that have been discontinued by the manufacturers.

15 WN Ultramarine Violet (ST) is a clear soft colour, nearest to that of a true violet flower.

COLOUR TESTING CHART – PURPLES

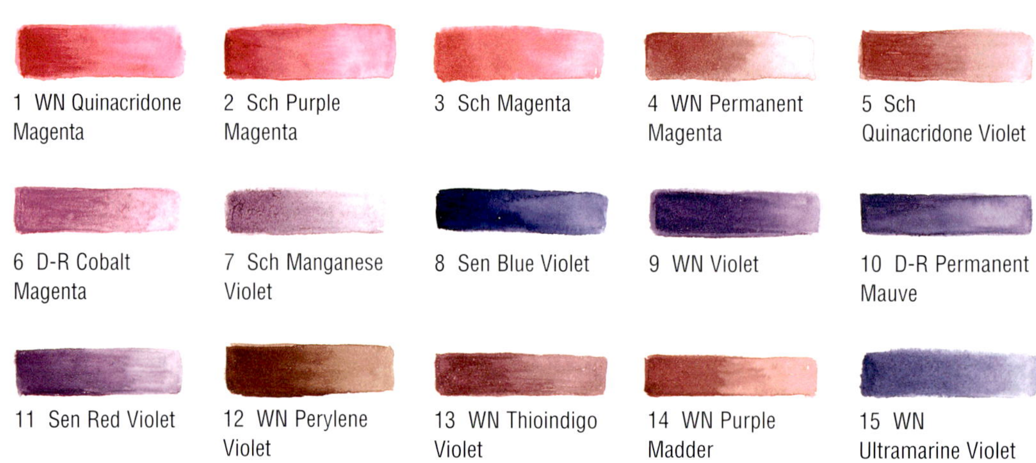

COLOUR TESTING THE BROWNS

1 WN Burnt Umber (T) is interchangeable with **2** Sen Burnt Umber (T).

3 Sen Burnt Sienna (T) is slightly less pink than **4** WN Burnt Sienna (T).

5 Sch Gold Brown (SO) is interchangeable with **4** WN Burnt Sienna (T), although a less transparent colour.

6 Sch Translucent Brown (SO), **7** D-R Transparent Red Brown (T), **8** WN Vandyke Brown (ST), **9** WN Sepia (O) and **10** WN Caput Mortuum Violet (O) are all very different from each other. These colours all have their place for use in painting foliage, bark, twigs and fungi, and as mixing pigments to produce a varying range.

11 WN Raw Sienna (T) has less depth of colour than **12** D-R Raw Sienna (T). **13** WN Raw Umber (T) and **14** D-R Raw Umber (T) are totally different colours, the latter being a much browner pigment.

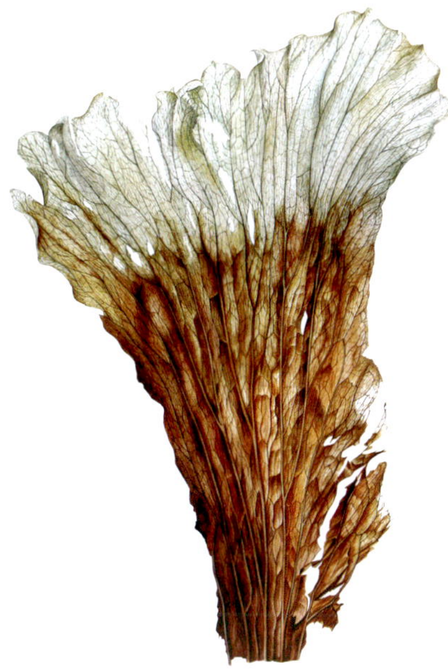

PLATICERIUM SUPERBUM (watercolour) 55 × 34 cm (21½ × 13½ in) ANITA WALSMIT SACHS SBA

COLOUR TESTING CHART – BROWNS

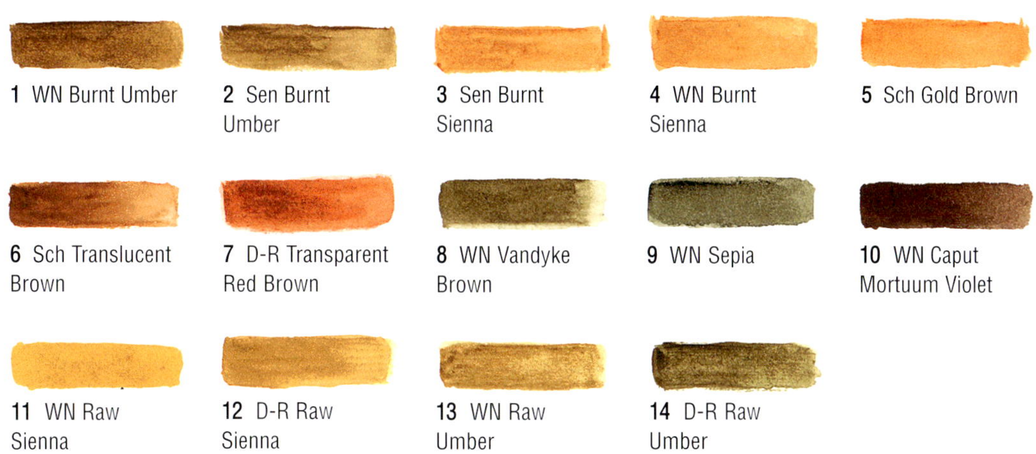

GALLERY

THE FOLLOWING pages show examples of work by Members of the Society of Botanical Artists, all of which were exhibited in a recent Westminster Exhibition. These paintings clearly demonstrate a wide range of subject matter, from humorous spring onions, looking like a collection of mauve 'welly' boots, to translucent grapes and saucy mandrake root – proof, were it needed, that botanical art is not just about the stiff, formal art of past times.

It is also worth noting that the true artist looks for the beauty displayed in less obvious subjects, as in the curvaceous lines of the Seeds of Magnolia × *soulangeana* by Jenny Jowett. However, there will always be a place for the classic flower portrait, of which Alister Mathews' Tulipa 'Texas Flame' is a splendid example. Looking at these pictures it is easy to see why botanical painting is enjoying a renaissance.

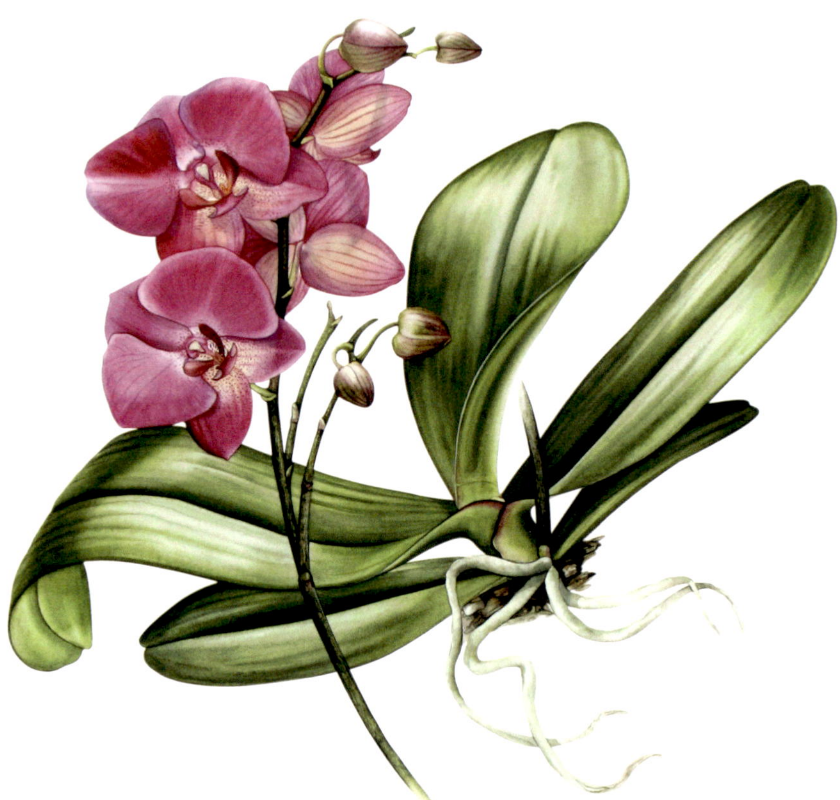

PHALAENOPSIS
(watercolour)
56 × 59 cm (22 × 23 in)
BILLY SHOWELL SBA

UGNI BLANC – WHITE GRAPE
(watercolour)
38 × 25 cm (15 × 10 in)
JACKY JOUSSON SBA

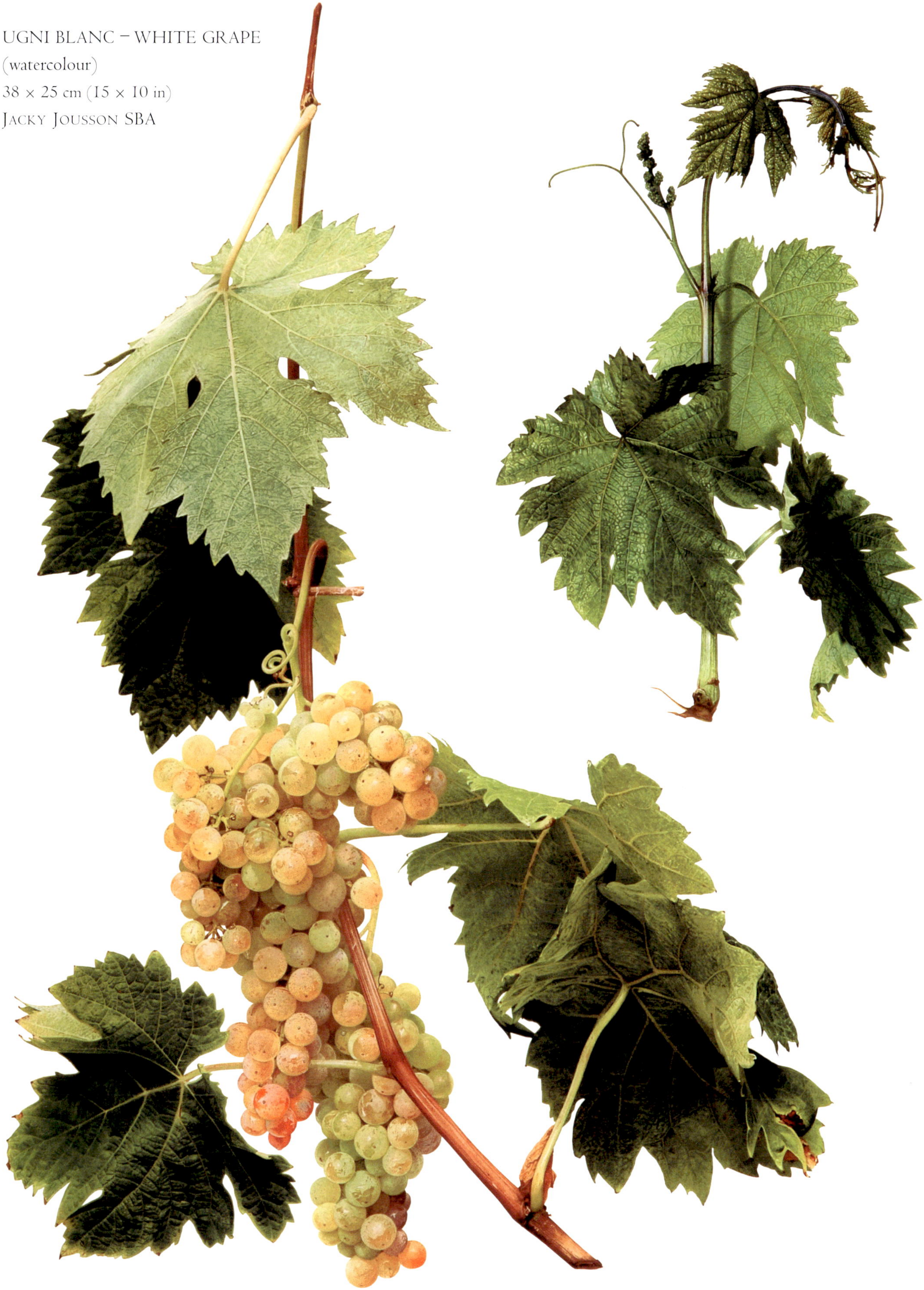

FLOWERING TEASEL
(watercolour)
86 × 46 cm (34 × 18 in)
Susan Dalton SBA

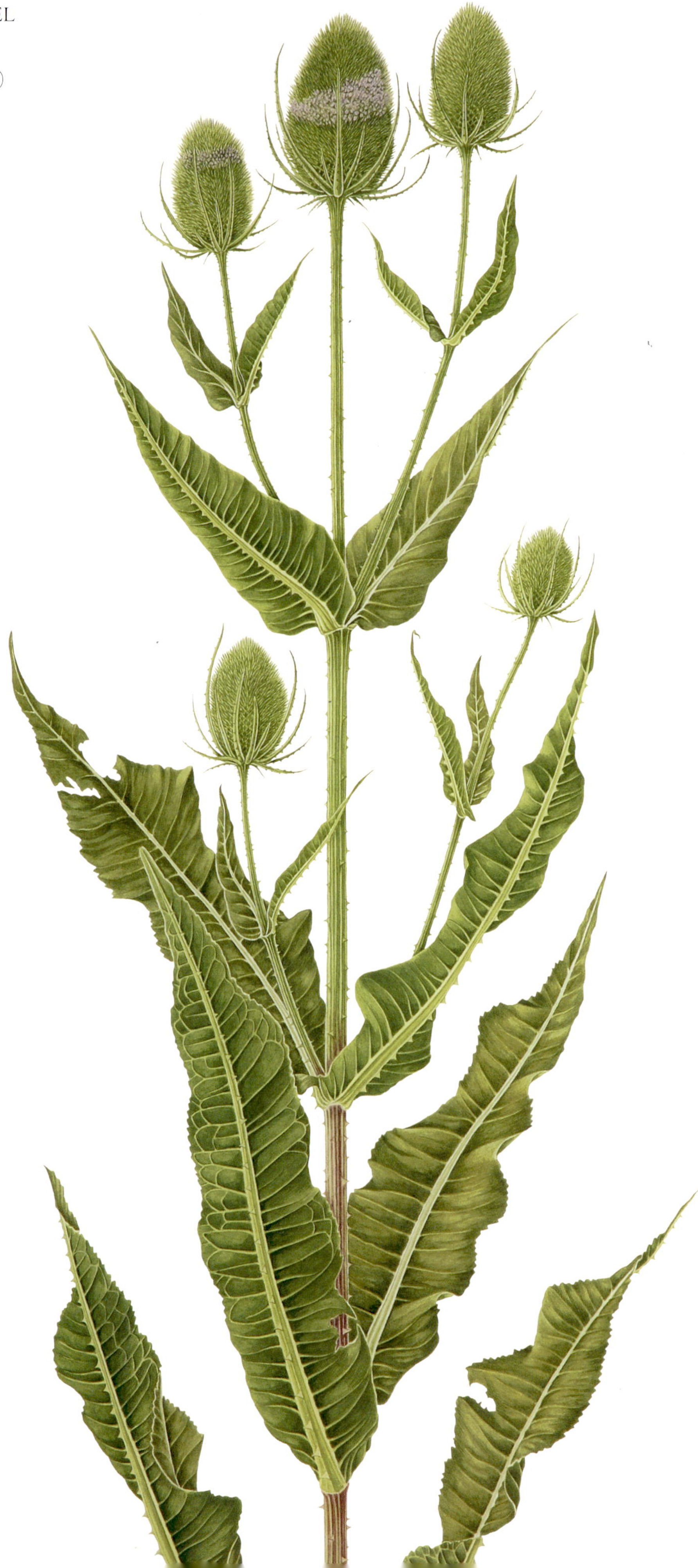

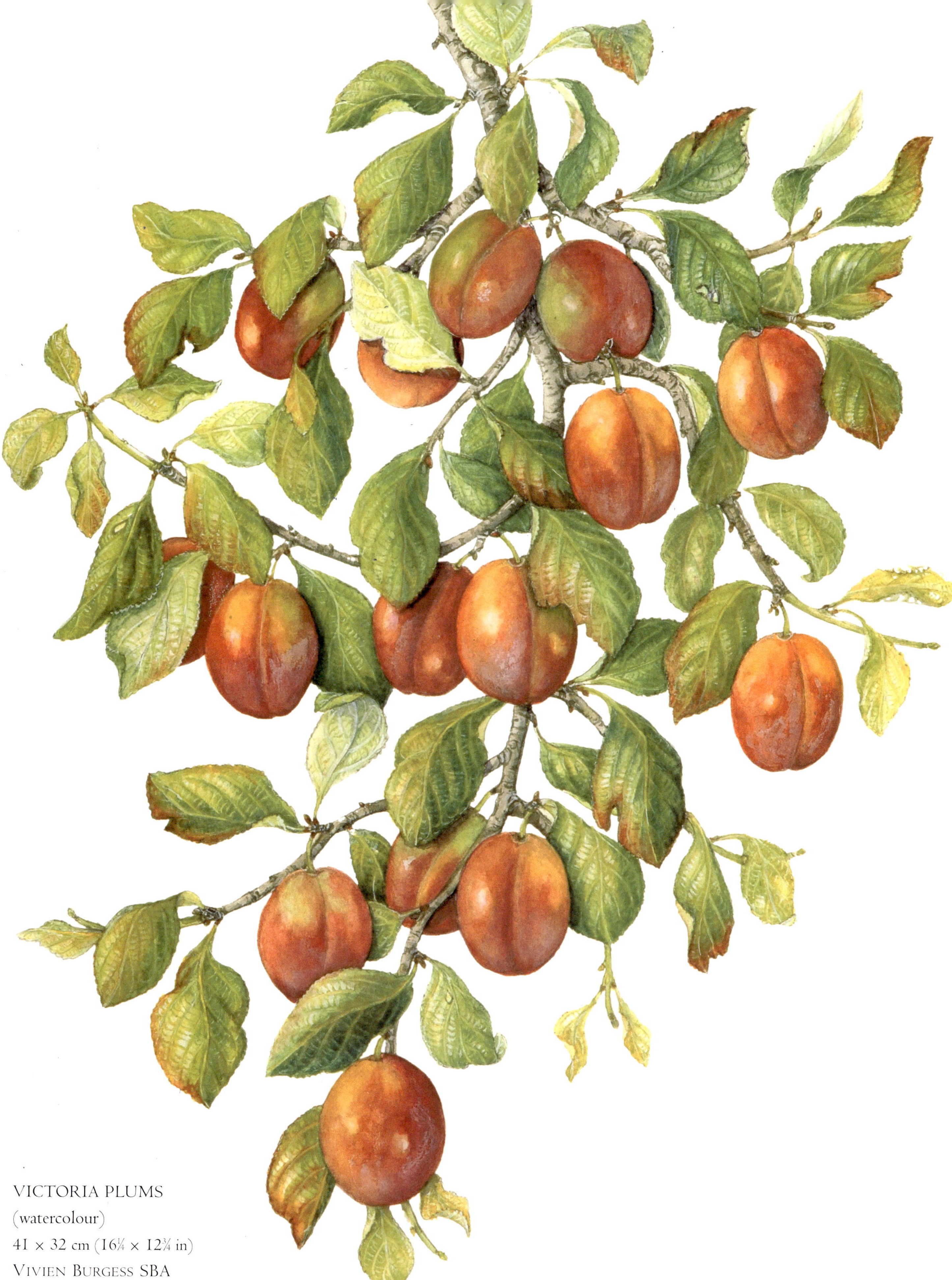

VICTORIA PLUMS
(watercolour)
41 × 32 cm (16¼ × 12¾ in)
Vivien Burgess SBA

RHODODENDRON
'LODERI PINK DIAMOND'
(watercolour)
69 × 57 cm (27 × 22½ in)
SIRIOL SHERLOCK SBA

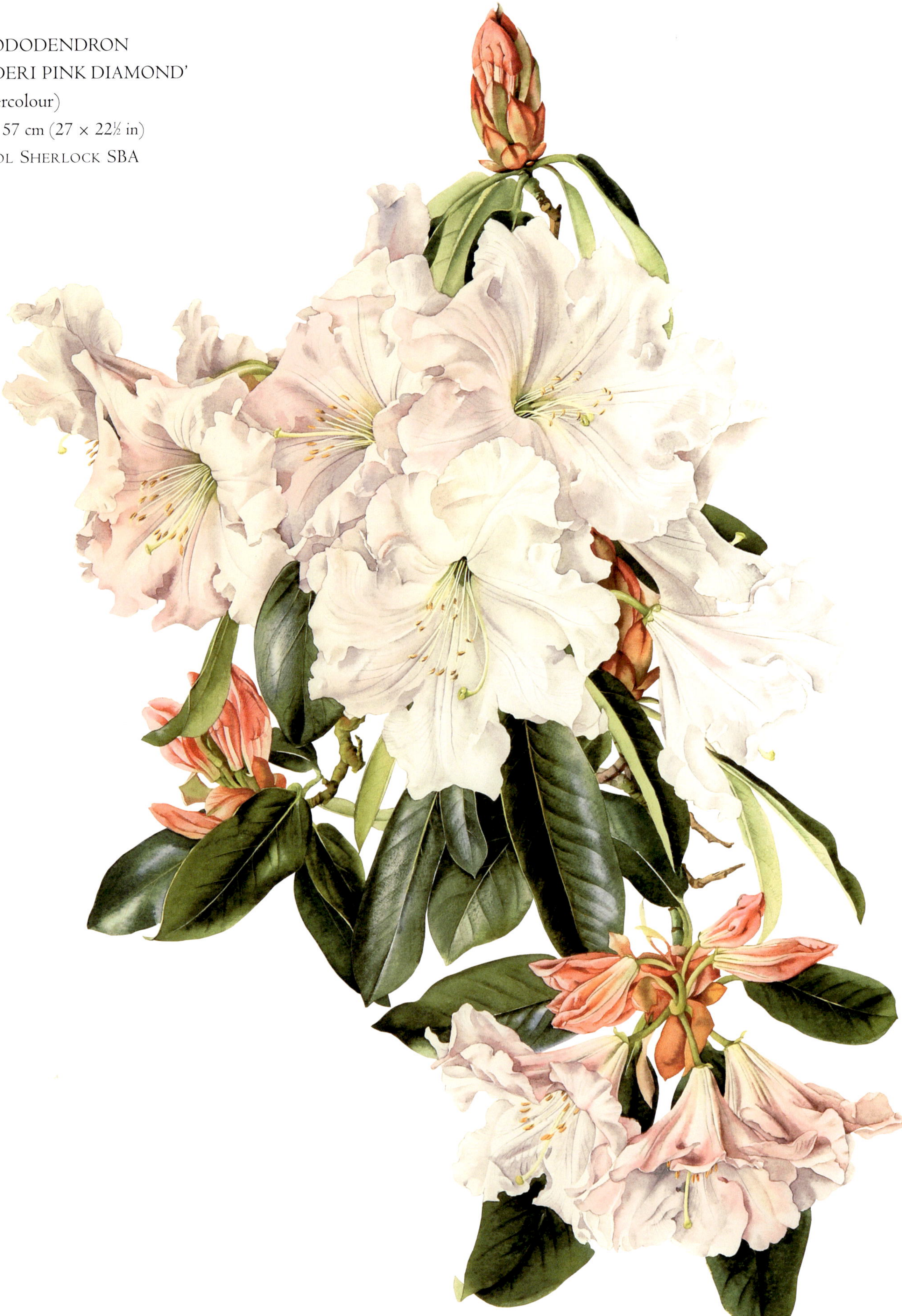

NERINES
(watercolour)
34 × 28 cm (13¼ × 11 in)
Sally Crosthwaite SBA

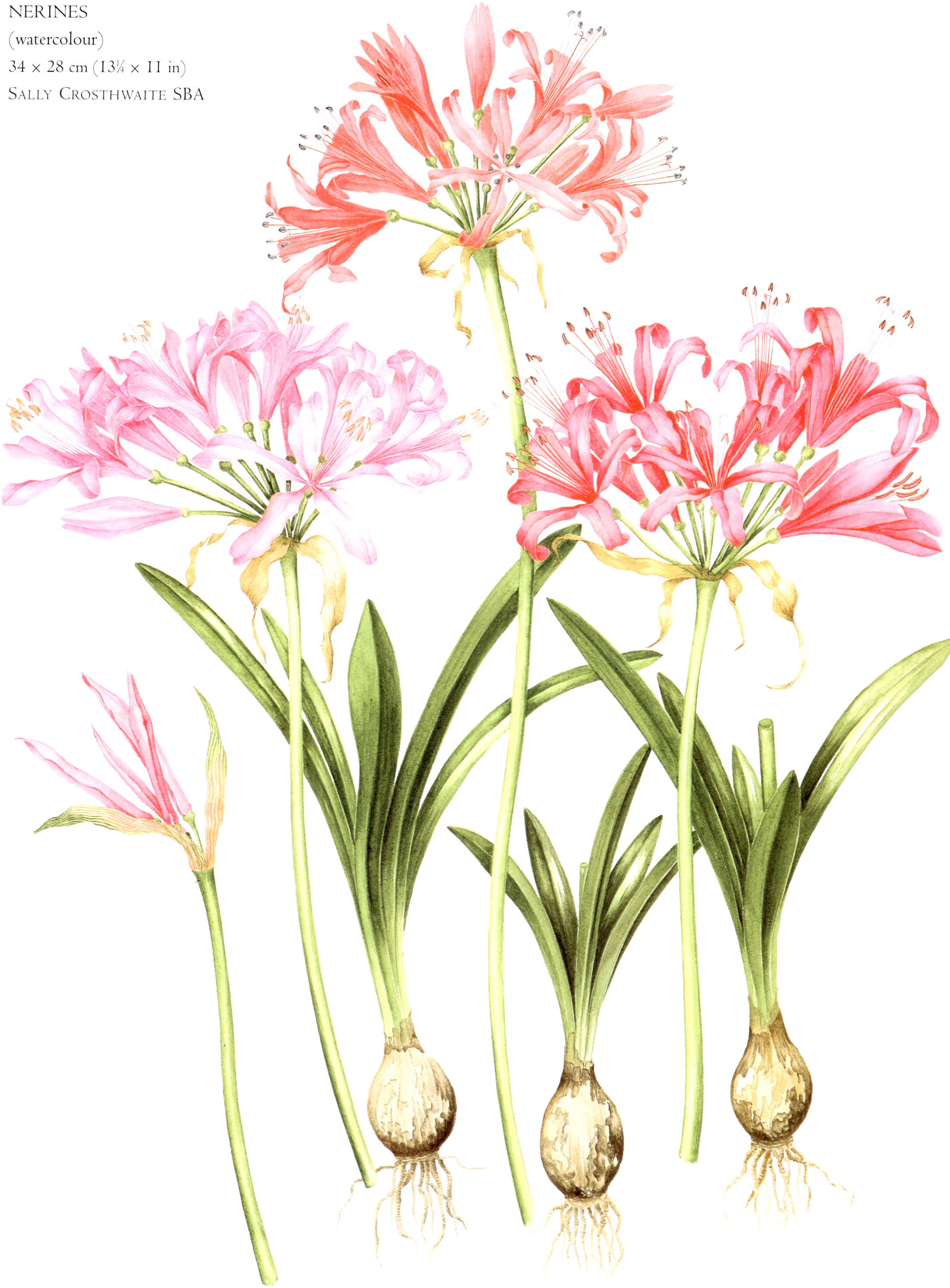

ECHINOPS
(watercolour)
58 × 46 cm (23 × 18 in)
Sandra Wall
Armitage SBA

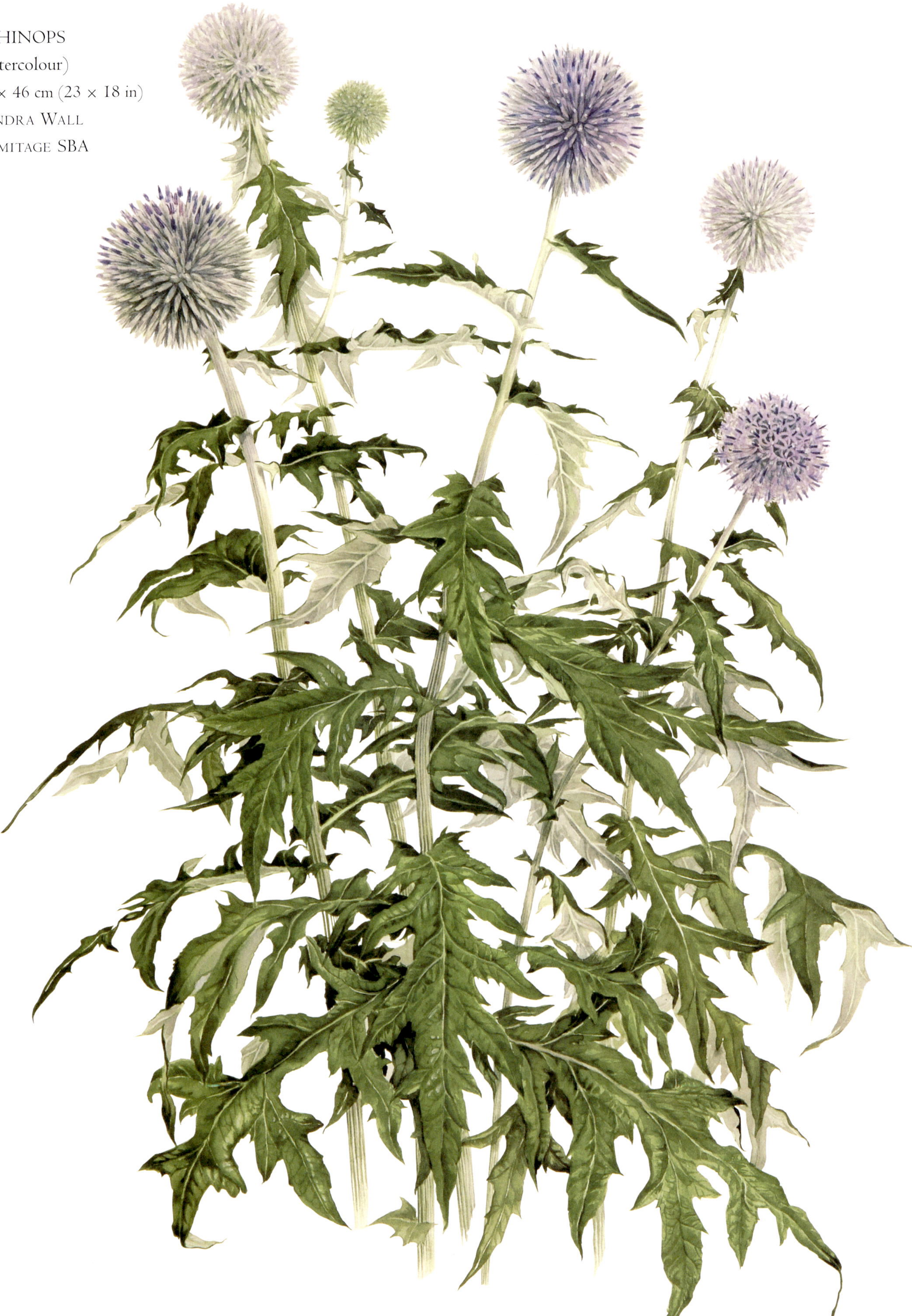

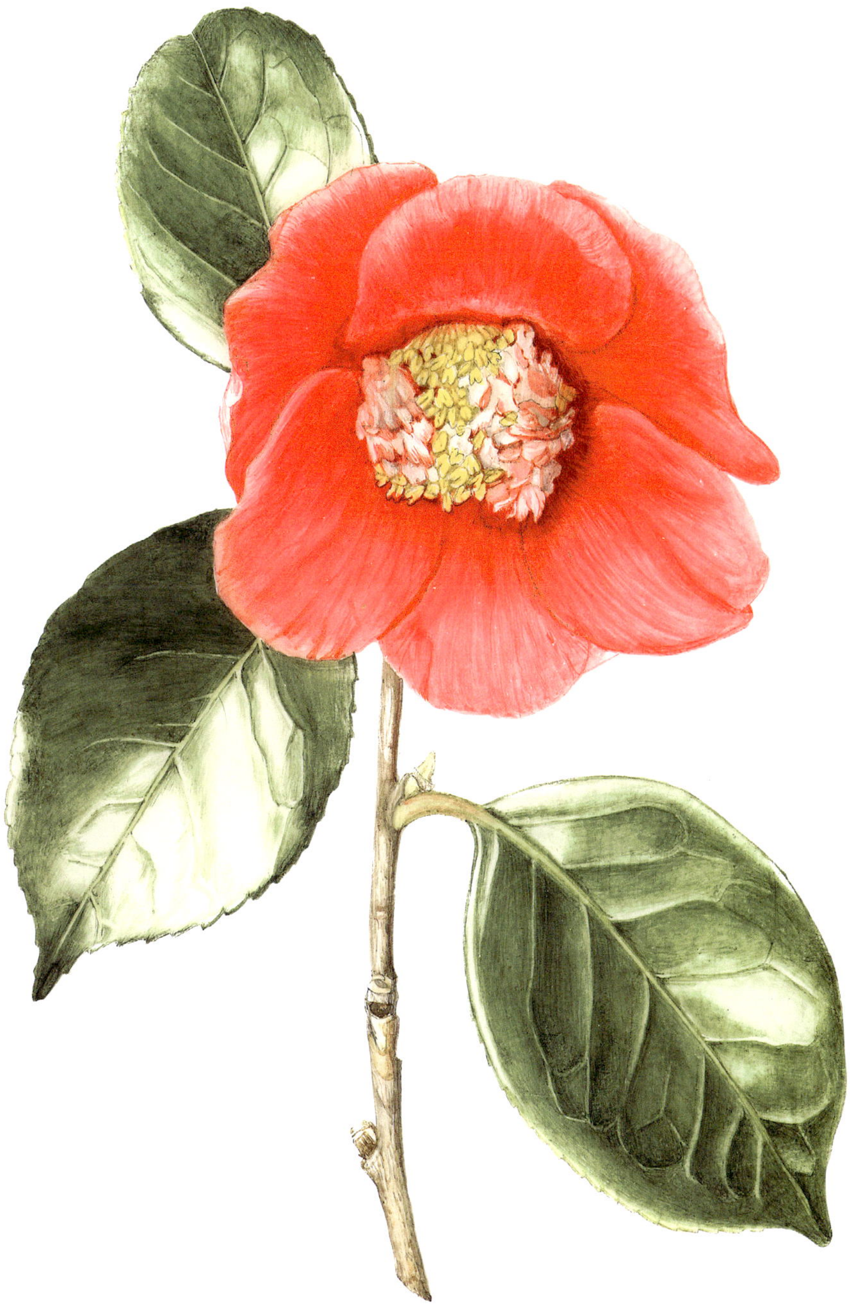

CAMELLIA JAPONICA
'ANEMONIFLORA'
(watercolour)
17.5 × 13 cm (7 × 5 in)
KAY REES-DAVIES SBA

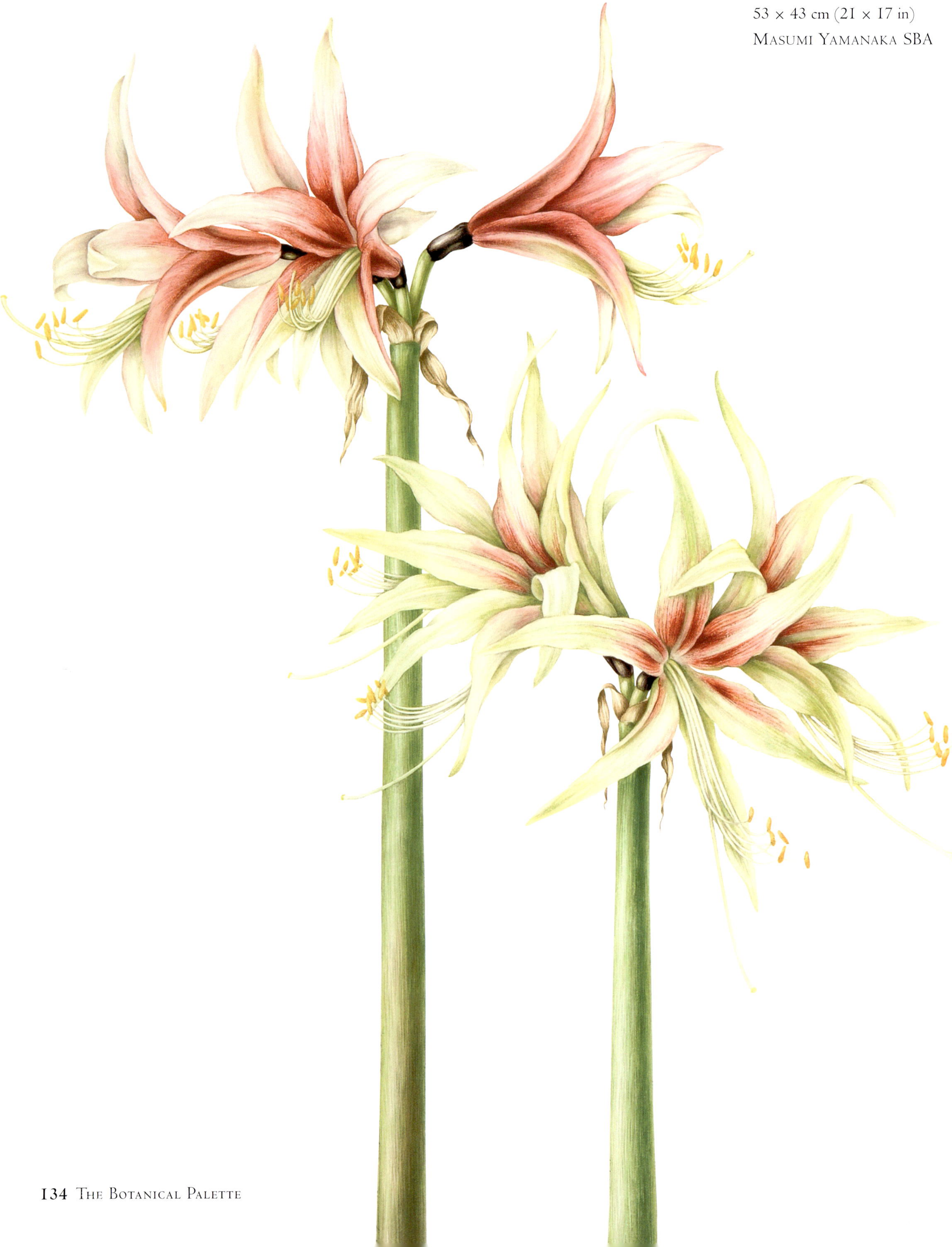

HIPPEASTRUM
(watercolour)
53 × 43 cm (21 × 17 in)
Masumi Yamanaka SBA

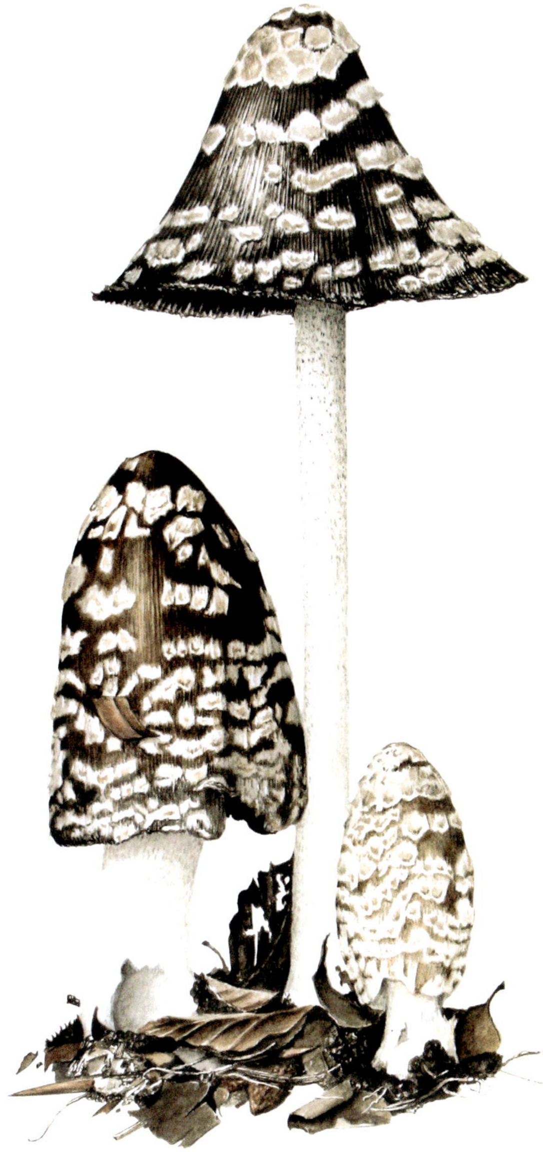

COPRINUS PICACEUS –
THE MAGPIE FUNGUS
(watercolour)
30 × 23 cm (12 × 9 in)
Roger C Reynolds SBA

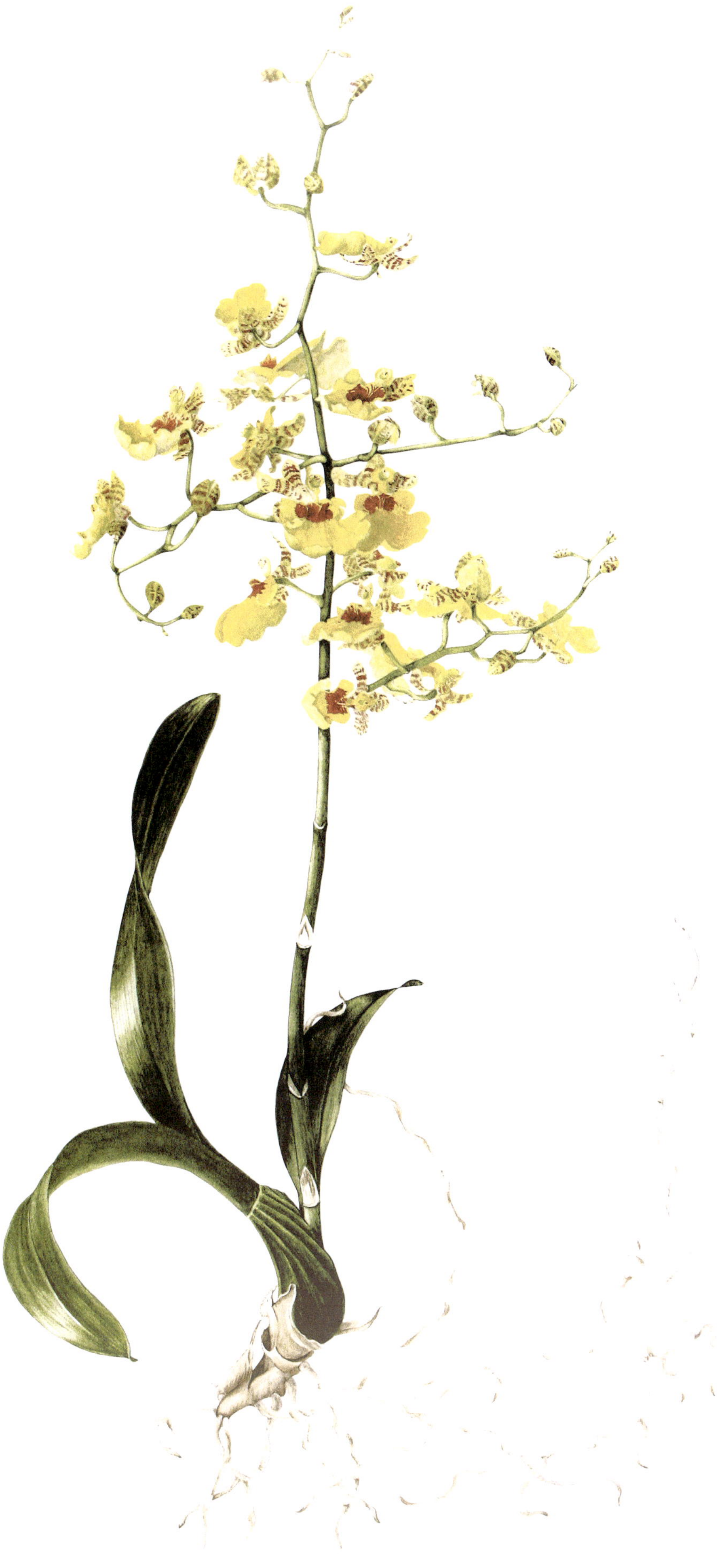

ORCHID 'GOLDEN SHOWERS'
(watercolour)
46 × 33 cm (18 × 13 in)
Ghreta Clegg Assoc. SBA

SEEDS OF MAGNOLIA × SOULANGEANA
(watercolour)
41 × 30 cm (16 × 12 in)
JENNY JOWETT FSBA

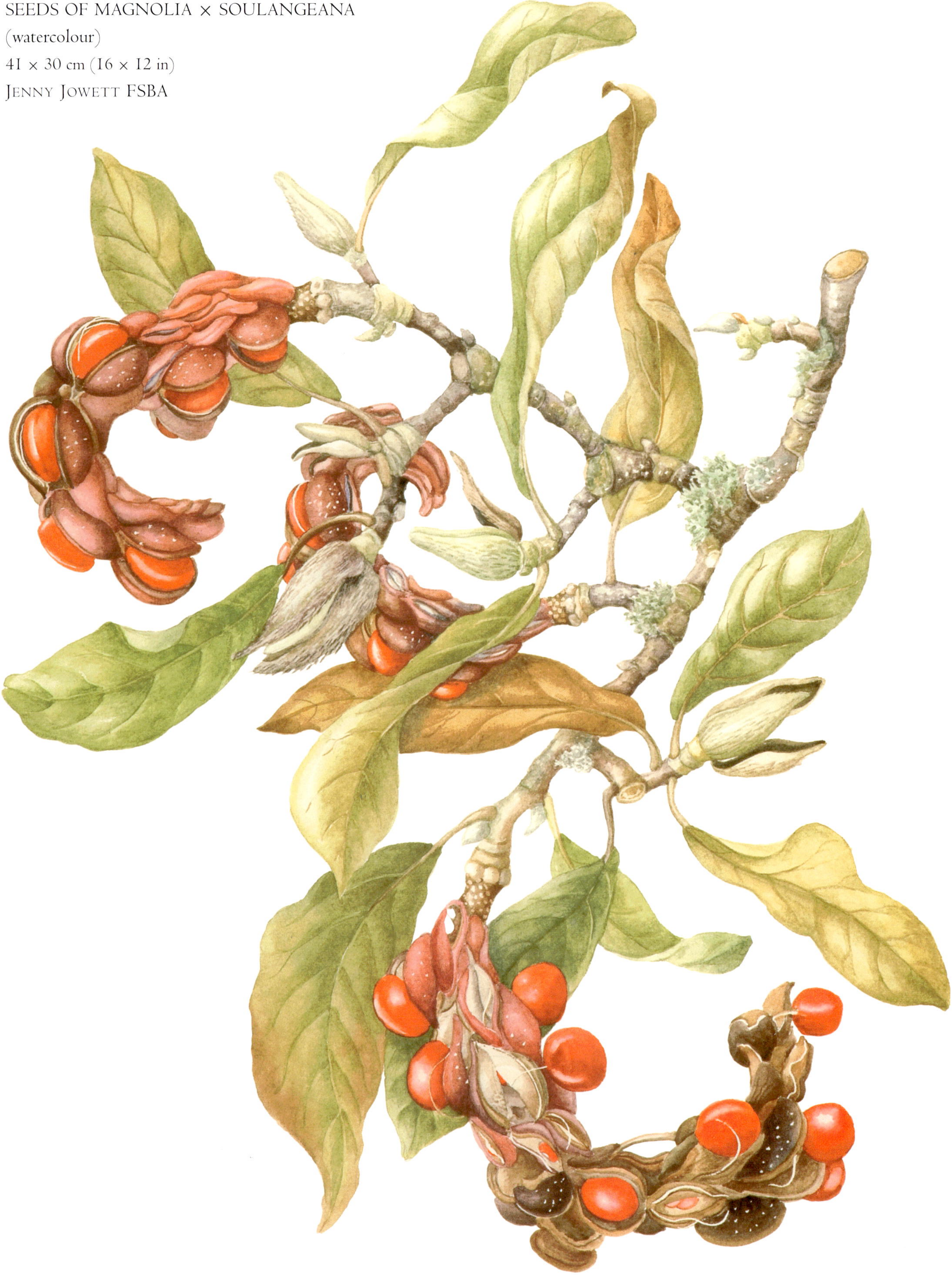

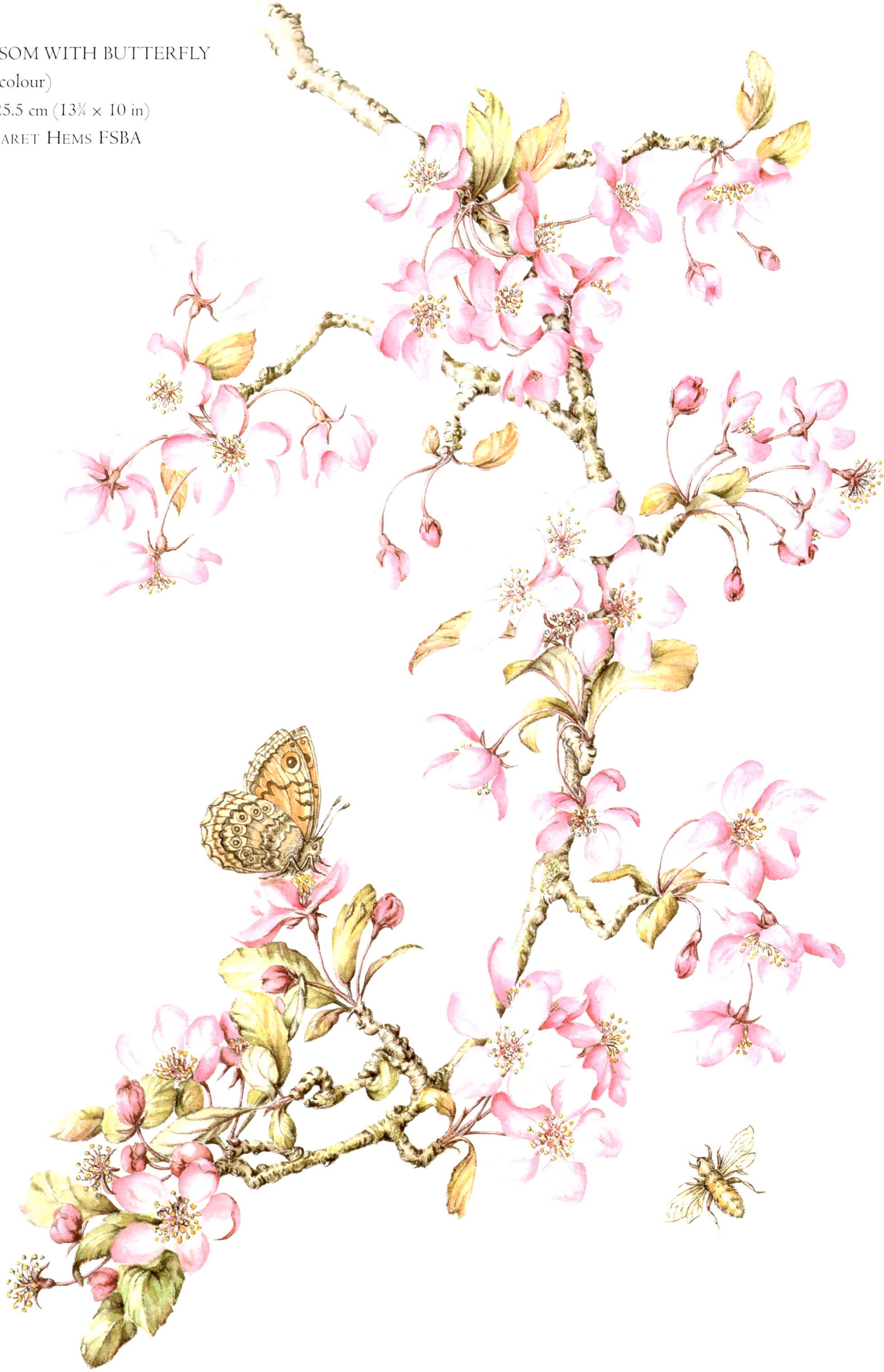

BLOSSOM WITH BUTTERFLY
(watercolour)
35 × 25.5 cm (13¾ × 10 in)
MARGARET HEMS FSBA

TULIPA 'TEXAS FLAME'
(watercolour)
24 × 17.5 cm (10 × 7 in)
ALISTER MATHEWS VPSBA

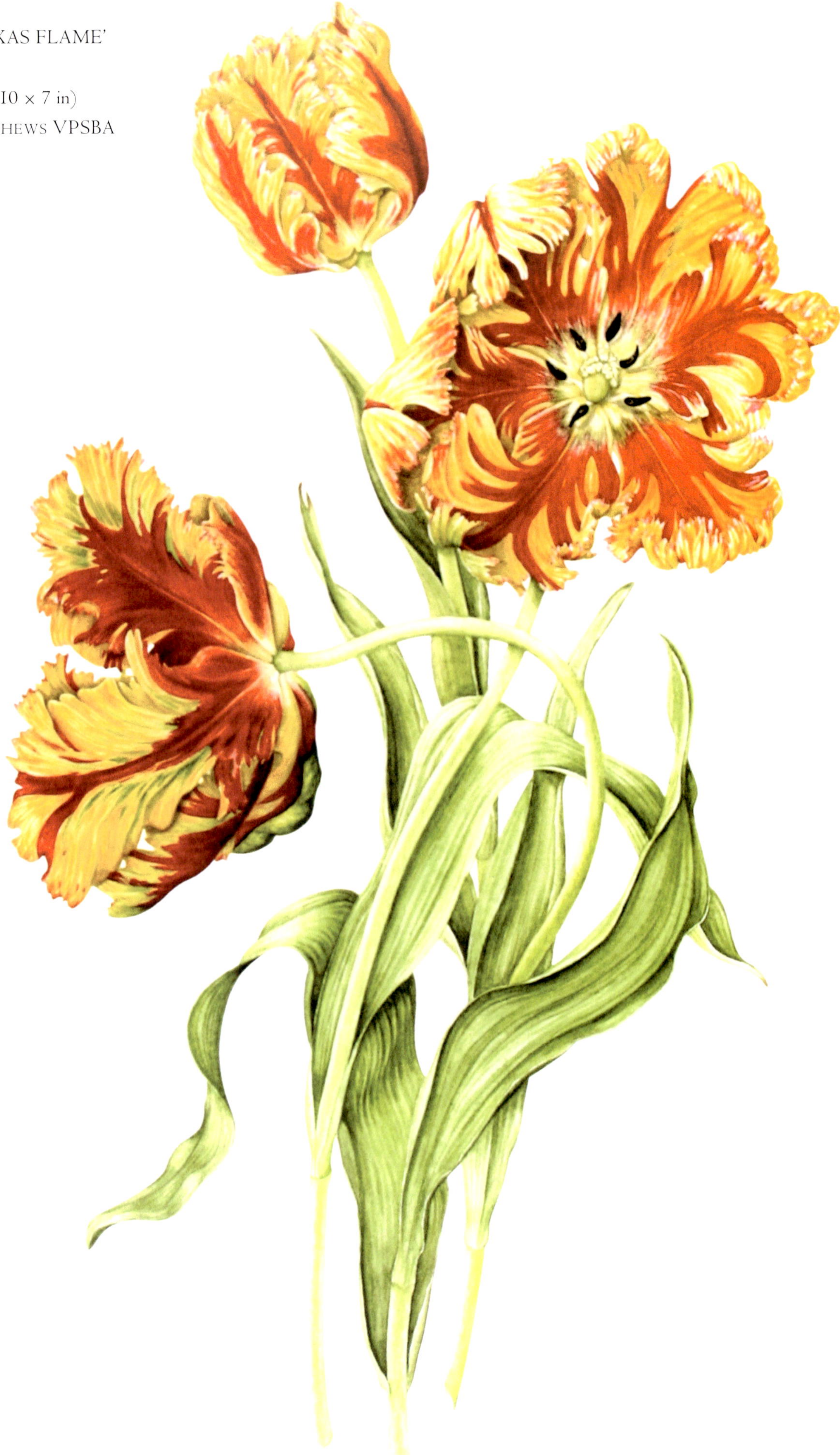

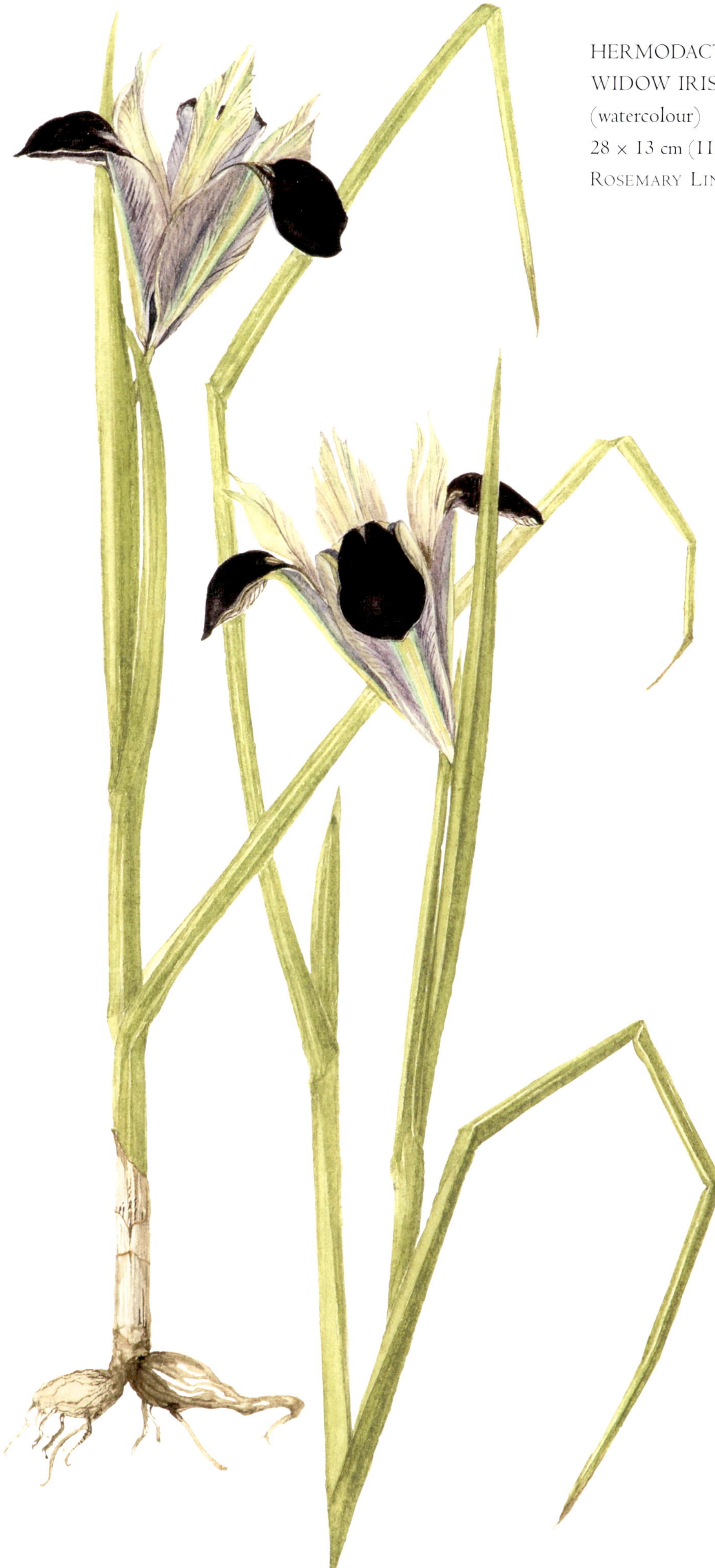

HERMODACTYLUS TUBEROSUS –
WIDOW IRIS
(watercolour)
28 × 13 cm (11 × 5 in)
ROSEMARY LINDSAY SBA

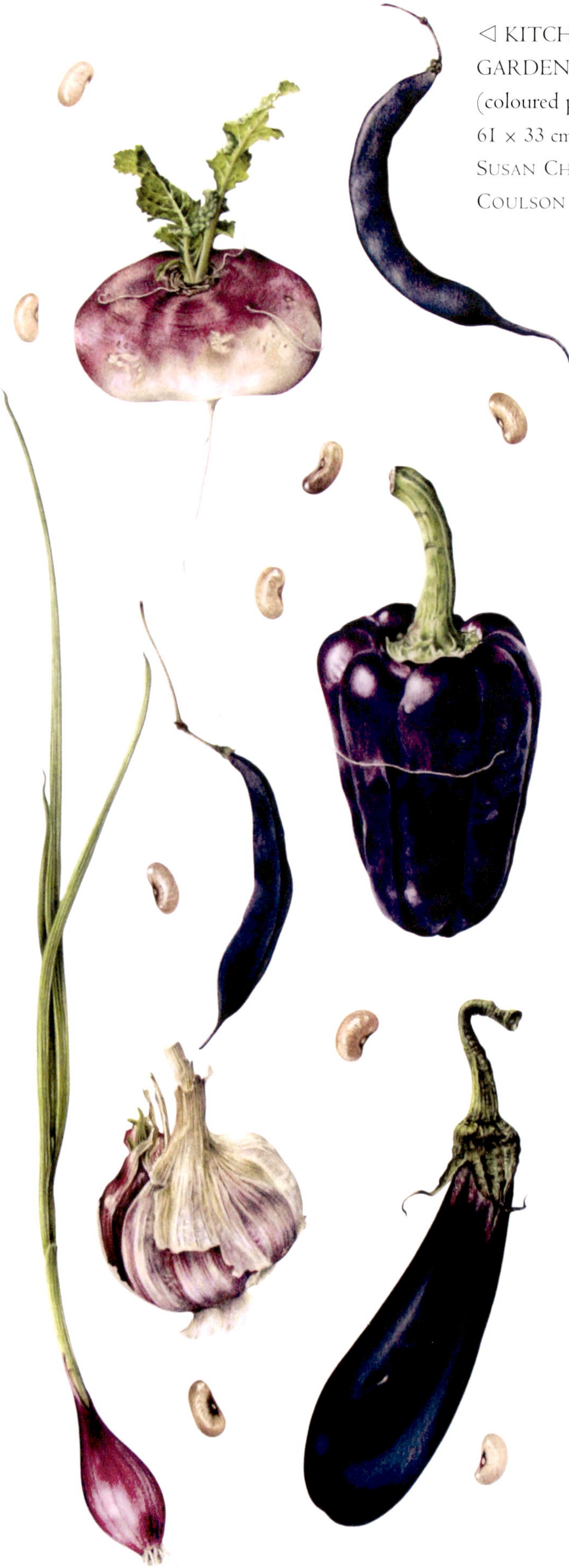

◁ KITCHEN GARDEN PURPLES
(coloured pencil)
61 × 33 cm (24 × 13 in)
SUSAN CHRISTOPHER-COULSON SBA

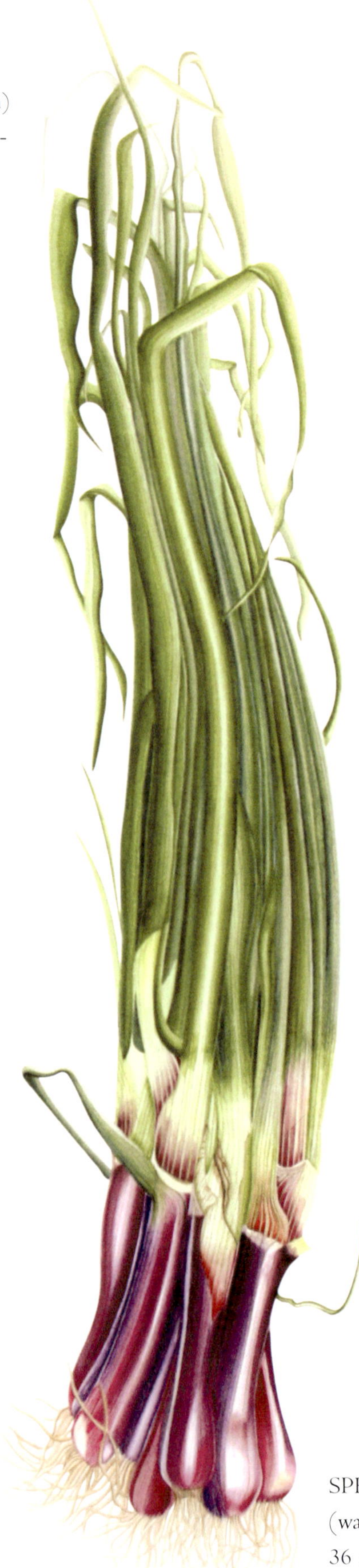

SPRING ONIONS
(watercolour)
36 × 30 cm (14 × 12 in)
VICKY MAPPIN SBA

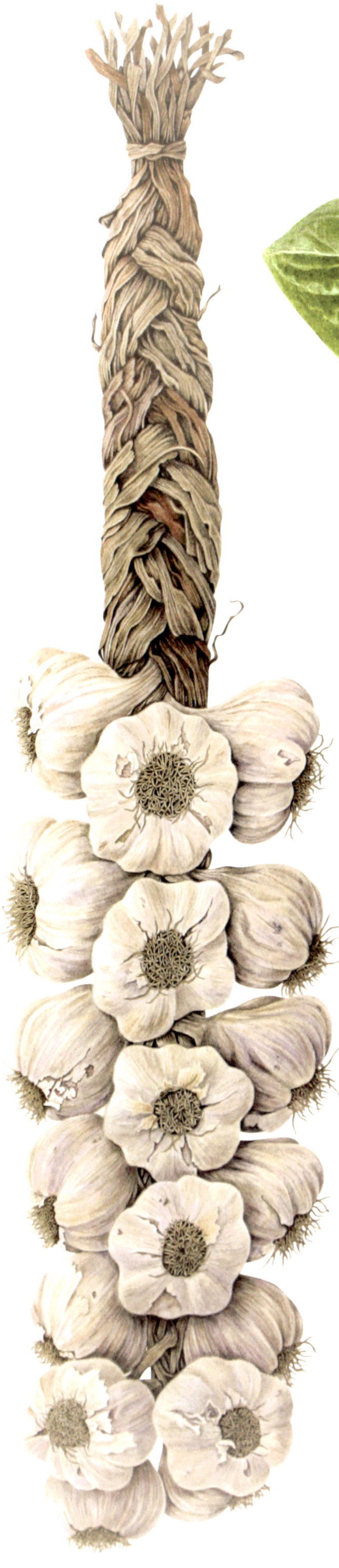

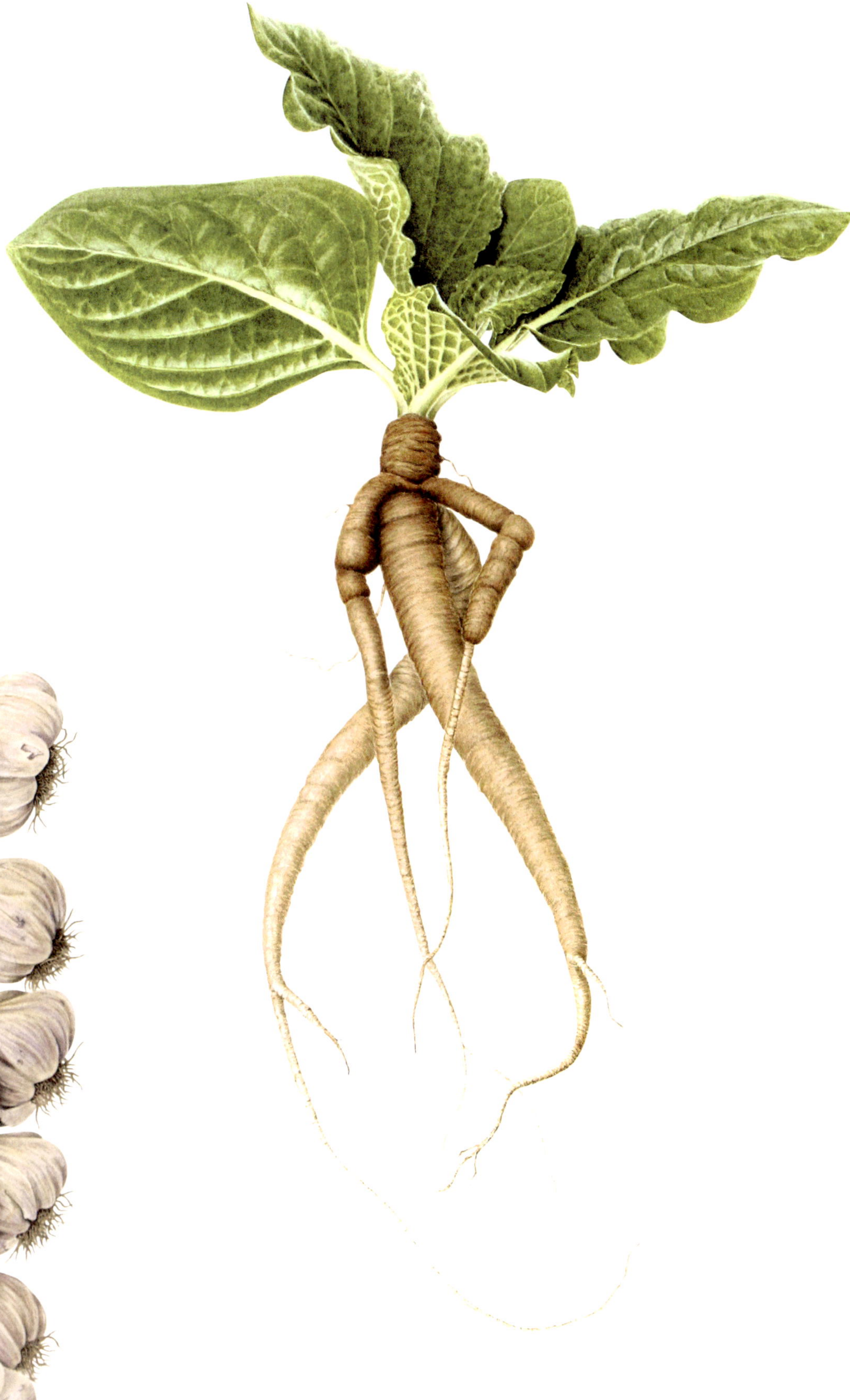

◁ GARLIC PLAIT
(watercolour)
69 × 23 cm (27 × 9 in)
SUSAN DALTON SBA

YOUNG MANDRAKE
(watercolour)
38 × 25 cm (15 × 10 in)
YVONNE EDWARDS SBA

THE LAST WORD

Botanical Painters work in quite a specialized area and their love of plants is generally linked to a passion for gardens and gardening. Even when advancing years and creaking joints prevent much active tilling of the soil I know that most older artists consider a regular trip around the garden centre to be essential. There they will find the inspiration for their next painting and the selected plant will be carried home like a cherished newborn infant. It will be the focus of their attention until its portrait is complete and ready for framing. Never mind if the plant cannot be accommodated in the artist's own garden as it will be passed on to a like-minded friend. Such is the fellowship between artist and gardener. Friendships are formed and sustained over many years, with societies offering a focal point both socially and by allowing the means for further education and exhibition. As President of the Society of Botanical Artists I have over twenty years' experience of this and now count some of the society's members amongst my oldest friends. The annual exhibition offers artists the chance to show their work in the finest surroundings and now the Distance Learning Diploma Course gives students the chance to participate as student members as well as improve their artistic ability. A student from California recently wrote to me as follows:

'*I am learning a great deal in this course with a surprising side effect. That is, a growing love and deep respect for plants. My life has become richer and more joyful as a result… Your dedication and commitment to Botanical Art and to creating the DLDC has certainly enriched my life and the lives of many others I am sure.*'

I hope that this book and the other books and magazines listed here, together with details of societies and courses, will benefit more aspiring artists worldwide so that they can share the pleasure that some of us already enjoy.

ART MAGAZINES

The Artist, Caxton House, 63–65 High Street, Tenterden, Kent TN30 6BD; tel: 01580 763315 www.theartistmagazine.co.uk

Artists & Illustrators, 26–30 Old Church Street, London SW3 5BY; tel: 0207 349 3150, www.aimag.co.uk

International Artist, PO Box 4316, Braintree, Essex CM7 4QZ; tel: 01371 811345 www.artinthemaking.com

Leisure Painter, Caxton House, 63–65 High Street, Tenterden, Kent TN30 6BD; tel: 01580 763315 www.leisurepainter.co.uk

The following magazines are also useful either because the photographs will inspire you to seek out different plants or show you which colours work well together in a well-planted border or in a well-composed painting!

The English Garden

The Garden – Journal of the Royal Horticultural Society

Kew Magazine – Journal of the Royal Botanic Gardens, Kew

ART MATERIALS

Daler-Rowney Ltd, PO Box 10, Bracknell, Berkshire RG12 8ST; tel: 01344 461000 www.daler-rowney.com

Great Art, 1 Nether Street, Alton, Hampshire GU34 1EA; tel: 0845 601 5772 www.greatart.co.uk

Sennelier paints: from Jackson's Art Supplies; tel: 0870 241 1849 www.jacksonsart.co.uk

Winsor & Newton, Whitefriars Avenue, Wealdstone, Harrow, Middlesex HA3 5RH; tel 0208 427 4343 www.winsornewton.com

ART SOCIETIES

Society for All Artists (SAA); tel: 01949 844050, www.saa.co.uk

Society of Graphic Fine Art, www.sgfa.org.uk

Society of Woman Artists, www.society-women-artists.org.uk

UK Coloured Pencil Society www.ukcps.co.uk

BOOK CLUBS FOR ARTISTS

Artists' Choice, PO Box 3, Huntingdon, Cambridgeshire PE28 0QX; tel: 01832 710201 www.artists-choice.co.uk

The Arts Guild, Hargreaves Road, Swindon, Wiltshire SN99 9XX; tel: 0870 165 0165 www.artsguild.co.uk

Painting for Pleasure, Brunel House, Newton Abbot, Devon TQ12 4BR; tel: 0870 4422 1223 www.readersunion.co.uk

BOTANICAL ART COURSES

A list of watercolour, monochrome and coloured pencils courses will be found on the SBA website: www.soc-botanical-artists.org.

FURTHER READING

Blunt, Wilfred and William T. Stearn, *The Art of Botanical Illustration*, The Antique Collectors' Club, 1994

Butler, Patricia, *Irish Botanical Illustrators and Flower Painters*, The Antique Collectors' Club, 2000

Gildow, Janie and Barbara Benedetti Newton, *Colored Pencil Solution Book*, North Light Books, 2000

Guest, Coral G, *Painting Flowers in Watercolour: A Naturalistic Approach*, A & C Black, 2001

Martin, Judy, *The Encyclopaedia of Coloured Pencil Techniques*, Headline, 1995

Sherlock, Siriol, *Botanical Illustration: Painting with Watercolours*, B T Batsford, 2004

Sherwood, Dr Shirley, *A New Flowering – 1000 Years of Botanical Art*, The Ashmolean, 2005

Showell, Billy, *Watercolour Flower Portraits*, Search Press 2006

Sidaway, Ian, *Colour Mixing Bible*, David & Charles, 2004

Walpole, Josephine, *Botanical Art: A History and Dictionary of British Flower Painters 1650–1950*, The Antique Collectors' Club, 2006

West, Keith, *How to Draw Plants: Techniques of Botanical Illustration*, A & C Black, 2004

Whittle, Janet, *Painting Flowers & Plants*, Search Press, 2003

SOLANDRA MAXIMA
(watercolour)
28 × 22 cm (11 × 8¾ in)
Marion Perkins SBA

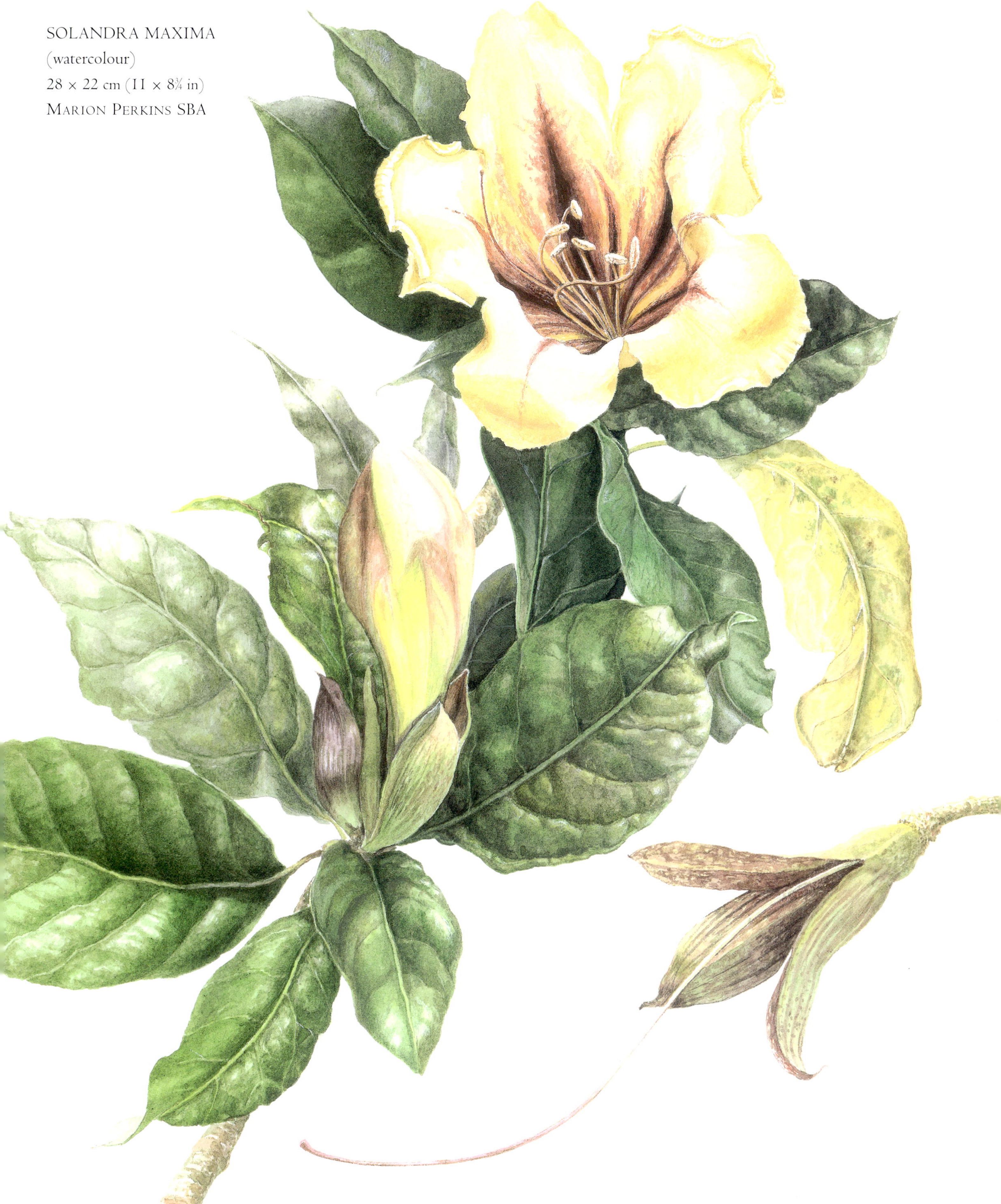

INDEX

Italic pagination indicates illustrations.